The Gun Book *for* Boys

Silvio Calabi, Steve Helsley & Roger Sanger

SHOOTING
SPORTSMAN
BOOKS

Copyright © 2012 by Silvio Calabi, Steve Helsley, and Roger Sanger

ISBN 978-1-60893-199-6

Library of Congress Cataloging-in-Publication Data available upon request

Printed in the USA

5 4 3 2 1

 Books

Distributed to the trade by National Book Network

Designed by Rich Eastman

Manufactured by Thomson-Shore, Dexter, MI (USA); RMA583KJ870, August, 2012

This book is dedicated to boys—and of course
girls—of all ages who are interested
in guns and shooting.

Contents

Lock & Load!

What This Book Is About & Why It's Important

All sorts of books have been written for boys. Maybe you've gotten some of them already. They tell us how to make paper airplanes and build treehouses and who won famous battles in history. It's all good, but when we were boys we wanted to know about guns and shooting, snipers and rogue elephants and man-eating tigers and blowing up stuff. How far will a bullet go, anyway? Were those $15 war-surplus guns in the magazine ads any good? Is my .22 enough for hunting deer? What about an old army rifle? Can I get ammo for that relic pistol Granddad gave me? Isn't shooting birds with clusters of pellets cheating? Does a bulletproof vest stop all types of bullets? Why is it dangerous to shoot at the water? Will firing a machine gun for a long time melt the barrel? Why is my mother so freaked out about BB guns?

In order, the answers are: It depends. Some of them. It can be. Sure. Probably not. No way. No way. Because it's like skipping a stone. Yes, sort of. Because she's your mother (and loves you).

We've been working on the answers to these questions—and a whole lot more—ever since we were kids ourselves. Then finally it seemed like a good idea to share them with you. No shooter knows everything, and all shooters have questions. Thanks to the Internet, answers are easy to find, but they aren't always complete answers or even the right answers. We're here to help you sort out the right answers from the junk.

You don't have to read this book from the beginning. It's set up like a box of chocolates: You can dip into it anywhere and find something interesting. However, you probably should read (or at least look at) the section called "Talking the Talk" first. It explains a lot of the language of guns and shooting. You may think you know this already, but even a lot of adults who've owned guns for years get some of the lingo wrong. Then later on, if you find a word you don't know while you're reading, flip back to that section and look for it. If the word isn't there, it's probably explained somewhere else. For example, if you don't know what a percussion cap is, it's not in the alphabetic listing; it's in "Making It Go Boom." Naturally.

GUNS ARE TOOLS

Some adults won't like this book. As you probably already know, to some people guns have become symbols of crime and violence, and a few people believe no one should own guns anymore.

However, from the days of the Pilgrims up until about when your parents were born, most of us regarded guns as everyday items. We seemed to get a lot more uptight about them after the Vietnam War, which ended in 1975. Also, at the same time, the population of our country was growing quickly and more and more people were living in cities, where they learned nothing about hunting or self-reliance, which is what guns were for during

A Russian SVD, the *Snayperskaya Vintovka Dragunova*, or Dragunov sniper rifle. Some people would call this a scary gun. Guns aren't scary, but what *is* scary are some people with guns. This book can make you a safe shooter who really knows his or her way around firearms.

most of America's history. (History is everything. In Japan there are almost no shootings. Japan has a culture of blademaking, though, that goes back more than a thousand years. When criminal violence occurs in Japan, it's usually with knives or swords.)

As a result, too many people are now afraid of guns. But guns are just tools, and *every* tool has a purpose. Use any tool, from a hammer to a lawn mower, the wrong way and it can become dangerous. No one has a problem with chain saws, but no one would use a chain saw to carve the Thanksgiving turkey, either. The same thing is true for guns. They don't belong in school. They're not toys. You don't use them to settle arguments.

Guns aren't scary, but what is scary are some people with guns—people who have bad intentions or who are just ignorant or careless. This book probably can't do much about your intentions, but it can make you a safe shooter who really knows his or her way around firearms.

You Can't Argue with History

Quick: What's the single most important manmade item in history?

You probably thought, *Oh, easy: the automobile.* Or maybe the computer.

Wrong. The most important manmade item in history, so far anyway, has been the gun. Some of the biggest breakthroughs in technology came about because someone wanted a better gun or ammunition, and then these breakthroughs were applied to making other things. You probably learned in history class that Henry Ford invented the assembly line, where mass-produced parts were put together in a standard way to produce the Model T car quickly and inexpensively. Ford may have been the first to build automobiles this way, but gunmakers like Eli

Whitney and John Hall beat him to the basic idea a century earlier.

(In fact, an 1882 report to the US Census Bureau on "The Manufacture of Firearms and Ammunition" declared that this "interchangeable system" of manufacturing "has been one of the chief influences in the rapid increase in the national wealth" in the previous 50 years.)

Here's another absolutely key advancement that came courtesy of the gun business: The most basic concept in precision manufacturing is the ability to shape things consistently to within a few thousandths of an inch. (A motor, for example, won't run if its parts don't fit together this closely.) The first person to work to such tight dimensions—he "invented" the thousandth of an inch—was Joseph Whitworth, an English engineer who was designing a more accurate rifle for the British army in the 1850s. Queen Victoria knighted him for his work.

The Bessemer process of smelting iron ore efficiently came about in part because the gun industry needed better steel. And so on and so forth.

It wasn't just manufacturing, either. The importance of guns in all of history is impossible to ignore.

The first Europeans known to have reached North America were Vikings who arrived in Newfoundland a thousand years ago. Their settlement failed. Some historians think the Norsemen were driven away because their swords, axes and bows were no better than the native Indians' weapons. Six hundred years later the Pilgrims landed on what is now Cape Cod. They had guns, though—a lot of guns. (By 1630 the Massachusetts Bay Colony required that all men, including servants, be "furnished with good & sufficient arms" and would provide guns to those who couldn't afford them.) The English settlers were able to hold off the Indians, and they stayed and prospered. The rest, as they say, is history—America's history.

In "You'll Put Your Eye Out!" you'll read about what might have been the single most important gun in American history: the air rifle that in 1804 was the Lewis & Clark Expedition's "secret weapon."

Going much farther back in time, the most important weapon in England's history (which, thanks to those Pilgrims and their guns, is where American history began) was the longbow, a fearsome and far-reaching killing device that was the forerunner of the rifle. It was the first weapon that allowed a peasant on foot to topple an armored nobleman from his horse—to stand up for himself, in other words, and refuse to be treated like a slave. This was the beginning of the end of the feudal system of kings, vassals and serfs. It took centuries—and proclamations like Magna Carta, the Constitution and the Bill of Rights—for the rights of the common man to be fully nailed down, but standing behind these rights was always the threat of armed resistance to the abuse of authority.

The first shots of the American Revolution were fired on April 19, 1775, when British troops marched out of Boston to seize colonists' guns and ammunition. Americans have been a bit touchy about this subject ever since.

Pilgrim John Alden's wheellock rifle. Alden sailed to America on the *Mayflower* in 1620, when he was 20 years old, and became a member of Capt. Miles Standish's Plymouth Colony militia. Without their guns, the colonists might have been forced to return to England. The rifle was found hidden in the walls of the Alden family home in 1924.

National Firearms Museum

It's Not Dangerous If You Know What You're Doing

The National Rifle Association, the Boy Scouts of America, the National Shooting Sports Foundation and other organizations across America have helped teach good gun-handling to millions of people. As a result, shooting has become one of the safest of all sports. There are many, many fewer accidents in shooting than in skateboarding or volleyball, for example, or weightlifting or even swimming.

In most places, before we can hunt or drive a car we have to take a course and pass a test. Driving leads to way more accidents than shooting, but you don't see people giving up their cars.

Read this book. Pay attention. Become a skilled, smart, safe shooter and represent our sport well. Hey, we're all in this together.

The National Rifle Association of America, the NRA, was created in 1871 to teach firearms skills. It's still doing that today. Thanks to the NRA and to other groups, including the Boy Scouts of America and the National Shooting Sports Foundation, shooting has become one of the safest of all sports. There are many, many fewer accidents in shooting than in, say, skateboarding or volleyball.

More Great Books on Guns

If you really get interested in shooting, you're eventually going to own a library of books on the subject. If this copy of *The Gun Book for Boys* belongs to you, your library is already off to a good start. Here are three more titles that you should pick up next:

Small Arms of the World, by Edward Clinton Ezell. This is one of the bibles of the shooting sports, with hundreds of pages of text and pictures. It's been around forever and is now in its 12th edition, but the older versions are just as interesting as the newer ones. You can get used paperback copies very inexpensively.

Frank Barnes's *Cartridges of the World* is another must-have-yet-low-priced shooting book. The current edition is the 10th, revised and expanded to include descriptions of more than 1,500 cartridges—American, British, European, new, old, military, wildcats, obsolete, for rifle, pistol and shotgun. All the editions are useful, but the newer ones have more information.

The Gun and Its Development, by W.W. Greener. The author was one of England's best-known and most-successful gunmakers. His book has been through at least nine editions since it was first published, in 1881, and has been reprinted over and over. It's long and sometimes difficult to follow, but no shooting library is complete without it. New or secondhand copies are available for just a few bucks.

There are hundreds if not thousands more books on guns, gunmakers, ammunition and shooting (competition, military and hunting) out there. Plus there are magazines and Websites that cover every one of the shooting sports, from collecting old guns to hunting big game and everything in between.

By the way, on the subject of books: Don't leave this one where Dad or Granddad can find it. They might get so wrapped up in it that you won't get it back for a while.

Talking the Talk

Learn the Language of Guns & Shooting

Shooting has its own vocabulary, and non-shooters often mix up words or use them incorrectly. A magazine, for example, is not the same thing as a clip, and a revolver isn't a pistol. Even shooters sometimes get confused about what is or isn't an assault rifle. If you run into a word in this book that you're not sure of, flip back to this section and look it up. If it's not here, go to the dictionary. Or to the Internet.

The word "gun" itself can be confusing. It actually means a shotgun, not a rifle or a pistol, but everyone uses it more loosely. In this book you'll be able to tell whether we're using "gun" to mean a shotgun or a rifle, some type of handgun, or something else (such as a ship's cannon, called a naval gun), or whether it doesn't matter.

We use **firearm** to mean a shotgun, rifle or handgun that launches a projectile through the ignition of an explosive (gunpowder), so a BB gun or a pellet gun is not a firearm because it uses compressed air or some other gas.

Federal law and most state laws also treat firearms and air guns as two different things for the

Is this a real gun? An orange plastic tip on the muzzle tells us it's an Airsoft replica, in this case of a US Army M4 carbine. In some places the law calls this a firearm; in others it's an air gun. You should know the difference, and which definition applies where you live.

same reason. But some towns and cities define "firearm" as something like "any instrument used in the propulsion of pellets, shot, shells or bullets by action of gunpowder, compressed air or gas exploded or released within it." This is important because (depending on where you live) it means you could get into legal trouble even with a BB gun. This is covered in the section called "Target Practice," so don't worry about it just yet.

RIFLES

Rifles are designed to fire a single projectile: a bullet. "Rifle" comes from rifling, the half-dozen or so grooves cut along the bore (the inside of the barrel) in long spirals. The bullet is a tight fit in the bore; the rifling grips the bullet and makes it spin in the air to make it fly accurately. (The feathers on an arrow do the same thing. So

does a spiral pass with a football.) A hunting rifle should be accurate enough to put its bullets into a one-inch circle at 100 yards. (This is known as minute-of-angle accuracy.) Target rifles and certain tactical rifles for police and military sharpshooters should put their bullets more or less into the same hole at that distance.

Dozens of terms describe this bolt-action hunting rifle. You can learn them and also something about the hundreds of years of history and technology that went into developing it.

There are four basic types of repeating rifles: bolt-action, lever-action, pump-action and autoloading. There are also single-shot rifles and double-barreled rifles. Turn to the section called "Guns, Guns, Guns" for explanations.

The power of rifles—the energy of their cartridges or, really, their projectiles—varies tremendously. At one end of the range we have "plinking" rifles like .22s, for shooting at tin cans or small game like squirrels. (As you'll see, though, .22s can be deadly.) At the other end are so-called stopping rifles, such as the .600 Nitro Express, which fire bullets the size of your thumb that can penetrate many inches of thick skin and heavy bone. In general, the more powerful a rifle, the heavier it is and the more it kicks (recoil).

On the military side there are long-range rifles that fire the huge .50-caliber Browning Machine Gun cartridge and even 20-millimeter rounds, which are far more powerful than any hunting or target rifle. But .50 BMG rifles weigh more than 20 pounds, and the old 20mm Lahti rifle from Finland weighs almost a hundred pounds, so these things are fired from bipods or other supports.

Cartridges (from left): A .22 Long Rifle generates about 125 foot-pounds of energy; a .223 Remington creates 10 times that much; and the .600 Nitro Express makes 65 times more than the .22, or 8,200 foot-pounds.

Steve Helsley

HANDGUNS

Handguns fire bullets too and also have rifled barrels. There are three types of handguns: revolvers, pistols and single-shots. "Pistol" is like the word "gun"—it's used for all sorts of handguns, but it now means a semi-automatic or a single-shot.

Being usually less powerful than rifles, handguns are mostly for target shooting or for self-defense at close range. A few, single-shots and revolvers, are specially set up for hunting, with longer barrels and more powerful ammunition. Single-shot handguns often have longer barrels too, for better accuracy. Most cops and soldiers carry semi-auto pistols.

The smallest common handgun is the .22. The largest is the .500 Smith & Wesson Magnum. Some single-shot hunting handguns take rifle ammunition, which is even more powerful. Shooting

A Colt Model 1917 .45 that was modified for fast-draw combat: The hammer spur and trigger guard were cut away and a carbine front sight was added. The owner carried it in the jungles of Malaya in WWII. If only it could talk!

CARTRIDGES

Cartridges are single units of ammunition, sometimes called rounds. A rifle or handgun cartridge has a bullet wedged into the mouth of a metal case, or shell, which holds the gunpowder. A shotgun cartridge contains either shot pellets or a single large projectile called a slug. (Sometimes the word "shell" is used to mean a loaded cartridge.)

A cartridge has a **primer** in its base—a tiny explosive that is struck by the gun's firing pin, to light the gunpowder that drives the bullet or shot down the barrel. If the primer powder is contained inside the rim of the case (like most .22 ammunition), it's called a rimfire cartridge. More powerful ammunition has a separate primer set into the center of the base of the shell. This is called centerfire ammunition, and these cases often can be reloaded and reused.

A cartridge should fit precisely into the **chamber**, which is the first section of the gun barrel. After firing, the empty cartridge case (or shell) has to come out before the chamber can be reloaded for the next shot. Each type of firearm performs this process differently.

these well takes some practice. At least one self-defense revolver can fire .410 shotgun shells loaded with buckshot, which are large pellets that spread out in flight.

Handguns come in a huge variety of calibers and styles. This is a super-precise Anschutz air pistol for 10-meter international-match competition like in the Olympic Games. The shooter can adjust the grip to fit his or her hand like a glove. The tube under the barrel is the compressed-air reservoir.

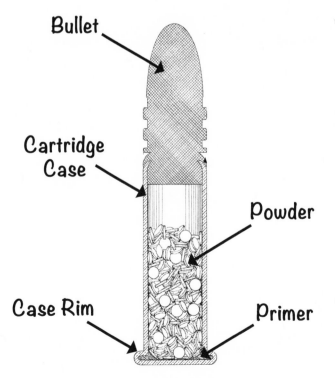

The different parts of a .22 rimfire round. The primer may be in a different place and the projectile may be one bullet or many shot pellets, but basically all cartridges work the same way.

As guns progressed from smoothbore muskets to modern rifles, projectiles evolved right along with them, from hand-cast lead balls to super-accurate bullets factory-made for specific purposes.

CALIBER

The caliber of a rifle or handgun is the diameter of its bullet, which is also the diameter of its bore (the inside of the barrel). This is written in millimeters for European rifles and handguns and modern military weapons (9mm, for example, or 5.56mm or 7.62mm) and in decimal fractions of an inch (.308, for example, or .45 or .303) for American and British guns.

Just to be confusing, however, a cartridge's official name and the diameter of its bullet aren't always the same. For example, the British .450 Nitro Express and the American .458 Winchester Magnum use the same bullet, which is in fact .458-inch across. This is because the Brits measure bore diameter between the tops of the rifling ridges (or "lands"), while Americans measure it between the bottoms of the rifling grooves. The difference is usually about .008", which just happens to be the difference between .450 and .458.

Sometimes, though, gun companies pick numbers just because they sound good or they're bigger than their competitors'. A .340 Weatherby Magnum bullet, for example, actually measures .338-inch in diameter.

Important: Caliber is also often used to mean cartridge. So we say, "Hey, what caliber is that rifle?"

If the reply is, "Three hundred," we have to ask again: "Which .300?"

The word "Magnum" generally means a more powerful version of a certain cartridge. But power is relative. This .44 Magnum round (left, shown actual size) is puny compared to the massive 4-bore big-game cartridge from the 1880s.

CALIBER CONFUSION

Since the self-contained cartridge was perfected, 150 years ago, a lot of different ones have appeared. To be clear about which one we mean, we usually have to provide more than just the bore diameter. For example, 7.62mm is a very common bore size, so we can tell cartridges apart by the lengths of their cases, also in millimeters. There's a 7.62x22mm, a 7.62x38mm, a 7.62x39mm, a 7.62x51mm and a 7.62x54mm. (There may be more.) The shorter ones are for handguns, the others for rifles. A couple of them have cases with rims that stick out, so they have the letter R attached. There's also a 7.63x25mm pistol round and two different 7.65mm pistol rounds: the German 7.65x22mm Parabellum and the 7.65x17mm Browning.

And then, just to make things more confusing, some of these European metric cartridges have different names in English. The 7.65x17mm Browning is the same as the .32 ACP (Automatic Colt Pistol).

Seven-six-two em-em (as it's pronounced) is the metric equivalent of .30-inch, and there are many more .30-caliber cartridges, from the old .30-30 Winchester and .30-40 Krag to the .30 M1 and .30-06 Springfield, the .308 Winchester and on and on. These terms all mean something: The 30 and 40 refer to grains of gunpowder. (A grain is a unit of weight. There are 7,000 grains in a pound.) M1 is the model of military carbine that this particular cartridge was invented for. The .30-06 is a round that was adopted by the American military in 1906.

Then, still in .30-caliber, there's a .300 Weatherby Magnum, a .300 Winchester Magnum, a .300 Holland & Holland (H&H) Magnum and a .300 Dakota Magnum. The shapes and weights of the bullets vary and their cases have different dimensions and hold different amounts of powder,

so they aren't interchangeable. A .300 Weatherby round won't chamber (fit) in a .300 H&H rifle.

"Magnum," by the way, just means "more powerful." An animal that is shot in the right place with a plain old .30-06 winds up just as dead as if it had been hit with a .300 Remington UltraMag, so the difference between a lot of these calibers is just theoretical—one company trying to outsell another.

"Factory loads" are standard cartridges manufactured to precise dimensions that we can buy over the counter. One brand of factory ammunition will fit another company's guns if they're exactly the same cartridge. Some people like to create their own cartridges by modifying a standard load (and chambering a gun barrel to fit). This is called a "wildcat" cartridge, and its name may be something like the .223 Ackley Improved. Sometimes a wildcat performs so well that it becomes a standard factory cartridge.

There's one more type of cartridge designation that you should know about. Most of these are British and date from the early 1900s, but some of them are still used. A .500/.450 x 3¼, for example, has a case that's 3¼" long and originally was meant for a .500-caliber (half-inch-diameter) bullet, but its mouth has been reduced ("necked down") to take a smaller .450 bullet. Other common examples include the .577/.450 and the .500/.416. The case length is needed only where there's a choice.

If you've followed this far, you already know more than many experienced shooters do. Don't let this confuse you. Just be aware that you need more than just one number to identify most cartridges. Over time you'll get comfortable with the lingo. In the meantime, just flip back to these pages if you have questions.

BULLETS

Bullets usually but not always contain lead (because it has a very high specific gravity, meaning that it's heavy for its volume) and have some sort of jacket, or outer layer, of a metal such as copper or nickel.

The Hague Convention on land warfare of 1899 prohibited "the use of bullets which expand or flatten easily in the human body." Ever since then, military bullets have had full metal jackets, which drill right through and leave behind fairly clean, small holes. This may reduce the slaughter on a battlefield, but in hunting the goal is to kill the game as quickly and humanely as possible. Most hunting bullets have only partial jackets and soft (or hollow) points so they "mushroom," or expand, when they hit in order to cut as many blood vessels and organs as possible.

Big animals with thick skin and heavy bones usually require heavier, stronger bullets. The lead may be mixed with other materials to make it harder. Bullets that don't expand at all—for punching through heavy bone—are called "solids." Over about two centuries of development, ammunition makers have learned to make bullets for different needs that perform very differently.

Like powder, bullet weights are also given in grains. A 450-grain bullet weighs almost exactly one ounce. (Dig five quarters out of your pocket; that's just about one ounce.) A hollowpoint rimfire .22 bullet may weigh only 37 grains. The US Army's standard 5.56mm rifle bullet weighs 62 grains. Most .30-caliber hunting bullets weigh 150 to 180 grains. The largest .500 Smith & Wesson Magnum revolver bullet is 500 grains. Most cartridges are available with several different weights and types of bullets for different kinds of shooting or targets.

A round musket **ball** isn't the same thing as a streamlined, cone-shaped rifle bullet. Bullets have two great advantages over balls: First, they are more aerodynamically stable in flight and so more accurate. And second, a bullet can be made heavier just by making it longer, while a lead ball of a certain diameter (or gauge—see next page) comes in just one weight.

BALLISTICS

The science of projectiles in flight is called ballistics. Shooters generally use two ballistic measurements to describe the performance of bullets: their speed (in feet per second) and the energy that they create (in foot-pounds). This is important, and there's more about it in "How Far & How Hard," but for now just know that a bullet of a certain weight, say 165 grains, might be traveling at 2,800 fps and generating 3,200 foot-pounds of energy. These numbers usually are measured at the gun's muzzle and sometimes 100 yards away in order to indicate how much the bullet has slowed down at that distance and how much power it has lost.

A bullet immediately starts to slow down (because of air resistance) and drop (because of gravity) when it leaves the gun, so it travels along a curve called the arc of trajectory. The bullet's velocity—the speed at which it flies—and shape determine how long it takes to get to the target, and this sets the trajectory.

A bullet that travels 2,000 feet in two seconds drops 64 feet in that distance! But if its speed can be doubled, to cover 2,000 feet in just one second, the bullet drops only 16 feet because gravity and air resistance have less time to affect it. The sights on a gun barrel are adjusted to tilt the barrel upward to compensate for the drop in trajectory.

Modern bullets achieve muzzle velocities of anywhere from about 1,000 to 4,000 fps. Their speed is measured using an instrument called a chronograph. The bullet's energy can then be calculated with a mathematical formula.

SHOTGUNS

Like all guns, shotguns come in many shapes and sizes. This is the five-shot 12-gauge Benelli Super 90 M4 tactical shotgun as issued to the US Marines. It's meant for instinctive shooting in close-quarters combat.

Shotguns are "smoothbores"; they have no rifling in their barrels. Shotguns are meant to shoot clusters of pellets, which spread out to make it easier to hit fast-moving targets such as birds in flight. Shotguns are short-range weapons.

The ounce or so of pellets in a normal shotgun cartridge needs a little distance to spread out, so inside of 20 feet a shotgun blast is highly lethal and destructive, no matter whether the gun is loaded with fine birdshot or large buckshot. Beyond that distance the spread of the pellets can be controlled somewhat by "choking" the barrel—shrinking its bore diameter slightly at the muzzle. A full-choke barrel delivers a tighter cloud of pellets downrange than an open-choke barrel; it should put nearly all of the shot inside a 30-inch circle at 40 yards.

Shotguns also can fire single projectiles called slugs loaded in special cartridges. Slugs are sort of halfway between a ball and a bullet in shape and will kill deer-size game out to about 125 yards. Some slugs are grooved to spin in flight, and it is possible to buy replacement rifled barrels for shotguns. Still, slugs don't have the range and accuracy of bullets.

Shotguns are measured in **gauge**. Gauge is the number of equal-size balls that could be made from one pound of lead that each just fits that diameter barrel. A 12-gauge gun barrel would fit a ball that weighs one-twelfth of a pound. A 20-gauge gun is smaller; it would fit a ball that weighs one-twentieth of a pound.

This comes from old cannon designations. A 12-pounder cannon from the days of the American Revolution fired a 12-pound ball; a 12-gauge gun is a $\frac{1}{12}$-pounder. (By the way, those cannons were guns—no rifling.) The designation was by weight instead of bore diameter, or caliber, because a lead ball that weighs X always has a certain diameter, while the weight of a bullet can be made more or less by changing its length, even though its caliber (diameter) stays the same.

A lead ball that weighs $\frac{1}{12}$ of a pound is 0.729-inch in diameter, so 12 gauge is .729 caliber. That's almost three-quarters of an inch, much bigger than any rifle or handgun caliber because of space needed for the hundreds of pellets in a shotgun cartridge. Twelve has been the most popular shotgun gauge for hundreds of years. The most common other shotgun gauges today are 20

A completely different sort of 12-gauge—a made-to-measure, double-barreled Rigby shotgun for hunting gamebirds. But it too is designed for fast, instinctive shooting without aiming.

and 28. There are also 10- and 16-gauge guns and the smallest common shotgun: the .410 bore, which is a true caliber, not a gauge size. (See "Shotguns for Birds.")

There are different kinds of shotguns for target shooting, hunting and tactical use (military, police and self-defense).

The parts of a modern shotgun cartridge: The primer, gunpowder and (in a plastic shot-cup wad) shot pellets are packed into the plastic-and-brass case, which is then crimped shut.

Steve Helsley

MAGAZINES

A magazine is a container built into a gun that holds the ammunition. A magazine has a spring in it that pushes the cartridges along so the action of the gun can grab each fresh one and feed it into the chamber for firing. A magazine is often called a clip, but this is wrong. A clip is a strip of metal that holds a row of cartridges so that they can be slid into the magazine or the cylinder of a revolver. (Filling a magazine by pushing each round in against its feed spring can be a pain.) Sometimes it's called a stripper clip or a charger clip.

Rifle and shotgun magazines can be tubes under the barrel that you fill from one end or the other. Or they may be rectangular boxes that fit into the action just ahead of the trigger. Box magazines may be hidden inside the stock or they may stick out, and they're either detachable or fixed in place.

A detachable magazine can be removed when it's empty and a fresh one snapped into place for quick reloading. Fixed-box magazines may have a floorplate that can be opened to dump out unused cartridges when it's time to unload the gun (instead of

Box magazines and their clips. These are for the .30-caliber M1 carbine from WWII. Even shooters get mixed up about "magazines" and "clips." A clip is a strip of metal that holds a row of cartridges so that they can be slid into a magazine or into the cylinder of a revolver.

Steve Helsley

working the action to cycle the cartridges through the gun, which might result in an accidental discharge). Box magazines on hunting rifles usually hold two to four rounds. Assault rifles and their look-alikes usually have long magazines that hold 10 to 30 cartridges.

A pistol magazine holds from six to a dozen or more cartridges. It fits into the butt, or handle, of the gun. If it sticks out farther than the end of the grip, it's an *extended* magazine for more ammunition.

Revolver magazines are called *cylinders*, which turn (revolve) to bring each cartridge in line with the barrel for firing.

A revolver's magazine is its cylinder; it swings out to the side for reloading. (On some old revolvers, the barrel and cylinder are hinged to tip down, so you can reload from above.)

MACHINE GUNS

A heavy machine gun lights up the night with a stream of .50-caliber tracer fire from the roof of a Humvee. The automatic gun changed warfare when it arrived on the battlefields of WWI.

Dept. of Defense

By law and by sporting tradition and ethics, a rifle, shotgun or handgun meant for hunting fires one round at a time; the trigger has to be pulled once per shot. A firearm that shoots as long as its trigger is held back is a *fully automatic* weapon—also known as a *machine gun*.

Before the National Firearms Act of 1934, Americans could own machine guns with no restriction. Civilians can still own and shoot machine guns if the guns are properly registered.

Full-auto weapons, including a few combat shotguns, come in all shapes and sizes. A *machine pistol* is a handgun that can empty its magazine with just one squeeze of the trigger. A *submachine gun* is a compact, short-range, two-handed machine gun chambered for a pistol cartridge. An *assault rifle* is a full-size shoulder weapon for military use that fires a more powerful round. Many assault rifles can be switched from full- to semi-automatic fire, and some fire in three-shot bursts.

Non-military versions of these rifles fire only *semi-automatically*, meaning that the trigger has to be pulled separately for each shot.

And then there are light, medium and heavy machine guns, which are increasingly more powerful and are operated by a crew of two or more soldiers. Medium and heavy machine guns are usually mounted in aircraft or boats or on trucks or armored vehicles.

PARTS OF A BOLT-ACTION RIFLE

Rifles, shotguns and handguns have many similar parts. Shown here are the parts of a commonly used rifle—the bolt-action.

Front Sight

Barrel

Muzzle

Chamber

Bolt Action

Rear Sight

Sling Swivel

Bolt Handle

Forend

Magazine

Comb

Trigger

Trigger Guard

Grip

Stock

Sling Swivel

Butt

Buttpad

GLOSSARY

Action—the machinery of a gun that loads and fires the ammunition and then ejects the empty case.

Action body—the housing for the action, also called the receiver.

Assault rifle—a medium-weight military rifle that can be fired continuously as a machine gun, as well as semi-automatically, one round at a time.

Assault weapon—a political term: An "assault weapon" may look like an assault rifle, but it does not function like one; as defined by law in some states, most assault weapons are semi-automatics.

Barrel—the long tube through which a bullet or shot charge is fired.

Blunderbuss—a short-barreled muzzleloading smoothbore gun with a flared muzzle that is loaded with heavy balls and meant for close combat; forerunner of the riot gun.

Bolt—the part of a gun's action that locks the cartridge into the chamber for firing.

Bore—the inside of the barrel.

Breech—the end of the barrel attached to the receiver, or action body, where the chamber is.

Breechloader—a firearm that is loaded from the breech, or the end of the barrel near the shooter. Successful breechloaders had to wait until one-piece metallic cartridges were perfected, around 1860. Breechloaders can be loaded and fired much faster than muzzleloaders.

Butt or **buttstock**—the part of a long gun (a shotgun or rifle) that fits against the shooter's shoulder.

Carbine—a compact, short-barreled rifle.

Centerfire—a cartridge with a separate primer in the center of the base of the case. These cases can be reloaded and reused.

Chamber—the first part of the barrel, where the cartridge fits.

Chamber pressure—a measure of the explosive energy of a cartridge. It's the pressure in pounds per square inch that the barrel, chamber and bolt have to withstand when the cartridge is fired.

Choke—in shotgun barrels, the constriction of the bore near the muzzle that helps control the spread of the shot pellets in flight.

Clip—a strip of metal that holds several cartridges so that they can be loaded into a magazine or, in a revolver, the cylinder.

Cylinder—see "revolver."

Damascus steel—strips of iron and steel heated and hammered together in a forge and then wound in a spiral around a long rod, or mandrel, to make a gun barrel. Damascus barrels faded away around 1910.

Steve Helsley

The many alternating spiral layers of forged metal give Damascus steel its unusual look. When steel-making and machining became cheaper, Damascus faded away. Today high-quality Damascus is prized. The action of this Sauer shotgun was engraved to complement the pattern on the barrels.

Double action—a revolver with a hammer that can be cocked and fired with one (long) pull of the trigger. See "single action" too.

Double rifle—a rifle with two barrels, either side by side or one atop the other.

Drilling—a gun with three barrels, usually two shotgun barrels side by side on top and one rifle barrel underneath.

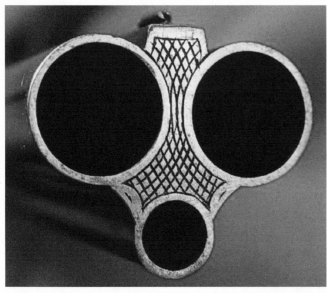

Three-barreled break-action guns called Drillings are popular in Germany. With shotgun and rifle barrels, the hunter is prepared for everything from birds to big game. *Dreiling* means triplet in German.

Dry-firing—working the action and pulling the trigger with no ammunition in the gun or with snap caps (dummy cartridges) in place of live ammunition.

Factory load—ammunition that can be bought over the counter in a store.

Flash hider—a cone-shaped device on a military rifle meant to cover up the muzzle flash of firing in the dark in order to keep the shooter from being blinded.

Flintlock—a muzzleloading gun whose powder charge is fired by sparks created by a piece of flint dragged across a steel "frizzen."

Full-automatic—a machine gun.

Hair trigger—a trigger that fires the gun with very little finger pressure. Dueling pistols often had hair triggers; now they're used on target rifles and handguns. A hair trigger is sometimes confused with a set trigger.

Iron sights—also called open sights; that is, not telescopic, optical or electronic. (They haven't actually been made of iron for more than a century.)

Kentucky rifle—a light, long-barreled, full-stocked smallbore (.32 to .50 caliber) flintlock from the 1700s when Kentucky was the frontier, where civilization ended and the wilderness began. Kentucky rifles were actually made by German gunsmiths who settled in Pennsylvania. They were beautifully built and highly accurate. America's reputation as a "land of riflemen" began with the Kentucky/Pennsylvania rifle.

A flintlock "Kentucky" rifle made by Mathias Miller of Pennsylvania around 1780. America's reputation as a "land of riflemen" began with these rifles, which helped win the American Revolution.

Lockwork—the part of the action that fires the cartridge; includes the hammer, spring and firing pin.

Machine gun—a gun that keeps firing as long as its trigger is held back (and ammunition is available).

Magazine—a container that holds the ammunition in a repeating gun. It can be a tube under the barrel or a rectangular box that fits into the action.

Magnum—a more powerful version of a cartridge; usually not interchangeable in the same gun.

Metallic cartridge—a one-piece round with its bullet and powder contained in a metal (usually brass or steel) case, or shell.

Musket—a long-barreled military shoulder gun. At first, a musket was a smoothbore muzzleloader. The word "musket" was still used in the early 1900s, even after the military switched to breechloading rifles, but then it became obsolete.

Muzzle—the end of the barrel from which the bullet or shot exits.

Muzzle brake—holes or slots at the muzzle of a gun barrel that bleed off or redirect some of the powder gas to reduce recoil. Some muzzle brakes are machined right into the barrel; others are attached to it.

These backswept channels in the Barrett rifle's muzzle brake help tame the recoil of the .50 BMG cartridge by bleeding off and redirecting some of the combustion gas.

Muzzleloader—a firearm that's not a breechloader; its powder and ball or shot have to be rammed down the barrel from the muzzle with wads to hold them in place. Before about 1850 nearly all firearms—handguns, rifles, shotguns, cannons—were muzzleloaders.

Pennsylvania rifle—see "Kentucky rifle."

Percussion lock—a type of ignition system for muzzleloading guns that uses a metallic or paper primer held where the hammer can hit it.

Pistol—a semi-automatic or single-shot handgun.

Plinking—shooting for fun at improvised targets, almost always with a .22.

Point-blank range—a distance at which the bullet has not yet dropped significantly.

Primer—the part of a cartridge that is struck by the firing pin to ignite the gunpowder.

Receiver—the housing for the action, also called the action body.

Recoil pad—a section of soft material at the end of a gun's buttstock that absorbs some of the recoil.

Revolver—a handgun with a cylinder-shaped magazine that turns (revolves) to bring each cartridge in line with the barrel for firing.

Rifling—the spiral grooves cut into the bore that grip the bullet and make it spin in flight for stability and accuracy.

Rimfire—a cartridge with its primer powder inside the rim of the case.

Riot gun—a short-barreled pump-action or semi-auto shotgun issued to police. The term isn't used any longer.

A 12-gauge Winchester Model 1897 riot gun. The US Army added bayonets and called them trench guns. This was the tactical shotgun of its day, meant to deliver a lot of firepower at close range.

Safety or **safety catch**—a mechanism that locks the trigger or action of a gun so that it can't be fired accidentally.

Self-loader—a full- or semi-automatic gun.

Semi-automatic—a firearm that reloads and cocks itself automatically and can be fired just by pressing the trigger. A machine gun is a fully automatic firearm that fires as long as the trigger is held back.

Serial number—today, by law, every gun has to be numbered by its maker to record its caliber and when and to whom it was sold. (Most makers record much more information than that.) Better-quality guns have had serial numbers for 200 years or more.

Set trigger—a trigger that can be "set" to fire at two different pull weights, for example four pounds and four ounces. The heavy setting is for normal hunting use. The light one is for extra-precise shooting from a rest at a faraway target. European hunting rifles often have set triggers.

Sights—the optical or mechanical fittings on a gun barrel that let the shooter aim precisely.

Single action—a handgun with a hammer that has to be cocked with the thumb before it can be fired with the trigger. See also "Double action."

Six-gun—a revolver with chambers for six cartridges; also known as a six-shooter.

Small arms—rifles, shotguns and handguns that are carried and used by one person.

Smoothbore—a firearm with no rifling in its barrel: a shotgun or cannon.

Snap cap—a dummy cartridge made for dry-firing.

Spitzer bullet—a modern-style bullet that comes to a point. The word comes from *Spitzgeschoss*, which is German for "pointy bullet."

Stock—the part of a long gun that holds the action and barrel and that the shooter holds. It can be wood, fiberglass, plastic or some other material. Stocks have been made of everything from rhino horn to mastodon ivory.

Submachine gun—a full-automatic weapon (machine gun) that fires a pistol cartridge.

Subsonic round—a cartridge with a reduced powder charge to drop the velocity of the bullet below the speed of sound (about 1,125 fps at sea level) to make it quieter.

Takedown—a rifle or shotgun that can be taken apart into two sections for easier transport or storage.

A takedown rifle or shotgun is one that can be taken apart for easier transport or storage. This is a Krieghoff Semprio.

Tracer round—a bullet with a tiny powder charge in its base that burns in flight so the shooter can see where it goes.

Wheelgun—another name for a revolver. (The cylinder turns like a wheel as the gun is fired.)

Wildcat—a custom-made cartridge, one that's not commercially available.

EVERYDAY SHOOTING EXPRESSIONS

Guns and shooting have played enormous roles in American history. They also have left their footprints all over our language. Here's a list of firearms-related words and phrases that almost everyone uses, even people who don't know where they came from.

All up in arms—outraged, excited; from a police, militia or other first-response unit grabbing its guns to answer an alarm.

Big gun—an important person.

Big shot—another important person.

Bite the bullet—go ahead, do it, even if it hurts. Old-time medics supposedly gave injured soldiers a bullet (more likely a piece of leather or wood) to bite down on while they were removing a bullet or hacking off an arm.

Bull's-eye!—you're right on target with what you were saying (or doing).

Bullet—used to describe anything really fast, like Japan's bullet train.

Butt (of a joke)—the butt end of a gun is where it hurts (recoil).

Caliber—meaning quality, as in "he's of the right caliber."

Cannon fodder—something or someone that's expendable or of so little value that they could be marched into the enemy cannons or could be fired out of a cannon.

Cocked and locked—all set, good to go, ready to rock and roll.

Dodge a bullet—escape the consequences.

Drop the hammer—go ahead, do it; fire!

Firing a broadside—giving it all you've got. Battleships that shot every gun on one side of the ship at an enemy fired a broadside.

Firing a shot across the bow—traditionally, a military vessel fires a round from a deck gun into the water by the bow of a ship they're trying to stop; this indicates that the next one won't miss. Used generally to mean any threatening or confrontational warning.

Flash in the pan—a minor event that comes and goes quickly, like the flash of priming powder in a flintlock pan.

Full bore—using all the power available, like a cartridge loaded full of gunpowder.

Give 'em both barrels—let 'em have it!

Going great guns—furious activity, like a warship firing all of its great guns in broadsides.

Going off half-cocked—doing something before you're completely ready, as in dropping the hammer on a gun before it's fully cocked.

Gun-shy—afraid of the recoil or noise of a shot; used to describe anyone who's nervous about repeating something that caused a problem before. ("He broke his leg, so he's gun-shy about skiing again.")

Hang fire—a shot that hasn't gone off even though the trigger was pulled is "hanging fire"; so it means an unexpected delay.

He can't hit the broad side of a barn—he's incompetent.

He's gunning for you—look out, someone's after you.

He has a hair trigger—he's short-tempered; could go off half-cocked.

He has you in his sights—he's coming after you; look out!

Hired gun—an assassin or a mercenary soldier; generally anyone brought in to do an unpleasant or difficult job.

Hit or miss—maybe it'll work and maybe it won't; erratic.

Hoist with his own petard—he's the victim of his own attempt to harm somebody else. "Petard" is a French word for a type of explosive.

Hotter than a $2 pistol—even a long time ago, $2 was very little for a pistol, but sometimes a pistol had to be gotten rid of quickly and was sold cheap. Used to describe something dodgy or of questionable background.

In the crosshairs—under close scrutiny, as though being watched through a riflescope.

The whole shootin' match—everything; the whole banana, enchilada, etc.

Jump the gun—start too early; like going off half-cocked.

Just a wild shot—a poor attempt; a shot in the dark.

Keep your powder dry—stay alert, be prepared; from the muzzleloading days when wet powder or primer meant a misfire.

Kentucky windage—adjusting to an unfamiliar situation; a guesstimate. Windage is how far a bullet is blown off course by the wind, and Kentucky windage was an unscientific guess about where to aim to compensate. Probably linked to the frontiersmen who used Kentucky rifles.

Loaded for bear—prepared for the worst; or really angry and looking for revenge.

Lock and load—get ready! Once you've done this, you're "cocked and locked."

Lock, stock and barrel—everything; the whole shootin' match.

Long shot—a difficult, possibly risky attempt that's unlikely to succeed.

Machine-gun speech—talkingwaytoofast.

On the right trajectory—heading in the correct direction, like a well-aimed bullet.

On target—absolutely right; bull's-eye!

Parting shot—the last word. Retreating troops fired a parting shot and left the scene.

Point-blank—at short range, used to mean blunt, or in your face. "I asked her point-blank why . . . ."

Potshot—an easy score or an unfair comment. From "shooting for the pot"—hunting up any animal for food as opposed to a challenging trophy.

A powder-keg situation—something that could blow up or go wrong any minute. When cannons were muzzleloaders, gunpowder was kept in kegs that could be blown up accidentally by sparks or even static electricity.

Quick on the draw—fast-reacting; almost the same as going off half-cocked. It comes from Western-style fast-draw handgun shooting.

Quick on the trigger—same as above.

Ramrod straight—usually used to describe a soldier's position at attention. A ramrod is used to push a bullet down a muzzleloader's barrel. Sometimes "ramrod stiff."

Riding shotgun—stagecoach guards in the old West were armed with double-barreled shotguns and sat next to the driver, so this means either sitting in the front passenger seat in a car or riding along as protection.

Right on target—absolutely correct; bull's-eye!

Shoot from the hip—instead of aiming with the sights, so it means to act quickly without preparing.

Shoot first, ask questions later—act too quickly.

Shoot off your mouth—talk foolishly or carelessly.

Shoot your wad—give it all you've got.

Shooting blanks—used to describe a male that's sterile.

Shot in the dark—a good-faith attempt that might or might not work.

Shotgun approach—trying everything possible; like spraying shot pellets all over a target.

Shotgun wedding—a forced or hurried wedding where the bride is pregnant and her father is supposedly holding a shotgun on the groom to make him marry her.

Smoking gun—evidence; a strong clue or hint, like a gun that's still smoking left at the scene of a crime.

Stick to your guns!—don't give up.

Straight shooter—a trustworthy, honest, reliable person.

Take a shot!—give it a try!

Trigger-happy—inclined to act too quickly, to shoot first and ask questions later.

Under the gun—under a lot of pressure to act, as though someone's forcing you to do something at the point of a gun.

Zero in—take careful aim, or close in on something. Zeroing-in your sights means adjusting them for zero error so the gun shoots accurately.

Zombie gun—Mossberg's lever-action .30-30 "black rifle" that mixes new and old with pure fantasy.

Making It Go *BOOM!*

A Short History of Firearms & Ammunition

For more than 500 years, black powder and lead balls were the standard diet of firearms. Through all of those centuries the quality of gunpowder improved and the round balls eventually became conical bullets, but the biggest changes were in how the powder was ignited and the shot was fired. The earliest "hand gonnes" (portable firearms) had no moving parts, or sights or shoulder stocks. They were basically small cannons—crude gun barrels loaded from the muzzle and either mounted on a pole or rested on a support. The gunner held a burning stick or something similar to a small hole in the barrel to light the powder charge.

Early in the 15th Century (1400s) came the first advancements in ignition. For the next 400 years, until the percussion cap was invented, every gun barrel had a "pan," which was a small cup attached alongside the barrel at the breech end to hold a bit of priming powder. A tiny hole in the barrel wall led from the pan to the chamber inside. Every gun also had some sort of mechanism called

A "hand gonne" was a smaller version of this—and this was a portable version of a cannon. The painting is from 1405; the downsizing continued until we had muskets and handguns.

a "lock" that set off the priming powder. The flash traveled through the hole and lit the main charge in the chamber.

EARLY GUNS: THE MATCHLOCK

An English royal .60-caliber matchlock. A clamp on the end of the curved arm (the serpentine) held the "match," which was a piece of smoldering rope. Pulling the trigger (that bent piece of wire underneath) released the serpentine to snap down into the pan, where the match lit the priming powder—most of the time. (Here the match cord is missing, and the serpentine is resting in the pan.) The matchlock was the first portable gun with a trigger and a stock, which helped aim and control the recoil.

The first gun with a priming pan and an action was the matchlock. It had a length of thick cord, the match, clamped in a pivoting S-shaped arm called a serpentine. Before the battle, the gunner lit the end of the cord—a fuse, really—that then smoldered. To fire, he pulled the trigger, which was sometimes the lower end of the serpentine, which pivoted the burning matchcord into the priming powder in the pan. A trigger and a stock allowed aiming and a steadier, two-hand grip on the gun. The matchcord was soaked in saltpeter, so when it dried it would burn evenly and slowly.

Some units of the Chinese army were still using matchlocks (as well as bows and arrows and spears) in the early 1900s, but the next step ahead in technology came around 1500 in Italy.

EARLY GUNS: THE WHEELLOCK

The wheellock's inventor was none other than the brilliant artist, engineer and scientist Leonardo da Vinci. Since it used friction to generate heat, the wheellock was the first true mechanical gun lock. It had a small steel wheel powered by a hairspring, and next to it was a pivoting arm (the "dog") that held a piece of iron pyrite for sparking. The shooter had to wind the spring with a special key before he put priming powder in the pan. Pulling the trigger released the wheel to spin and pressed the pyrite against it. Like a cigarette lighter, this made a shower of sparks that dropped into the pan to set off the charge—most of the time, anyway. It took the skills of both a watchmaker and a gunmaker to build a wheellock, so it was too expensive for armies. Kings and princes and dukes and that sort ordered them. Since they could be fired with just one hand, the first pistols were wheellocks.

A wheellock with two locks on the same barrel. The shooter loaded two charges, one behind the other, and then fired the front one first (or tried to, hoping that both didn't go off together). Under each round cover is a steel wheel; the two arms, the "dogs," held chunks of a mineral called iron pyrite. After loading the gun, the shooter used a key to wind a spring on each wheel. Pulling the trigger released the wheel, so it could spin, and let the dog snap down onto it. The friction of the pyrite against the edge of the spinning wheel created sparks, which fell into the pan, inside, and lit the powder.

Tower of London Collection; George Swenson

EARLY GUNS: THE FLINTLOCK

Fast-forward another hundred years to the end of the 16th Century: Gunmakers in Holland invented the snaphance (pronounced "snap-hantz"), a simpler and more reliable lock that didn't need a wheel. It had a hammer, called the cock, that held a piece of flint. The gunner thumbed back the hammer against a spring to "cock" it. When he released the hammer by squeezing the trigger, the spring snapped it down onto a piece of steel called the frizzen. Once again sparks were created that set off the priming charge.

Meanwhile, in Spain, gunmakers came up with a slightly different form of snaplock called a miquelet ("mick-elet"). Like the snaphance, it was much cheaper to make than a wheellock, but it was still too expensive to supply to ordinary soldiers. So the matchlock stayed in service for a few more years. (As did the longbow, which was a lot faster and more accurate.)

The snaphance and the miquelet both had flaws, but they were soon fixed—this time by French gunmakers, who began to perfect the flintlock early in the 17th Century. As you might guess, the flintlock also struck flint against steel to produce sparks. A well-made flintlock proved to be very reliable. The first troops to be armed with true flintlocks were five regiments of King Louis XIV's army of France in the middle 1600s. The US Army used flintlocks into the 1840s.

Hammer ("Cock") · Flint (Missing) · Frizzen · Flash Pan

Aquila Services Group

A flintlock. The hammer, or cock, had a piece of flint (missing) clamped into it. The curved piece on the right is the frizzen, or steel. When powder, wad and ball had been rammed down the barrel, the shooter pushed the frizzen forward (as shown) and poured priming powder into the flash pan under it. Then he pulled the frizzen back, to bring it into striking range of the flint. (This also covered the pan to shield the priming powder from wind or rain.) Thumbing the hammer all the way back against its spring "cocked" the lock. Pulling the trigger let the hammer snap forward, which dragged the flint down along the face of the frizzen, and the resulting shower of sparks fell into the flash pan, lighting the priming powder. The flame traveled through a tiny hole in the barrel and lit the main charge in the chamber. Over 200 years of fine-tuning, the flintlock became very reliable and effective.

But no matter how the priming charge in the pan was lit or how well protected it was against the elements, dampness was a real problem. Soggy powder won't ignite. What's worse, just keeping the rain off the gun wasn't enough; gunpowder attracts moisture from the air. (Wet bowstrings wouldn't pull, either. Swords and spears, however, worked fine in the rain. So did bayonets, which arrived on the battlefield around 1640.) A better ignition method was needed, and it was a scientifically minded Scottish clergyman named Alexander Forsyth who came up with it around 1805.

EARLY GUNS: PERCUSSION FIRE

Reverend Forsyth was looking for practical ways to use explosives such as fulminate of mercury (fulminate comes from the Latin word for lightning, *fulmen*). This was sometimes risky; according to family legend, one of Forsyth's experiments blew him out of his workshop. He discovered a "fulminating powder" that could be set off by whacking it with a hammer. Since he was a shooter and a hunter, Forsyth realized that this might be the better ignition method, so he designed and patented new gun locks for it that didn't required flint and steel.

Other inventors went to work with Forsyth's fulminating powder too, looking for the most convenient and reliable way to use it in a gun. The big breakthrough was the percussion cap, which appeared early in the 1800s. Several gunmakers claimed the credit, but it showed up in America and Britain at about the same time. A percussion cap is a tiny copper cup with fulminate in its base. The shooter presses it onto a nipple, where the hammer strikes it. A hole through the nipple conducts the flash down to the gunpowder in the chamber.

The percussion cap proved safe, reliable, easy to use and reasonably weatherproof. It worked equally well on rifles, shotguns and handguns, and percussion locks were robust and easy to produce. It really was a breakthrough, and percussion guns and caps are still made today.

A percussion cap on the nipple of a double-barreled shotgun made in 1848. This was the first more or less weatherproof way to fire a gun; the next step was to put the cap directly into the cartridge.

Percussion Cap

Steve Helsley

EARLY GUNS: NEEDLEFIRE & PINFIRE

fter this, advancements in guns and ammunition started coming thick and fast. Before too much longer, guns were being loaded from the breech instead of the muzzle, with one-piece rounds that had powder and ball and percussion caps built into them. At first there

The next step was pinfire cartridges. The pins stick up through notches in the ends of the barrels. The hammers drove the pins onto percussion caps, or primers, inside the cartridges. You didn't want to fall down with a dozen of these in your pocket.

A 12-gauge needlefire shot cartridge with a metal base and a thick paper case. The "needle" was a long firing pin that punctured the bottom of the case and set off a percussion cap buried in the gunpowder. The white strip is the wad that separates the powder and shot.

were two kinds of these cartridges, called needlefire and pinfire. Needlefire ammunition came in paper cases and turned out to be a technological dead-end. Pinfire cartridges had metal cases or

just bases, and these evolved into shell cases with primers in their bases.

Then in the 1850s and '60s gunmakers in America, Britain and France introduced cartridges in metal cases with percussion caps set into their bases. It was all coming together, and finally two army officers, one British and the other American, brought the primer to its modern centerfire forms. (Centerfire, as opposed to rimfire, because the primers are set into the centers of the shell bases.)

MODERN GUNS: PRIMERS & METALLIC CARTRIDGES

ol. Edward Boxer was an ammunition designer and the superintendent of the military arsenal at Woolwich, in London. The primer that bears his name is a little disk that contains an

anvil and *explosive compound.* This is pressed into a pocket in the bottom of the shell case. The firing pin detonates the primer by hammering the compound against the anvil, and the flame reaches the powder charge through a hole in the bottom center of the case.

Gen. Hiram Berdan set up the famous Union Army sharpshooter regiments in the American Civil War. Along with being a marksman, he was also a firearms and ammunition inventor. His primer (Patent No. 53,388 of 1866) was a little different from Boxer's: The anvil is part of the shell case, not the primer, and there are two small flash holes leading to the gunpowder.

Left: Gen. Berdan's primer on its cartridge case, which has two flash holes on either side of the anvil pin. Right: the Boxer primer, which has its anvil built in and is pressed into a cartridge case that has just one hole. Both kinds are still used, but the Boxer is much easier to reload.

Ironically, since the English Boxer primer is easier to remove and replace, it's most used in the United States, where many shooters reload their own ammo. And the American Berdan primer is the standard in European and other countries, where shooters usually don't reload their cases.

Just so you know, there are two primer sizes: large and small rifle, and large and small pistol. Also, modern priming compound is more "gun-friendly" than what Boxer and Berdan had to work with in the 1870s. The mercury fulminate and potassium chlorate (salt) in their primers weaken shell cases and rust gun barrels. These chemicals were replaced in commercial American ammunition by 1930, but some military primers were made with potassium chlorate until the late 1950s. A lot of foreign ammunition, especially military surplus, still has "salted" primers too. This type of ammunition shoots fine, but the gun barrel must be cleaned afterward.

What you've just read is hardly the whole story of how gunpowder was exploded over the centuries; we've only covered the methods that were successful enough to become popular. Here are a couple of other ways you might not have thought of: Around 1810 a gunmaker named Johannes Samuel Pauly, in Paris, detonated cartridges with compressed air. (Compressed air gets very hot.) And in the 1870s and '80s the British government gave patents to at least seven different gun locks that used electricity to fire cartridges. Electric ignition gets reinvented every few decades, but it has yet to catch on.

Rifling & the Devil

With the wheellock came rifling. Gunmakers knew it made guns more accurate, but not why. From *The Age of Firearms*: "The Bavarian necromancer [wizard] Moretius (Herman Moritz) found the explanation in 1522. A bullet fired from a rifled barrel flew true because no devil could remain astride a spinning object, as witness the rotating heavenly spheres (devil-free) and the stationary earth (devil-infested)."

MODERN GUNS: THE CARTRIDGE CASE

Today high-quality rifle and pistol cartridge cases are made of brass, while shotgun shells are plastic or coated-cardboard tubes tucked into brass bases. It seems simple, but the cartridge took as long to improve as the gun. The two had to develop more or less together over hundreds of years. A better cartridge led to a better gun, and a better case meant a better cartridge.

Then: Paper cartridges with their ends tied off. One has buckshot over the gunpowder, the other has a Minié ball; both are for muzzleloading guns and could only be loaded by hand. The shooter tore the paper with his teeth, dumped the powder down the barrel, and then pushed the bullet or shot cluster after it with the ramrod. The paper became the wad.

Already by the end of the 16th Century, cartridges had been invented for muzzleloaders: paper tubes filled with powder and ball with the ends tied off. The shooter tore open the tube with his teeth, poured the powder down the barrel and followed it with the ball; the paper served as the wad. The cartridge stayed in this basic form until the 1860s, when breechloading guns finally became practical. This was partly because cartridges had been invented; paper tubes don't work well in a breechloader (and not at all in a repeater with a mechanical action).

England's King Henry VIII (1491-1547) had a collection of guns that included early breechloaders.

One type used German *Eisenpatronen*, or iron cartridges. The iron case was loaded with powder and ball or shot. If it was for a matchlock or a wheellock, the case had a built-in pan that held the priming charge. A breechloading flintlock's Eisenpatrone had a complete pan and frizzen assembly. As you can imagine, these guns and their ammo were complicated and very expensive. And like all muzzleloaders they suffered from leaking combustion gas.

Now: Flimsy paper cartridges won't work in mechanical repeating-rifle or machine-gun actions. These are military .338 Lapua Magnum rounds with brass cases and full-metal-jacketed bullets that won't mushroom.

Muzzleloading gun barrels need a vent hole so the flash of the priming powder or percussion cap can get to the main charge. Holes go both ways, though, so some of the main explosion came out this hole too, at least with a flintlock. This robbed the gun of a little of its power, and it left ash and other junk in the vent and all over the lock. A percussion cap should seal the vent hole, but too heavy a main charge could blow back hard enough to break the hammer. Vent-hole ignition didn't work well in rainy or even just damp weather, either. Although for centuries gunmakers worked to improve gunpowder, triggers, locks, rifling, sights, bullets, barrels and gun stocks, the number-one challenge was to come up with a barrel-and-cartridge arrangement that completely sealed the breech when the gun fired.

(Hand-in-hand with this, however, was the *other* number-one problem: priming powder and ignition. We've described how the metallic primer evolved, but without a practical case to put it in, it would have been worthless.)

In addition to iron and paper, over the centuries people tried making cartridges with cardboard, varnished fabric, collodion (something like cellophane), pig gut, silk, metal foil, linen, rubber, copper and steel. The first breechloaders were generally single-shots, revolvers or break-action doubles. Shooters loaded them by hand, one cartridge at a time, so the cases could be fairly flimsy. But repeaters—guns with mechanical actions to load and eject cartridges—had to have ammunition with stronger cases that could be yanked around without coming apart.

By the 1860s and '70s, engineers had settled on brass as the ideal material for cartridge cases. Brass can be drawn (formed) into the right shapes, and it's both strong and slightly elastic. The body of the case expands when the cartridge fires, so it fills and seals the chamber snugly, and then it retracts a bit, which makes it easier to pull out the empty. Brass is even somewhat self-lubricating, so the gun's action can handle it easily. Brass cases may also be reloaded and reused.

Then Col. Boxer and Gen. Berdan came up with their metallic primers to be added to the new brass cases, and the modern cartridge with all its advantages was born. Since then ammo companies have used aluminum and plastic too, but nothing works as well as good old brass. However, to keep prices down a bit, many cartridges now come in less-expensive steel or aluminum cases, lacquered or brass-plated, for shooters who don't want to reload their ammunition.

"Enemies of the Gun Barrel"

A trigger is squeezed, primer struck. Gunpowder ignites and a projectile is launched. In that brief instant one of the most hostile places on earth is also created. Inside the gun barrel is a place that at the same time has the highest pressure, and highest temperature, and the strongest winds of anywhere on the planet. Accompanying these conditions is an atmosphere of poisonous and corrosive gasses . . . . The burning powder creates a mixture of toxic waste that includes: ammonia, water, carbon monoxide, carbon dioxide, methane, and hydrogen sulfide." —*George E. Kontis*

EVOLUTION OF THE BULLET

Lead is heavy and fairly soft and melts at relatively low temperatures. In many ways it's the perfect metal for bullets. Until about 1900, with a few exceptions it was the only metal used in bullets. And for centuries most bullets were just round lead balls that were loaded into the gun barrel from the muzzle.

The streamlined, pointed shape of the modern bullet seems obvious now, yet it was anything but. The first elongated bullets in wide use, around 1840, were shaped like eggs. Others had projections on their bases to tie a paper cartridge onto. The modern cone shape didn't become standard until the Minié bullet came along in the 1850s. (See "Gunsights: Then & Now.") This, especially in a rifled barrel, made shooting much more accurate at longer ranges. It also allowed the weight of the bullet to vary without changing the caliber (just make it longer or shorter).

However, lead bullets have limits, even if they're hardened. They can't be fired at really high speeds without being damaged, and they tend to leave residue in the barrel, which destroys accuracy. Then smokeless gunpowder arrived in the 1880s, and this was able to drive bullets much faster than black powder.

Swiss gunmakers began to experiment with bullets that were jacketed, or coated, with harder metals. But then instead of lead in the barrel, deposits from the jacket metal became the problem. People tried different types of jacketing, wrapping bullets in paper, even greasing them with tallow or beeswax. Nothing completely eliminated the fouling, but it has been much reduced.

In 1898 the French designed a revolutionary bullet called the *Balle D*. Instead of a flat nose, it had a sharp nose, which made it much more aerodynamic, and two other revolutionary features: It was solid brass, and it had a tapered "boattail" base, which reduces aerodynamic drag in flight and therefore increases the range. This turned out to be especially valuable for machine guns, which could be used for very-long-range area fire. Area fire means they were used like artillery, dropping rounds into a general area instead of sighting on specific targets. This is what made the boattail so useful for crew-served machine guns, as opposed to infantry rifles.

The world's major armies redesigned their ammunition. The United States adopted a spitzer

The evolution of the bullet. Left to right: a .60-caliber, 314-grain musket ball; a 460-grain, .58-caliber Minié ball; a 240-grain, .44-caliber pistol bullet with red wax lubricant; a copper-jacketed, soft-nosed, 170-grain .308 hunting bullet; a 300-grain hollowpoint .45-70 bullet with a flat nose that can be used in a tubular magazine; a soft-nosed 175-grain 8mm hunting bullet with a spire point; and a 232-grain jacketed 8mm French bullet with a tapered boattail base for the Hotchkiss machine gun. The last one is a 168-grain .308 hunting bullet with a polymer tip and a boattail.

(pointed) bullet in 1906, England in 1910, Russia in 1909 and Germany in 1905. For more about the differences between military and hunting ammunition, read the section about bullets in "Talking the Talk."

Warfare calls for a lot of special ammunition, such as incendiary, tracer, door-breaching or armor-piercing rounds, which fire bullets with steel, tungsten or even (in calibers 20mm and up) depleted-uranium cores. (Depleted uranium is waste fuel from nuclear reactors and is extremely dense and heavy; it not only can punch through thick steel plate, it also will explode when it does. Yes, it's radioactive too.)

Still, the shape of bullets and how they are constructed hasn't changed much in the past century. Most bullets are still mostly lead, hardened somewhat by adding tin or a metal called antimony, and have copper or nickel jackets that vary in thickness depending on the speed at which they're to be fired and the resistance of the target. For greatest "mushrooming" (expansion), a bullet will have a hollow point, which might be filled with a little plastic tip to get the aerodynamic benefits of a point.

In recent years, however, concern about the effects of lead (which is toxic) on wildlife and the environment has forced ammo companies to come up with new materials. For hunting waterfowl, in many places traditional lead shot has been replaced by pellets made of steel, bismuth or tungsten. Some rifle and pistol bullets are now (like the Balle D) solid brass, and others are made from sintered metals, which are certain metallic powders fused together under pressure and heat.

Perhaps the most "striking" new trend in bullets is the popularity of .17- and .20-caliber cartridges. These tiny bullets can be driven at very high velocities, because they're mostly jacket and very little lead, and are very accurate. (Some rounds, like these and the .308 Winchester, seem to be inherently very accurate, and we don't necessarily know exactly why.) Since they're so small, they have the added benefit of producing almost no recoil.

Guns, Guns, Guns

Basic Types of Guns & How They Work

A picture, they say, is worth a thousand words. So on the next few pages we're going to show you a common example of each of the basic types of long guns and handguns, with their actions open and closed. Study the photos and captions, and flip back to the general explanations on this page as needed. Don't forget you can also look up certain definitions in the chapter "Talking the Talk."

• Most firearms have hammers, which either hit the primer directly or drive the firing pin into the primer, to detonate the cartridge. Some guns have external, or outside, hammers, which can be cocked manually by pulling them back with your thumb. Hammerguns usually don't have safety catches; you can prevent them from firing just by de-cocking them (lowering the hammer) with your thumb.

Lever-actions, which don't all have outside hammers, generally do have safety catches.

• Guns with internal hammers are cocked mechanically when the shooter opens or closes the action. You can't see or touch these hammers, so safety catches are needed to keep the gun from going off accidentally. Different guns have their safety catches in different places, but they should be easy to reach with a finger or thumb.

• Except for revolvers, every repeating gun has a bolt (or breechblock) that the action moves forward—to push the cartridge into the chamber and lock (bolt) it in place for firing—and then pulls backward, to extract the empty case. Bolts are moved by different sorts of levers or handles, which is what gives each type of gun action its name. The bolt also contains the firing pin.

• It's fairly easy to see when bolt-actions or lever-actions are open and the guns are safe. It's harder to tell with semi-automatics and pump-action guns. You can spot an open (safe) break-action gun from a long way off, which is one reason some shooters like them.

• Break-action guns usually have two barrels, but some have three or even four— or just one. The lever or other device that unlocks these guns and allows them to "break" open may be on top of the action body, under it or alongside it.

So many different guns have been made by so many clever people over so many centuries that just about *every* idea has been tried at least once. What you'll see here are the *basic* types of firearm actions, the most successful and popular ones.

Somewhere in this collection is every imaginable type of gun—and plenty of other weapons.

SINGLE-SHOT VS. LEVER-ACTION

*T*hese actions may look similar, but they're not. Lever-actions are repeaters and can shoot faster; single-shots are considered to be more accurate.

SINGLE-SHOT

A single-shot gun has to be reloaded every time it's fired; there's no magazine for extra ammunition. There are many different single-shot actions. This Ruger No. 1 rifle is a "falling-block" type: Pushing the lever forward lets the breechblock—as this kind of bolt is called—drop down; it also extracts the empty shell and recocks the hammer. The shooter pushes a fresh cartridge into the chamber with his fingers and closes the lever, which raises the breechblock and locks it into place. Good to go!

LEVER-ACTION

This Marlin Model 336 has a tubular magazine inside the wooden forend that is loaded through the little door in the side. Pushing the lever forward after firing drives the bolt backward, which pulls the empty shell from the chamber and kicks it out through the slot on the side; it also re-cocks the hammer. A spring in the magazine tube pushes a fresh round backward into the action; closing the lever pushes the bolt forward again, which shoves the new cartridge into the chamber and locks up everything for firing.

BOLT-ACTION VS. DOUBLE RIFLE

These are shown together because rifles for dangerous game are almost always one type or the other. A big-bore bolt-action holds three or four cartridges; the double rifle holds only two, but it can fire them faster.

BOLT-ACTION

Turning the knobbed handle of this Winchester Model 70 upward unlocks the bolt so the shooter can pull it back, extracting the empty case and throwing it aside. A spring in the box magazine (inside the stock in front of the trigger) raises a fresh cartridge so it lines up with the barrel. The shooter then pushes the bolt forward, shoving the cartridge into the chamber, and then turns the bolt downward to lock the action so the rifle can be fired.

DOUBLE RIFLE

This old Holland & Holland rifle has two single-shot barrels side-by-side and a locking lever under the trigger guard. Pushing the lever to the side unlocks a hinge, which lets the barrels drop open. The shooter pulls out the empties, slides in two fresh cartridges, and then closes the barrels and swings the lever back to the trigger guard, to lock everything up. This rifle's hammers have to be cocked by hand (pulled back with your thumb), and it has two triggers, one for each barrel.

SEMI-AUTO VS. PUMPGUN

These actions look somewhat alike and operate basically the same way, but a pumpgun has to be worked ("pumped") by hand.

SEMI-AUTOMATIC

The bulge in front of the trigger guard in the bottom of this Browning semi-auto rifle is a magazine box. The shooter pulls back the cocking lever to open the bolt and let a cartridge rise up from the magazine; a spring then snaps the bolt forward, to load the round into the chamber and lock the action. When the rifle is fired, the force of the explosion shoves the bolt backward and ejects the empty. Then the return spring takes over, and the process repeats itself every time the trigger is pulled until the magazine is empty. A semi-automatic requires one trigger pull per shot; a full-automatic (machine gun) fires as long as the trigger is held back.

PUMPGUN

A pump- or slide-action gun works the same way as a semi-automatic, except that the shooter has to operate the action by hand, pulling the forend backward and then pushing it ahead again. The tube under the barrel of this Remington Model 760 rifle is *not* the magazine but rather the rail that the pump slides along. (This rifle has a box magazine.) The slot in the action body is the port through which empty shells are ejected.

SIDE-BY-SIDE VS. OVER/UNDER

Mechanically, these actions are the same. There are some subtle differences in how the two types of guns feel, however, so some shooters prefer one or the other.

SIDE-BY-SIDE

Like the Holland & Holland rifle and the over/under, this shotgun (a Boswell) has two single-shot barrels joined together and is a break-action gun. Pushing the lever (this one is on the top of the gun) to the side unlocks the hinge so the action can "break" open for reloading. Like the double rifle, it has a trigger for each barrel. The front trigger often fires the right, more-open-choked, barrel first.

OVER/UNDER

Double guns and rifles may have their barrels arranged horizontally or one above the other, like this, but the basic operating principle is the same. This Browning Citori shotgun has a single trigger, which fires first one barrel and then the other. (A "selector" on the safety lets you choose which barrel to fire first.) Unlike the double rifle but like the side-by-side shotgun pictured here, its hammers are inside the body of the gun; opening the action cocks them mechanically for firing.

REVOLVER VS. SEMI-AUTOMATIC

*T*hese are the two most common types of handguns. Revolvers are more popular for hunting, while semi-autos are generally for police, military or self-defense use.

REVOLVER

The cylinder in this Smith & Wesson Model 19 swings out to the side for loading. Most revolvers hold six rounds, so they're also called six-guns or six-shooters—or even, because the cylinders turn to line up each round with the barrel, wheelguns. If the hammer has to be cocked with the thumb, it's a single-action revolver; if pulling the trigger can both cock and release the hammer, it's a double-action. The M19 is a double-action revolver.

SEMI-AUTOMATIC

This Glock 17 pistol works the same way as the Browning semi-auto rifle, but instead of a cocking lever, it has what's called a slide, which the shooter pulls back. This lets a cartridge rise out of the magazine, which is hidden inside the grip, or handle, and on most pistols this also cocks the action. Releasing the slide lets it slam forward, loading the chamber and making the pistol ready to fire. The little "finger" on the trigger is Glock's safety catch, which the shooter has to press to release the main trigger.

Gunsights: Then & Now

Taking Aim and Hitting Your Target

Two hundred and seventy years ago, Lt. Col. Sir Andrew Agnew's advice was right on target, so to speak. He actually said (or, more likely, roared at the top of his lungs, as one did on a battlefield), "*Dinna fire till ye see the whites of their e'en!*"

That is, "Don't shoot until you see the whites of their eyes!"

Sir Andrew led the 21st Foot of the Scots Fusiliers Regiment of the British Army, and he probably gave his famous order in their own Scottish accent. Fusiliers were infantry armed with *fusils*, French for muskets, muzzleloading smoothbore guns.

After the first volley, a battlefield was covered with a dirty white fog of smoke that smelled like rotten eggs. Unless the wind blew it away, troops couldn't see to aim, and they had to breathe the nasty stuff too.

The occasion was the Battle of Dettingen, in Germany in 1743, during the War of the Austrian Succession. The 21st Foot was being charged by French "heavy horse"—armored cavalry. Sir An-

drew had devised the unusual tactic of splitting his soldiers into two columns with an open lane in between. The French galloped right into this trap, and the Fusiliers turned and caught them in a dreadful crossfire. (Cavalry of all armies were famous for their dash and bravery, not their brains.) Sir Andrew had to keep his troops from giving away the surprise by opening fire too soon, and thus his famous order about holding fire till the very last second.

Steve Helsley

The crude front sight of a big-bore French *fusil*. (The end of the ramrod, underneath, is shaped to fit over a Minié bullet without flattening its point.) Many military muskets had no rear sights at all, but they were so inaccurate that it hardly mattered.

(Supposedly, at the end of the day, when the victorious British were mopping up, King George II came by and said, "Sir Andrew, I hear the French rode through your regiment today." Agnew is said to have replied, "Aye, yer Majesty, but they dinna git oot again.")

Sir Andrew knew that his men had to make their first volley count, and that also meant letting the enemy get close. Soldiers then were not trained in marksmanship as we know it, but just to stand in rows and load, aim and fire, over and over again, in the direction of the enemy. The enemy, if they were infantry also, would do the same thing. The loser was the army that broke and ran first.

At a hundred yards, military muskets were likely to miss a target the size of a man's head and probably the man himself. Not only that, but after the first volley a battlefield was blanketed with a foul-smelling, whitish fog of blackpowder smoke. Accuracy was impossible.

Everyone knew muskets were far less accurate than muzzleloading rifles, but they cost much less and, because the balls were a sloppy fit in the barrels, they could be reloaded and fired much more quickly. Most muskets had only a front sight that was little more than a bump near the muzzle and no rear sight at all.

Just point, grit your teeth and yank the trigger. Reload and do it again. And again and again and again.

In 1814 Gen. George Hanger wrote in his book, *To All Sportsmen, Farmers, and Gamekeepers*: "A soldier's musket, if not exceedingly ill-bored and very crooked, as many are, will strike the figure of a man at 80 yards; it may even at a hundred; but a soldier *must be very fortunate indeed* who shall be wounded by a *common musket* at 150 yards, PROVIDED HIS ANTAGONIST AIMS AT HIM; and, as to firing at him at 200 yards with a common musket, you may just as well fire at the moon and have the same hopes of hitting your object. I do maintain, and I will prove, whenever called on, that NO MAN WAS EVER KILLED, AT TWO HUNDRED YARDS, by a common soldier's musket, BY THE PERSON WHO AIMED AT HIM."

Cutting spiral grooves, rifling, into a gun barrel to spin the ball or bullet in flight greatly improves accuracy. The notion of rifling was understood, although the technology was still crude, by the end of the 16th Century. From then on, both front and rear sights were installed on rifles. Two sights let the shooter line up his barrel just so, for aiming. But, with a few exceptions, it wasn't until the mid-1800s that American soldiers had rifles instead of muskets.

Around 1856, a Frenchman named Claude Étienne Minié got his name on a projectile that changed the way wars would be fought. It was a true bullet, conical in shape, but its base was hollowed out. It could be rammed down a gun barrel easily because it didn't fit too tightly in the bore; yet the hollow base made the soft lead expand when the bullet was fired, to grip the rifling. It proved accurate

A highly accurate 1863 Sharps buffalo rifle (converted from a percussion carbine) with an aperture sight that could be adjusted precisely up and down for distance and also moved sideways to make up for crosswinds that might blow the bullet off-target.

Steve Helsley

out to 500 yards. To take advantage of this, more sophisticated sights were installed on infantry rifles.

(In Europe Minié is pronounced *min-yea*. Americans, however, say *minnie*. Many modern muzzleloader shooters still use "minnie balls.")

Target rifles were changing too. As interest in long-range competition—matches were shot out to 1,100 yards—grew, rear sights evolved quickly. Traditional sights were some sort of small pyramid shape at the muzzle and a crude vee at the rear of the barrel a few inches in front of the aiming eye. As the bullets, wads, powder, barrels and rifling for target shooting got more and more sophisticated, the rear sight was moved farther and farther back— from the barrel to the receiver and then behind the action, just an inch or so in front of the eye. (The farther apart the front and rear sights, the more precise the aim can be.) The sight itself became a disk with a fine hole (known as an aperture or peep) centered in it that could move up and down on a calibrated frame called a vernier. This was capable of very precise adjustment for elevation, to compensate for the drop of the bullet at long ranges.

Target rifles also got precision front sights that could be adjusted sideways, to move the impact of the bullet right or left. This would compensate for a steady wind pushing the bullet aside.

Rear sights got most of the attention since that's where the shooter's eye is, but one of the challenges of shooting open sights is the size of the front sight. At long range, the dot on a front sight covers up a lot of the target, which makes precise shooting difficult, but making the sight dot smaller makes it harder to see. This is another area where lots of shooting experience makes all the difference.

Military rifles stayed with barrel-mounted rear sights until World War I (1914-1918), when Britain and the United States adopted versions of the same bolt-action rifle with an aperture (peep) sight on its receiver. From then on both countries, and many others, put peep sights on military rifles. (The aperture in these sights, the aiming hole, was not as small as the one on a target sight.) It was thought that a soldier could get his "sight picture" more quickly than with the traditional barrel-mounted vee sight. That is, it was faster on target.

Gunsights with glass lenses go back at least as far as 17th Century Germany. Telescopic sights, which magnify the target, became available in the US in the 1840s. They were used by snipers on both sides in the American Civil War (1861-1865), but they were too cumbersome and fragile for general combat duty. That began to change only in the 1970s, when Britain put an optical sight on its main battle rifle, the L1A1. Now it's common to see things like the ACOG, the Advanced Combat Optical Gunsight, on American military rifles too.

An Advanced Combat Optical Gunsight, which not only magnifies the target but also draws the shooter's eye to it quickly. The sight proved so valuable in Iraq that the Marines decided that "every rifle and every carbine in the Marine Corps inventory will have an ACOG optic."

After World War II (1939-1945), "scopes" surged in popularity for target shooting and for hunting. The diameter of scope tubes was standardized, along with how they are mounted on rifles and handguns, and since then scopes have been improved in about every imaginable way. Scopes are easier to use than open "iron" sights and, naturally, they are a tremendous help to shooters with vision problems. In addition to making the target look a lot closer, they're now available with built-in features that were just science fiction a generation ago: laser

A front sight for long-range shooting matches. The bead, inside the hood, could be changed for different targets; the bubble level was to keep the rifle from canting to one side or the other, which would throw the bullet off; and the shooter could adjust the bead horizontally to compensate for wind. These sights were too complicated for hunting, warfare and even sniping.

rangefinders, night-vision capability, reticles (crosshairs) that light up, even digital cameras. And now there are the so-called red-dots: optical sights that create a lighted red dot in the center of the tube. The shooter simply puts the dot on the target and fires. Some red-dot sights magnify, many do not. Some rely on battery power; some use sunlight to make the dot glow. There are green ones, too, and triangles instead of dots.

Battery-powered laser sights are something different again. They project their aiming dot—it's the end of the laser beam—right onto the target.

Modern TRUGLO handgun sights with glow-in-the-dark Tritium dots that are visible even at night. Line up the front bead between the two dots on the rear sight and squeeze. These can be put on many pistols.

But their range is limited, so they're useful only for close-in shooting.

Over the past 150 years, iron sights have not changed as much as optical sights have. Match-grade aperture sights are now fabricated on computer-controlled machinery and are the most precise of their type ever made, but a target shooter from the Leech Cup match at Creedmoor in 1874 (see "Competition") would recognize them instantly and know how to use them. They are still found on target rifles used at 1,000 yards, and they are also on super-accurate pellet guns used at 10.9 yards—that's 10 meters, the distance at which Olympic air rifle and air pistol competition is shot.

A Burris scope with a built-in battery-powered rangefinder that measures distance precisely with a laser beam. A bullet drops as it leaves the barrel, so you can't count on hitting a target if you don't know how far away it is. Even if they have rangefinders, shooters should learn to gauge distance by eye.

ARE YOU A MARKSMAN?

Today, when almost everyone shoots rifles with scopes that make the target look closer (and sometimes even give you the range, so you know how to aim to compensate), it's easy to forget how accurate an expert can be without them. Later on we'll tell you about Billy Dixon and his true shot at the Battle of Adobe Walls. Dixon was an Indian fighter, buffalo hunter and cavalry scout—a plainsman who pretty much lived with a rifle in his hands. He had learned how to take into account distance, crosswinds, heat mirages, the size of his front sight bead and so on in his aiming. His famous shot was so unusual that it's still remembered today, but by about 1860 marksmen in America and Europe were competing in long-range shooting matches at distances of up to 1,100 yards.

Highly accurate muzzleloading Whitworth rifles with iron sights, for quick shooting, on top of their barrels and scopes mounted alongside the barrels for more precise aiming. These rifles were made in England but used by Confederate snipers during the American Civil War.

George Swenson

During the American Civil War Confederate marksmen armed with super-accurate British Whitworth rifles that had been smuggled past the Union blockade reportedly killed a few Union officers at long range, but at least some of these rifles had scopes on them. One of the most famous shots of that time was made on May 9, 1864, when Sgt. Grace of the 4th Georgia Infantry killed Union Gen. John Sedgwick at a distance that was reported to be anywhere from 800 to 1,000 yards.

On the other side of the war, to qualify as one of Gen. Hiram Berdan's Union Army sharpshooters, a man had to be able to put 10 consecutive shots "from the shoulder"—not firing off a fixed support—into a 10-inch circle at 200 yards with iron sights. Next time you're out with your .22 rifle, or even a BB gun, see if you can safely sight on something that far away (with your gun unloaded). If you have to pace off the distance, figure one giant step is a yard. Impressive, isn't it? Some of Berdan's men used scopes, but the point is that they already were deadly without them.

Iron, optical and electronic sights all have their advantages and disadvantages, but none of them can make up for poor shooting. It's a good idea to learn the basics with iron sights, and then those skills will transfer to scopes and dots. It's like learning to drive a car with a manual transmission and a clutch. You may never have to do it again, but it's nice to know how—and it makes you a better driver, and shooter.

SNIPERS: 1.3 SHOTS, ONE KILL

The modern sniper is a marvel. Every piece of his gear seems to have been built for just one purpose, and he is a highly trained specialist. A sniper team—one shooter, one or more spotters and sometimes, especially in city fighting, a protective platoon—can pin down an entire enemy unit or throw a curtain of deadly accurate covering fire over a friendly unit.

Everyone's got the sniper bug now, and the word gets tossed around like "assault rifle." It's applied to almost any kind of unseen shooter, including a juvenile delinquent with a BB gun on a freeway overpass. And then there are terms like "counter-sniper" and "designated marksman." We'll get back to them. Meanwhile, let's stick with this definition: A sniper is a soldier or a police officer who specializes in shooting from a concealed position and over longer ranges than normal, often with a specially designed or modified rifle. A sniper is skilled in marksmanship, camouflage and fieldcraft. Military snipers also have to be experts in infiltration, reconnaissance and observation.

Americans earned a reputation as sharpshooters by picking off "redcoats," especially officers, under conditions that astonished the British. But these weren't true snipers; they were woodsmen with accurate, long-barreled hunting rifles. Ordinary infantry muskets firing round balls were hardly long-range weapons. It wasn't until the 1850s, when conical bullets and rifled barrels became standard, that regular soldiers had guns capable of real accuracy. The telescopic sight appeared about then too. Sniping with scope-equipped rifles may have begun in the Crimean War (1853-1856) in Europe. Ten years later, as mentioned, both sides in the American Civil War had snipers equipped with scoped rifles.

By the 1890s, the range of army rifles—now bolt-action repeaters—had once again greatly increased, thanks to smokeless powder and jacketed, pointed bullets. Then, in late 1899, war broke out in South Africa, where British troops faced rebellious settlers called Boers. Like the American colonists of more than a century earlier, the Boers were mostly farmers,

During WWI not only was the German Model 98 Mauser sniper rifle more effective than what the Allied forces had, but also German snipers started out better trained.

Snipers have become the "tip of the spear" in today's desert and urban warfare, but for most of our fighting history snipers got very little official attention. During the Revolutionary War, some

and a lot of them were experienced hunters and shooters. In response, Lord Lovat, the chief of Scotland's Clan Fraser, raised companies of what he called Scouts, men who were also hunters and riflemen. They brought their ghillie suits, the bushy camouflage clothing they used for hunting in the brush and heather at home in the Scottish Highlands. This was the first known military use of the ghillie suit.

The British won, but at great cost: 20,000 killed, 22,000 wounded and, because of how they treated Boer prisoners, a huge blow to their international respect. The Lovat Scouts went on to become the British Army's first true sniper unit.

National Firearms Museum

A WWI Springfield Model 1903 sniper rifle with a crude Warner & Swasey scope and a 20-round magazine borrowed from a BAR (Browning Automatic Rifle).

Back home in Europe, the Great War broke out just a few years later, in 1914. It's said that "Generals always fight the previous war," and this was especially true then, in what later was called World War I. Allied military leaders were confused by all sorts of new challenges, ranging from machine guns and tanks to trench warfare, poison gas and lots of snipers. Their enemies, the Germans, were much better prepared for the war. They had, for example, built 15,000 scope-sighted Mauser bolt-action rifles and requisitioned many more hunting rifles, also with scopes, and trained soldiers to use them. These German snipers dominated the trenches in the early part of the war. England and later the United States, when it joined the war, had to cobble together sniper rifles and training programs as best they could. (The Lovat Scouts were experienced hunters who were recruited into the army but still had to be trained as snipers.)

Wars eventually end, and WWI was predicted to be the last big one, "the war to end all wars." Just as after the Revolu-

The White Death of WWII, Simo Häyhä, with his Finnish M28 Mosin rifle. Häyhä was wounded on March 6, 1940, which means he racked up his incredible body count in less than a year. He recovered and lived a quiet life until dying in 2002.

tion and the Civil War, national defense became low priorities in America. And so, when the next global conflict began—World War II this time, in 1939—once again the United States had no sniper program or sniper rifle. The US Marine Corps picked the Model 1903A1 Springfield with an 8-power Unertl scope; the US Army chose a different version of the Springfield as its sniper rifle and put ordinary Weaver and Lyman hunting scopes on them. By the end of the war, the new semi-automatic M1 Garand rifle was also being fitted with scopes. But low-power civilian sights weren't right for long-range shooting.

In the early days of WWII, the Russian Red Army invaded Finland in what was called the Winter War. The Russians outnumbered the Finns by at least three to one, but the Finns resisted furiously. (A joke went around Finland: "We are so few and they are so many. How will we bury them all?") One Finnish sniper, Simo Häyhä, nicknamed "White Death," killed 505 Russian soldiers with his rifle. (He killed another 200 enemies at close range with a submachine gun.) Camouflaged in white winter gear, Häyhä used a basic service rifle, without a scope, and tricks like putting snow in his mouth so that his breath wouldn't give away his position.

Häyhä was a perfect example of a sniper. Shooting skill is about 20 percent of what it takes, with the rest being patience, discipline, observation and the ability to use cover and estimate range and wind.

Only five years after World War II ended, Communist North Korea invaded democratic South Korea in 1950. The US military and its allies went to the rescue. The landscape sometimes let snipers see their enemy at very long distances, so it was here that the fearsome .50 BMG round was used for sniping for the first time. The "rifles" were Browning M2 heavy machine guns fitted with Unertl 8X scopes and set up for single fire.

In the early 1960s, the United States found itself fighting Communist forces in Asia again, this time in Vietnam. The US Army had set up a sniper school in 1955, after Korea, but the program had to be reinvented almost completely because Vietnam's jungles were so different from Korea's mountains. (Remember what we said about armies always being prepared for the previous war?) The Marines handed the job to Capt. Jim Land. The Corps already had a supply of Winchester Model 70 hunting rifles

During the Vietnam War, the US Marines began to get serious about their sniper-training program. This is Sgt. Carlos Hathcock shooting a Winchester M70 with a heavy target barrel and a high-powered (for the time) scope. The North Vietnamese Army called him "White Feather" and promised $30,000 to anyone who killed him, but he survived the war.

with the 8X Unertl scopes that were being used as match rifles, but he started the process that finally led to the 7.62x51mm M40 sniper rifle, built on a Remington Model 700 action.

Some of this gear couldn't stand the rain and heat of the jungle, and many different rifles, cartridges and scopes were tested. While their equipment could have been better, two Marine snipers, Carlos Hathcock and Chuck Mahwhinney, became famous for their performance in Vietnam. Hathcock's book *Marine Sniper: 93 Confirmed Kills* is a good read for anyone who wants to understand the challenges they faced.

One of the problems with snipers is that military commanders traditionally didn't know what to do with them. Detailed planning and logistics are necessary for units of troops—not to mention coordinating artillery, ships, aircraft or armor—but not for a few lone-wolf dudes who prowl through the bush with rifles and face paint. Yet their spectacular results made snipers impossible for the brass to ignore. According to the Department of Defense, it took an average of *50,000* rounds to kill one enemy soldier in Vietnam in battle. American snipers, on the other hand, killed an enemy with every 1.3 rounds they fired. That amounted to $23,000 per kill for the average infantryman versus 17¢ for the sniper.

After Vietnam, defense officials figured the next war would be fought with tanks against the Soviet Union in Europe, or maybe with airborne volleys of nuclear missiles. Wrong again. Instead, our military is facing (once again) "highly motivated Muslim warriors" in the deserts of Iraq and the mountains of Afghanistan. They have neither airplanes nor tanks nor formal battle units, just a strong will to fight, an endless supply of improvised explosive devices and the ability to fade into the civilian population. If this is the future, special-operations forces and especially snipers will play huge roles in wars to come.

The Secret Service has "countersnipers" who defend against all threats. Those are the shooters on top of buildings when the President makes a public appearance. They don't stalk other snipers. (The German-versus-Russian sniper duel in the movie *Enemy at the Gates* may have been made up by the Soviets to boost morale.) Carlos Hathcock did have a couple of one-on-one encounters with North Vietnamese shooters, but that was before the USMC sniper program had a plan or rules. If two snipers duel, which one is the "countersniper"? The real question is: If an enemy sniper is causing trouble in Iraq or Afghanistan, how should he be dealt with? Artillery or an air strike?

A "designated marksman" is a soldier trained to shoot at longer ranges than his squad mates and armed with a DMR (Designated Marksman Rifle),

Times, training and weapons have changed a lot. The Army rates this semi-automatic .50-caliber Barrett M107 effective at nearly twice the range (1,500 meters) of its .308 sniper rifles (800 meters). Snipers often reach much farther than that range with the .50, though. See the empty case in the air?

Dept. of Defense

which is usually capable of automatic fire. He's part of an infantry platoon, like a machine-gunner, not a single specialist.

Some police officers carry rifles in their patrol cars. The best information we can find is that these rifles are used at an average range of about 35 yards, while a police sniper's typical shot is about 70 yards—at, for example, someone who's holding a knife to a hostage's throat in a house across the street.

Civilian interest in long-range military-style shooting has grown tremendously, and along with it the market for sniper gear. Today's sniper (and sniper wanna-be) has a dizzying array of special rifles to choose from. There are bolt-action and semi-automatic "platforms" in calibers ranging

The British Army's Model L115A3 in .338 Lapua Magnum. This is the type of rifle used by Cpl. Craig Harrison to kill two enemies in Afghanistan at a range of more than a mile and a half.

from 5.56mm to .50 BMG, with finely tuned ammunition for each. The sniper also has night-vision scopes, laser rangefinders and palm computers to help determine his "firing solutions"—how to set his scope to compensate for bullet drop, wind, temperature and other variables, even the earth's rotation while the bullet is in flight.

The days of the old-fashioned .30-06 sniper rifle with a 2½X (power) Lyman Alaskan scope are long gone. Gone too are the days when snipers were treated as afterthoughts. Today they can stand off at incredible distances and launch API (Armor Piercing Incendiary) rounds from a .50-caliber Barrett M107, or coordinate with other teams to identify and take out an HVT (High Value Target).

Carlos Hathcock used fieldcraft to move through the jungle. Navy SEAL Chris Kyle is the top sniper from the Iraq and Afghanistan wars, with 150 confirmed kills. Kyle's fieldcraft didn't involve jungles; often he put himself deep into the shadows of city neighborhoods.

Kyle's longest kill was 2,100 yards with a .338 Lapua Magnum. That's 1.2 miles. Hathcock's longest in Vietnam was 2,000 yards with a .50 BMG. The combat record now belongs to Corp. Craig Harrison of England's Household Cavalry regiment. In November 2009, Harrison used a British-issue L115A3 rifle in .338 Lapua Magnum to drop two Taliban machine gunners in Helmand Province, Afghanistan, at a range of 2,707 yards—2.47 kilometers, or 1.53 miles. Incredible.

You'll Put Your Eye Out!

BB Guns, Pellet Guns, Paintball & Airsoft

Yes, you just might, if you're not careful. Put your eye out, that is—yours or more likely someone else's. Or worse. Three weeks before this was written, a boy in California died almost instantly when a pellet fired at very close range got past his ribs and went into his heart. It was an accident, but he's still dead, and his friend who was holding the air pistol will remember this awful thing for the rest of his life.

Here is the problem with guns that fire "only" BBs or pellets instead of "real bullets": It's too easy to treat them like toys. Even a small-caliber firearm (powered by gunpowder) makes a loud *crack!* when it goes off, which gets our attention and respect. A pellet gun (powered by compressed air or carbon dioxide) just goes pop! But what's important isn't the noise; it's the energy of the projectile.

A BB is a plain round ball; a pellet is cylindrical, precisely shaped for accuracy and with either a pointed or flat nose for hunting or target shooting.

Most air rifles in the United States are either .22 or .177 caliber. A .22-caliber pellet for hunting small game and shooting pests like rats typically weighs only about 15 grains (0.034 ounces, or the weight of a paper clip), but it's traveling at 600 to 850 feet per second or more when it leaves the gun. That's 410 to 580 miles per hour. Anything that moves carries energy with it, and that energy is transferred to whatever it hits. Energy comes from both mass (weight) and velocity (speed), so something light moving fast can have as much energy as something that's much heavier but traveling more slowly.

The energy of any projectile (whether it's a bullet, an arrow, a snowball or an airgun pellet) can

Modern Firepower BBs—gold-colored but hard steel. They'll ricochet like crazy off a hard surface.

Hollowpoint .177-caliber BSA pellets designed for hunting—that is, for penetration and killing.

be measured in foot-pounds. Energy can do work. One foot-pound is a measure of the energy needed to move a one-pound mass one foot. Get a one-pound can of something from the kitchen; raise it 12 inches. Nothing to it, right?

But a .22-caliber pellet at 850 feet per second creates about 22 foot-pounds of energy. Now lift a stack of 22 one-pound cans and think of that much energy being applied by a pellet instead of your hand.

Pellets fired from this Sheridan Blue Streak air rifle severely dented the steel sheet and went right through the wooden board.

A .177-caliber target pellet has less mass (usually 7 to 11 grains), but if it's fired by a similar blast of compressed air or other gas, it travels much faster—up to 1,200 fps. As a result, it delivers just about the same amount of energy.

(These velocities are measured at the gun's muzzle, the end of the barrel. As a pellet travels downrange from there, air resistance makes it steadily lose velocity and gravity pulls it toward the ground. If it hits something before then, its energy will be less than it was when it left the gun because it has slowed down. Its mass won't have changed, though.)

At point-blank range, almost any air-rifle pellet will punch through a one-inch-thick wooden board. Fired across your living room and into bare skin, it will go anywhere from four to eight inches deep in human tissue. A bone will stop it, with lots of pain— but an eye will hardly slow it down at all, and the pellet may go through the back of the eye socket and into the brain.

They're not toys. And there's a more complete explanation of energy in "Hollywood and Newton's Third Law."

HISTORIC AIR GUNS

A big-bore air rifle from the flintlock era. The ball is the compressed-air tank. The lock doesn't ignite gunpowder; the shooter thumbs back the hammer to cock the firing mechanism.

Guns powered by blasts of air instead of gunpowder are not new. The first one probably appeared in Germany around 1560. Three hundred and forty years later, in London, Sherlock Holmes narrowly missed death at the hands of an assassin armed with a near-silent air rifle. Holmes was a fictional detective, but large-caliber air rifles capable of killing humans at a distance were real.

In America the best-known historic air rifle is the Girandoni that was Lewis and Clark's "secret

weapon" on their expedition across the American wilderness from 1804 to 1806. According to the National Firearms Museum, in Fairfax, Virginia, that rifle might have been the single most important gun in our history.

An Italian named Bartolomeo Girandoni invented the air rifle that bears his name in the 1770s. It was used by the Austrian Army from 1780 until about 1815, principally against Napoleon Bonaparte's French Republican forces, which

Lewis & Clark's "secret weapon" was a Girandoni rifle. Here's one with its buttstock air tank detached. There was no flint or percussion cap, because there was no gunpowder to ignite; the shooter cocked the hammer (pulled it back till it clicked into a notch) in order to arm the air valve and set the trigger.

National Firearms Museum

were then trying to conquer all of Europe. Most firearms at that time were single-shots that had to be loaded from the muzzle by pushing gunpowder, wadding and a lead ball down the barrel with a ramrod. In favorable conditions a trained infantryman could load and fire his musket three or four times in a minute. Muskets were smoothbores—no rifling—so they were very inaccurate. They also made clouds of dirty white smoke, and the military versions recoiled horribly.

The Girandoni must have seemed miraculous by comparison. No smoke, less recoil and, thanks to its rifled barrel, impressive accuracy. Even more amazing was that it had a tubular magazine next to its barrel that could hold 20 to 30 rounds, and it could be fired as fast as the shooter could flick the loading lever, cock the hammer with his thumb and aim. It threw a heavy lead ball (.46 to .51 caliber, which is about a half-inch diameter, depending on the model) at around 800 fps—enough to kill an enemy at a hundred yards or more.

There were problems, though. The rifle's buttstock—hollow, made of metal and covered with leather—was the tank that held the compressed air. An Austrian soldier was issued three of these, which screwed onto the gun. A full load of air

could fire 30 to 40 shots before the power began to drop off noticeably. Then the empty tank had to be unscrewed and a fresh one put on. Each rifle came with a hand pump to refill the tanks, which could take an exhausting 1,500 strokes. Keeping that much pressurized air bottled up with the primitive materials of the day was difficult too, so there was a lot of leakage.

Advanced as it was in some ways, the Girandoni was too expensive and impractical to be a reliable military weapon. Technologically, it was years ahead of its time. But this didn't stop some well-to-do hunters and, in the case of Meriwether Lewis and William Clark, gentlemen explorers from making good use of it. In the journal of their trip, the air rifle is mentioned 39 times, and on the very first page of his own diary Lewis describes it as a "wonderment to the crowd."

Whenever their Corps of Discovery met an Indian band, Lewis and Clark and their officers (there were never more than 38 people in the company, including Sacajawea, the teen-age Shoshone girl who was their interpreter) dressed up in their military uniforms and put on a shooting demonstration—with the air rifle. It seems the Indians were always impressed with this powerful, accurate and rapid-firing weapon. Perhaps assuming that each of the whites had one of these deadly rifles, they let the party continue onward. Had the expedition been wiped out and the Indians seized its powder and shot, pistols, rifles, muskets, shotguns, blunderbusses and one swivel cannon, American and possibly even European history could have developed very differently.

BB Guns: 'It's a Daisy!'

By 1900, though, smokeless gunpowder and many other advancements had made firearms so much more effective that air-powered guns all but disappeared. With one exception.

In 1888 the Plymouth Iron Windmill Manufacturing Company, in Michigan, came up with a cheap air gun as a giveaway for the farmers who were its customers. It was a big hit—in the slang of those days, "a daisy." The name stuck, and within a few years the Daisy Manufacturing Company was born and windmill production stopped. Daisy BB guns spread all over the world, even to China, which for a while accounted for almost one-third of the company's overseas business.

There's a story that the Daisy's resemblance to a real rifle worried the Chinese government. The Daisy salesman offered the seat of his pants as a target to prove that the gun wasn't harmful. We don't know what the range was, but we do notice that he didn't face the gun. He probably was wearing a suit, too. Had he been bare-assed this would have been a genuine "pain in the butt."

For many shooters in America, their first gun was a Daisy. This is the classic BB gun, and it is different from a pellet gun because it fires round shot. BB (from "ball bearing") shot was originally for shotgun shells, and Daisy settled on it because it was a useful size and also cheap and plentiful. BB shot are supposed to be .180-caliber, but birdshot aren't made to the same strict size tolerances that bullets are, and variations meant they didn't always fit in an air gun. So around 1905 Daisy began to make its own BBs, carefully sized. This solved the fit problem and also gave Daisy a new product to sell.

At first BBs were soft lead coated with copper or zinc. Today, though, they're made of coated steel, which offers one big advantage and one big disadvantage.

Modern BB guns are .177-caliber smoothbores, with no rifling in the barrels. BBs themselves are only .171 to .173 inch in diameter, so a BB would just roll out of the barrel if the gun were tilted downward. Daisy solved this problem by putting a magnet in the piston that drives the BB—a magnet strong enough to hold the steel BB in place but not strong enough to hold back its launch. This magnetic feature is the advantage of steel.

The disadvantage is that steel, being much harder than lead, doesn't deform and slow down or stop when it hits a hard surface; it bounces off and keeps going. These ricochets are part of what makes even cheap, low-power, spring-air BB guns dangerous.

So they're still not toys.

The days when a kid could wander the neighborhood plinking with a BB gun (knocking down toy soldiers or protecting Mom's laundry from birds) are all but gone. But BB guns are still important when it comes to learning to shoot. A Daisy can be important in other ways too, as this note from a grownup friend about his BB gun indicates: "I've stood nose-to-nose with Cape buffalo, I've ridden a good mountain horse in the Rockies, I've dived with sharks, but I've never been as excited as I was when I opened that long, slim box on that Christmas morning 53 years ago!"

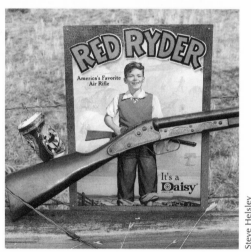

Steve Helsley

The rarest of all Daisy BB guns is this double-barreled Model 104 from the 1940s.

PELLET GUNS: SPRING-AIR, PNEUMATIC & CO₂

There are three basic kinds of air guns. The first two, spring-air and pneumatic, are powered by air compressed by the shooter. Most BB guns are spring-air, or single-stroke, types: Cocking the action compresses a spring, which when it's released (by pulling the trigger) pushes a piston into a chamber with a tiny vent at its other end, creating the blast of air that shoves another piston that shoves the BB down the barrel.

A Gamo Whisper spring-air rifle that fires .177-caliber pellets at 1,200 fps. The barrel is hinged at the end of the stock; "breaking it" opens the breech so you can load a pellet and also cocks the action.

Most lever-action air guns have springs soft enough for kids to compress, so they fire a BB at only about 275 fps. Some full-size adult spring-air guns, however, are true single-shot rifles that shoot .177 or .22 pellets at 600 fps or more. The barrels of these guns are hinged at the end of the stock, and "breaking" the barrel (cranking it downward) cocks the spring and exposes the breech so you can load a pellet into the barrel.

Benjamin's .177-caliber Model 397 pneumatic air rifle can fire pellets up to 800 fps, depending on how many times you pump the handle under the barrel.

Pneumatic air guns don't have springs. By pumping the action with a lever or handle, the shooter raises the pressure in the air cylinder inside, which powers the piston that fires the BB or pellet.

Feinwerkbau's super-sophisticated single-shot Model 800, a $3,000 Olympic-class target rifle. Its pre-filled air tank (under the barrel) fires .177-caliber pellets at 570 fps.

More pumping increases the air pressure and thus the velocity of the round.

The third kind of air gun is powered by compressed CO_2, or carbon dioxide. This saves having to pump, but it means buying the cylinders. Even the small 12-gram cylinders that fit into a pistol grip have enough charge to fire dozens of rounds, usually at velocities of 400 fps or more. If you put the gun away before using up the charge, the leftover gas eventually will leak out

Crosman's semi-automatic, 18-shot .177-caliber C11 Tactical BB pistol is good for up to 550 fps. This one has a suppressor, an accessory rail and an aiming laser. The replaceable CO_2 cartridge is in the grip.

and be wasted. This also leaves the gun able to be fired just by loading a round into it.

Some gas-powered guns—Paintball guns, for example—have large built-in cylinders that last much longer and can be refilled.

As mentioned, serious air guns pretty much disappeared early in the 1900s. But after World War II things changed again. In 1950 the National Rifle Association established a Junior Qualification Course for air rifles as a way to teach firearms safety.

In Europe, where laws about owning firearms were becoming more and more restrictive, air guns became especially popular. And then, in 1984, air guns entered Olympic competition. As a result of all of this, the velocity, accuracy and sophistication of air guns have increased tremendously. So have their prices. Daisy still sells a lot of inexpensive spring-air BB guns, but now it's also possible to spend thousands of dollars on a target rifle that will put match-grade .177 pellets into the same hole all day long at 10 meters.

They're all good. Still not toys, though.

Shooting BB Guns & Air Rifles

• **Why:** Shooting any BB gun is a great way to learn to shoot and to learn good safety habits. Regardless of what type of rifle you move on to—whether it's a Barrett .50, a Westley Richards .577 Nitro Express or a Remington .30-06—the basics are the same.

• **Where:** Your basement. The attic. A spare room. The back yard. Anywhere that you have more than 20 feet of range and a back wall that won't let BBs or pellets fly onward.

• **Aiming:** Adult pellet rifles may have fine scopes or Olympic-quality open sights, but BB guns generally have crude post-and-Vee sights. Experience will show you where your gun shoots (high, low, left, right), and then you just compensate. Shoot with both eyes open so you have a better view of the target. You'll also glimpse the BB in flight.

• **Targets:** A cardboard box stuffed with crumpled newspapers. Tape a bull's-eye or picture to the box, or hang something appropriate in front of it and use the box as a backstop.

• **Avoid:** Metal targets that make steel BBs or pellets ricochet; also things made of glass that might shatter (if they don't make the round ricochet).

• **Safety – Yours:** You don't need hearing protection with air guns, but you should wear shooting glasses in case of ricochets or if somehow your gun develops a leak that blows air or gas back into your face.

• **Safety – Theirs:** Don't shoot at your friends. Or enemies. Cats and dogs are not fair game either; want to explain to the neighbors how you blinded or killed their pet?

• **Uh-oh:** How'd that BB-size hole in the basement window get there? Good luck blaming it on your little brother; better to get out in front of this and confess *before* your parents see it and raise hell. Then they'll be impressed instead of ticked off.

• **The Bottom Line:** No air gun is a toy unless it fires NERF balls. (NERF, by the way, stands for Non-Expanding Recreational Foam.)

PAINTBALL: IS THIS THE DARK SIDE?

You're probably wondering, *What about Airsoft and Paintball? Aren't those air guns?* Yes, they are, and here you'll see why we put them in a different section.

As you know, adults have a tendency to see problems where kids don't. Sometimes this is bogus and sometimes it's a matter of opinion, but often it is the result of painful experience. So while you may think Paintball and Airsoft are fantastic because they're like stepping into a video game, this is exactly why a lot of experienced shooters worry about Paintball and Airsoft. Allow us to explain . . . .

First the background. Hard-skinned balls of wet paint to be used as markers (mostly by foresters and ranchers to identify certain trees and livestock) have been around since the 1950s. At first they contained paint, but this was replaced by dye that could be washed off. Modern paintballs are non-toxic, biodegradable, food-grade gelatin, like bath-oil beads. They are around .69 caliber, almost three-quarters of an inch in diameter, but they weigh only about one gram, or 15 grains. Regulation Paintball guns fire them at about 300 fps and, since they're large compared to a BB or a .177 or .22 pellet, they slow down quickly. A paintball bursts on impact, so it won't penetrate flesh, but it does leave a welt on bare skin and will destroy an eye.

Like pellets and BBs, paintballs are propelled by compressed air or CO_2. The guns may be pump-action types, which have to be re-cocked between shots, or self-loading semi-automatics or even fully automatic machine guns. Some Paintball guns have hoppers that hold a lot of ammunition and large gas reservoirs so shooting can go on and on. The gun barrels are generally short, and forget about precision sights or well-aimed fire. Most Paintball players rely on "spray and pray" shooting.

The Daisy company made the first paintball gun, a CO_2-powered bolt-action pistol called the

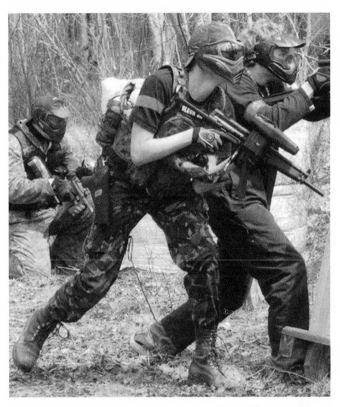

These days, Paintball is played by about 10 million people in the US alone. The trouble is that Paintball (just like Airsoft) can teach dangerous firearms handling, and the guns can be mistaken for the "real" thing.

Splotchmaker, in 1970. But this was for commercial use (those ranchers and foresters), and Paintball the game didn't arrive for another 11 years.

PAINTBALL IS BORN

To settle an argument about survival instincts—whether someone who worked in an office in the city was still as sharp a predator as someone who lived on the land and hunted—a friend of ours named Charles Gaines, a writer living in New Hampshire, organized a contest.

On June 27, 1981, he and 11 other guys walked into a hundred-acre section of woods at different points. Each of them was wearing camouflage and goggles and carrying a compass, a supply of paintballs and CO_2 cartridges, and an industrial-grade Nel-spot 007 paintball pistol. (These were actually Splotchmaker guns, made by Daisy for the Nelson Paint Company.) Each man also had a map showing four places in the woods where a dozen flags hung. The goal was to reach home base with four different flags and without having been shot by another player.

Everyone thought the game was tremendously exciting. The winner was a professional forester—the only player who never fired a shot and who was never even seen by anyone else.

As it happened, along with Gaines there were three other writers in that first game. One of them, another friend of ours named Bob Jones, wrote a story about it called "Survival" for *Sports Illustrated*. Then the other two wrote it up also, for *Time* and *Sports Afield*. Suddenly people all over the country wanted to play. Gaines and his friends cre-

ated a company called the National Survival Game, wrote a rulebook and began to sell Nel-spot guns and gear. The first commercial playing field opened in 1982, in Rochester, New York. In 1983 the first National Survival Game national championship was held, with a cash purse of $14,000.

The craze was on. Competing leagues and team play were created, the name changed to Paintball (with a capital P), and more and more companies got involved, supplying high-performance guns and all sorts of gear, from facemasks and body armor to special clothes and footwear. Paintball has become a global game, played indoors and out, informally or with referees and rules and sometimes with professional players, to capture objectives or reenact famous battles. Supposedly about 10 million people, mostly males between the ages of 12 and 24, now play Paintball just in the US.

AIRSOFT: MORE DARK SIDE?

Airsoft guns are much more sophisticated and real-looking than Paintball markers. They fire a 6mm (.236-caliber) plastic BB from a smoothbore barrel at 300 to 600 fps, depending on the type of gun and limits set by law or game rules. Airsoft began in Japan, where owning firearms is all but impossible, and then spread to Europe and the United States. Airsoft skirmishing has become a competitor to Paintball and requires the same sort of closed-off area for "combat."

There are four kinds of Airsoft guns: single-shot spring-powered types that have to be cocked manually; repeaters powered by CO_2 cartridges; guns fired by "green gas," which is basically propane with a small amount of silicone oil added for lubrication; and guns operated by built-in electric motors. The motor drives a piston that compresses air to blow the BB out of the barrel. Electric

Airsoft machine guns can fire up to 900 plastic BBs a minute.

About every type of tactical firearm—from pistols to submachine guns and assault rifles, combat shotguns, sniper rifles, even grenade launchers and heavy machine guns—is available as an Airsoft replica. (Some of these cost thousands of dollars.) You can't tell most of them from the real thing until you pick them up, and this is both their great attraction and their fatal flaw. A lot of Airsoft guns look like real guns that are illegal to own.

In the United States, Airsoft guns have high-visibility orange tips on their barrels to set them apart from firearms, but many owners remove the tips. Some European countries require Airsoft guns to be made of see-through plastic or painted in ridiculous colors for the same reason—but a few genuine firearms are also available in colors like pink. Britain has strict laws governing replica firearms that apply to many Airsoft guns. And Airsoft clubs and fields everywhere have their own rules about how to carry and handle the guns.

None of this, however, changes the fact that, to the general public, these things look frighteningly real. There have been some awful cases where police officers felt forced to shoot kids fooling around with what turned out to be Airsoft "toys." A lot of firearms experts think Airsoft is the worst of both worlds: useless as guns but so realistic that they can create very dangerous situations.

Like Paintball, Airsoft can also teach deadly firearms handing. One of the first rules of shooting is to never point a gun at something or someone you're not willing to kill. Any kid who lives in the World of Warcraft and has an Airsoft Heckler &

Koch MP-5 replica can learn everything wrong in a very short time.

Most Paintball and Airsoft players grow up, move on to other hobbies and never handle real guns. Many real shooters, on the other hand, never play these games. They're scared by them and the lessons they can teach.

If you absolutely have to have a Magpul Masada or a Barrett, wait till you can get the genuine article. And in the meantime learn how to shoot for real, well and safely. If you have fantasies about "special ops" and being a covert warrior, wait till you're old enough to enlist in the military. And then let's see if you have the right stuff.

The Echo1 USA full-size Gatling-type "Minigun" is one of those Airsoft models that look like real guns that people generally can't own. It weighs 33 pounds, fires thousands of pellets per minute and is driven by an electric motor with a separate power pack. It costs about $3,500.

Safety First

It's Easy to Be a Safe Shooter

THE 15 COMMANDMENTS OF GUN SAFETY

1. ALWAYS ASSUME THAT A GUN IS LOADED AND TREAT IT ACCORDINGLY.

2. EVERY TIME A GUN IS HANDLED FOR ANY REASON, CHECK TO SEE THAT IT IS UNLOADED. ALWAYS OPEN A GUN'S ACTION WHEN YOU PASS IT TO SOMEONE ELSE. ALWAYS OPEN A GUN'S ACTION WHEN SHOOTING IS DONE.

3. KEEP THE GUN POINTED IN THE SAFEST-POSSIBLE DIRECTION, AND ALWAYS BE AWARE OF WHERE IT'S POINTING. A SAFE DIRECTION IS ONE WHERE AN ACCIDENTAL DISCHARGE OF THE GUN WILL NOT CAUSE INJURY OR DAMAGE.

4. DON'T POINT A GUN AT ANYTHING YOU'RE NOT WILLING TO DESTROY.

5. ALWAYS KEEP YOUR FINGER OFF THE TRIGGER AND OUTSIDE THE TRIGGER GUARD UNTIL YOU'RE READY TO SHOOT.

6. KEEP THE SAFETY CATCH ON UNTIL YOU'RE READY TO SHOOT.

7. BE SURE YOUR TARGET IS WHAT YOU WANT TO SHOOT. NEVER SHOOT AT A TARGET THAT IS ONLY A MOVEMENT, COLOR, SOUND OR UNIDENTIFIABLE SHAPE. BE AWARE OF YOUR SURROUNDINGS BEFORE YOU SHOOT.

8. ALWAYS REMEMBER THAT IF THE BULLET MISSES OR PASSES THROUGH THE TARGET, IT COULD HIT SOMETHING OR SOMEONE BEHIND IT.

9. IF IN DOUBT, DON'T SHOOT.

10. USE ONLY THE PROPER AMMUNITION.

11. KEEP THE GUN UNLOADED UNTIL YOU ARE READY TO USE IT.

12. DON'T RELY ON THE GUN'S SAFETY CATCH TO PREVENT IT FROM FIRING.

13. KEEP THE BARREL CLEAR OF OBSTRUCTIONS AND THE GUN CLEAN AND FUNCTIONING.

14. BE COMPLETELY FAMILIAR WITH YOUR GUN AND KNOW HOW TO OPERATE IT, INCLUDING HOW TO LOAD AND UNLOAD IT AND CLEAR A MALFUNCTION. MANY GUNS ARE DIFFERENT; NEVER ASSUME THAT WHAT APPLIES TO ONE MAKE OR MODEL IS THE SAME ON ANOTHER.

15. WHEN THE GUN IS NOT IN YOUR HANDS, SAFETY IS STILL IMPORTANT. STORE YOUR GUN SAFELY AND SECURELY. PUT AN APPROVED SAFETY DEVICE, SUCH AS A TRIGGER LOCK OR CABLE LOCK, ON THE GUN SO IT CANNOT BE FIRED. STORE THE AMMUNITION SOMEWHERE ELSE THAT IS EQUALLY SAFE AND SECURE.

The 'Law of Three'

Accidents with guns can have awful consequences that change lives in an instant. Handling guns properly is not complicated. You just have to learn a few common-sense rules. Once you've programmed these rules into your subconscious mind so that they're habits, accidents with guns will be extremely rare—and when they do happen, their consequences should be minor.

Accidents often turn out to be the result of three smaller mistakes, all building on each other. It seems to be true for all sorts of things, whether it's riding your bicycle, slicing up a sandwich for lunch or shooting.

Think about it. You jump on your bike, fly down the street, cross over to a friend's house and get flattened by a car. Mistake No. 1: You weren't looking. Mistake No. 2: You were going too fast. Mistake No. 3: You didn't signal your turn. If you hadn't made any one of these three mistakes, the accident wouldn't have happened. You would have seen the car, or the driver would have seen you.

Here's how the "Law of Three" can apply to shooting:

On a pheasant hunt one of your authors got hit with a charge of shot from a 12-gauge gun. His shooting glasses saved his eyes and maybe his life, and some pellets were slowed down by his heavy vest, but it took a surgeon hours to dig pellets out of

The author's Ranger shooting glasses, covered with blood that dripped down from pellets that struck his forehead. One lens stopped several 12-gauge shot meant for pheasants.

his face, upper body and right hand and arm. The man who shot him, by accident, made three mistakes. First, his gun was still loaded when the group was done hunting and standing around chatting. Second, he fired low. And third, he failed to see the author standing beyond the bird that he was trying to kill, which suddenly appeared out of nowhere. (See Commandments 1, 3, 7 and 8.) Had he not made just one of these errors, the author wouldn't have pellets in his chest still today, 20 years later. The ones that are too deep to remove.

Some True-Life Stories

Here's an accident that was the fault of one of your authors. He was about 14 at the time and preparing to open fire with his .22 rifle on a woodchuck that was raiding the vegetable garden. He stood just inside the kitchen, holding the rifle pointing straight up, and pumped a cartridge into the chamber. The plan was to ease the screen door open, slide the barrel out, aim and shoot. What happened was that the rifle went off the instant the round was chambered, and the bullet blew a nasty gouge in the wooden door frame.

He made two mistakes. He had his finger on the trigger when he closed the gun's action, and the safety wasn't on. (You could also say that he

A Model 61 Winchester .22 like the one that put a hole in the author's kitchen-door frame. One good habit saved the day; a third mistake could have caused a serious problem.

shouldn't have loaded the gun in the house. There are times when it has to be done, but protecting vegetables isn't one of them.)

This scared the hell out of everyone, especially the author, and caused some damage. But he made just two mistakes, and one safety habit saved the day: He was pointing the rifle in a safe direction. Otherwise, someone could have been shot.

Sometimes guns just malfunction. Once in Africa the same author and a Professional Hunter were getting out of their Land Rover. As he slid out the door, the PH reached back to get a pump shot-

gun from the rack behind the seats. The moment he grabbed it, the gun went off, blowing a hole in the roof of the safari car. The man hadn't touched the trigger; the gun was worn out and needed to be set right by a gunsmith. Again, the good news is that it was pointing straight up when it went off.

Do not think, though, that since you're only going to make one or two mistakes, nothing bad will happen. Instead, build up so many good safety habits that when you do screw up, there are layers of protection that prevent something truly awful.

THE CARDINAL RULES OF GUN SAFETY

1. **Always assume a gun is loaded.**
2. **Never load a gun until it's time to use it.**
3. **Never point it at anything you don't wish to destroy.**
4. **Keep your finger off the trigger until you're ready to destroy your target.**

If you learn these simple habits, then if you happen to trip and fall with a gun in your hands or something else goes wrong, you'll just feel clumsy and scared for a moment instead of guilty for the rest of your life. Or injured, paralyzed or dead.

WHAT ABOUT THE SAFETY CATCH?

You can't trust a safety catch. Safety catches are switches that slide, levers that pivot, or buttons to push before a shot can be fired. Whatever its shape and wherever it is on the gun, the safety catch locks the trigger.

But in most firearms that's all it does. The action itself, which is cocked and ready to fire, is not locked. So dropping the gun or even just acciden-

tally banging it into something—a rock or a tree, for example—might possibly jar the action so that it fires the round in the chamber without the trigger doing anything.

Some safeties come on automatically when you close the action. Most, however, have to be switched on manually. Some specialized competition guns don't even have a safety catch, but

A double-barreled gun usually has its safety catch on top, where the shooter's thumb can operate it. This is a "bolted" safety—it has its own catch, the little lever that locks it in place. But it's still not foolproof.

they're loaded and cocked only when they're about to be fired and they're used only in highly controlled situations.

One of your authors once hunted with a rifle that seemed to have a mind of its own. Two or three times a day he found that the safety had mysteriously slid to the off position, even though it didn't seem loose and he didn't think he'd scraped it against

anything. Since he was sometimes crawling through brush with the rifle on his back, a twig could have found its way into the trigger guard and given everyone a nasty surprise.

A safety catch is not foolproof. It's just one of those layers of protection that add up to help prevent accidents. Here are some others:

• Don't chamber a round until you expect to shoot.

• Don't cock the gun until then, either.

• When you do load and cock, make sure the safety catch is engaged. (It's not foolproof, but that's what it's for.)

• Keep the gun pointed in a safe direction.

• When it's time to aim and fire, bring the gun up so that it doesn't swing across another person, or a vehicle, or your dog or anything else you wouldn't want to shoot.

How NOT to Hold a Gun

Even when a gun is unloaded, uncocked and completely safe, and its action is open, muzzle control—meaning where the gun is pointing—is still important.

It's not enough to tell yourself, "Right, the gun can't fire, so it's OK to wave it around in any old direction" because it's too easy to forget the details. ("Did I really unload?")

The only way to build up proper safety habits is to treat every gun as though it were loaded all the time, no exceptions. The bottom line: Never point even an *empty* gun at anything you wouldn't want to shoot. This includes your own foot or hand as well as people, cars, buildings or whatever or whomever might be nearby. Look at these three photos

Left: "It's OK, I've got another foot." This shows very poor muzzle safety, and the shotgun's action is closed too! What if the gun is loaded? *Right:* Where is the rifle pointing? And this bolt is closed too. Again, not good.

of common mistakes. In each case, how would you hold the gun?

Left: More bad muzzle control. What's in the line of fire? This over/under shotgun should be pointed at the ground—and its action should be open! *Right:* One reason many bird hunters like double guns is that the actions can be opened, which lets everyone around know that the gun is completely safe, even with cartridges still in the chambers. Here the gun muzzles are pointing at the ground too.

I Found a Gun!

If you find a gun at home, even if it's something a member of your family brought home long ago and it's in your attic or basement, assume it's loaded. Don't touch it. Leave the area. Tell your parents or another responsible adult.

If you're at a friend's house, get out of there and go home. Tell your parents or another responsible adult.

A gun found in the street or some other public place could have been used in a crime. Don't touch it. Call 9-1-1 on your cell phone and tell the dispatcher what you found. The dispatcher will ask you where you are and will send the police. When they arrive, don't pick it up! They will think they're being confronted with someone holding a gun.

If you find a gun in the woods, don't touch that either. But there may be an injured hunter nearby. Look and listen. Call 9-1-1 and follow the dispatcher's instructions. You might have to wait for the police or a game warden to arrive.

Don't take a chance with what seems to be a lost or abandoned gun. Leave it alone and tell one of your parents or another responsible adult about it.

Things We Never Forget

Most of us never forget accidental discharges or other close calls with guns. The author whose .22 went off in the kitchen remembers it like it happened last week, not 50 years ago: "The silence in the house afterward was deafening. And I've never loaded a gun, any gun, in the house, any house, since."

Another one of us had two accidental discharges with .22s: "I shot my parents' car. I was emptying the magazine by pumping the rounds through the action, and I put my finger on the trigger—dumb, dumb, dumb.

"Even worse, though, was that I once shot a hole in my pants when attempting a fast draw with my .22 revolver. My parents never found out about that one. Scared the crap out of me. It could have gone into my leg. Really dumb."

Serious First Aid

If you or anyone gets shot or otherwise seriously hurt, don't panic. Call 9-1-1. If you can, leave the phone on for instructions or to tell the emergency operator what's going on. Then:

1. Make sure that all guns are unloaded or in a secure place.

2. Stay where you are unless it's not safe.

3. Now you have to act quickly because time is critical. The victim could lose consciousness or die if he or she loses too much blood. Find the injury and see how badly it's bleeding. There may be two wounds: one where the bullet went in and another where it came out again. Put a compress (your T-shirt, coat, bandana, whatever) over the wound and press firmly to try to stop the blood loss. If the gunshot is in an arm or leg, raise it above the level of the victim's heart and apply a tourniquet—your belt, a gun sling, a piece of clothing, whatever. Don't worry about whether the compress or tourniquet is sterile; just stop the bleeding.

4. Don't let the victim eat or drink anything.

5. In addition to blood loss, remember the ABCs of emergency care. A = airway: Make the victim comfortable so that his airway (mouth, nose, throat) is open so he can breathe. B= breathing: Make sure the victim is breathing. C= circulation: Check for a pulse either at a wrist or the side of the throat. If the airway is open but the victim isn't breathing and you can't feel a pulse, start CPR (chest compressions). The 9-1-1 operator should be able to help you with this.

6. If you're outdoors, keep the victim warm. Hypothermia, or cold, can also lead to death.

With most gunshot wounds, getting the victim to a hospital is critical. Reaching a 9-1-1 operator as soon as possible improves the chances of survival.

It isn't just gunshots either. A gun that somehow blows up can cause serious injuries too. This is very rare and almost always preventable, but it can happen if the barrel gets plugged or if the wrong ammunition is used. Read "Keeping Guns Clean & Safe."

Dumb Things

What NOT to Do with Guns

GUNS AT SCHOOL

This one is really simple: Don't do it. Or, to put it another way, *Are you crazy?*

Sure, we all want to show our cool stuff to our friends, and what's cooler than a gun and being able to shoot it well? You may be a responsible person and already an experienced shooter with a good understanding of safety— but most of your friends in school are not. You can't risk one of them grabbing or sneaking the gun away from you. And don't even think about swearing them to secrecy. No kid (and few adults) can keep that kind of secret.

It's like that unwritten rule in the movies: If a gun shows up anywhere in the story, you know that somehow, sooner or later, it's going to be used. Same thing in school—and if it isn't used, it will be talked about. Then you'll be in real trouble with the police, not just the principal and your family. The federal Gun-Free School Zones Act of 1996 generally prohibits firearms on and within 1,000 feet of any private or public school property, kindergarten through 12th grade, except in the possession of a po-

DRUG FREE GUN FREE ZONE

Bring a gun to school, even if it's in a locked case in a car, and you'll be in trouble with the police, not just with the principal, your teachers and your family—and that's if nothing bad happens with it, like one of your friends "borrowing" it.

lice officer, a licensed school security guard or someone who is authorized by the state to carry a gun.

If you're lucky, you'll only be expelled for a while. You will lose your gun and your shooting privileges, and you could be charged with a crime.

The federal law applies to firearms, but state or local laws may include BB and pellet guns, Airsoft and Paintball guns, and even in some cases toy guns.

Even if you're old enough to have a driver's license, and you drive yourself to school, and it's hunting season and you're planning to go sit in your duck blind that afternoon— you still will be in violation of the law, even if your gun is in a locked case in the locked trunk. Go home after classes end and get your gun and gear, and then go hunting.

A few schools have organized, supervised shooting teams, usually for smallbore-rifle or for sporting clays, trap or skeet competition. (If your school does, you should be involved.) These schools have plenty of rules and regulations covering every aspect of this, and the guns probably aren't even kept at school.

AMMUNITION IN A FIRE

It usually goes like this: You're at the lake or camping, and everyone is sitting around a campfire. Someone's been shooting and has a pocketful of leftover .22s or some such. And then some idiot says, "Hey, I wonder what would happen if . . . ?"

If you don't stop him (it's always "him"; girls don't do this stuff) and he really does toss the ammo into the fire, here's what you can expect. First, never mind what you once saw in a movie; the cartridges won't do what they would in a gun. But they will explode. It'll take a few seconds for them to overheat, and then *pop! pop! pop!*

Because the detonations aren't enclosed in a gun barrel, and the bullets aren't directed by a bar-rel, the bullets won't do any damage. No, this time it's the casings that are dangerous. The force of the explosions will burst the brass cases, which can send hot fragments of metal flying in all directions like shrapnel.

With .22 rimfire ammunition, this is *probably* not going to be dangerous, but it's unpredictable and a genuinely stupid thing to do. And if more powerful cartridges, like any sort of .30-caliber rifle ammunition, winds up in a fire, the shrapnel is just about guaranteed to be hazardous.

LINE OF BORE VS. LINE OF SIGHT

Take a good look at any rifle that has a telescopic sight on it. See how the scope sits well above the barrel? This means that where the bullet comes out is that much below where you're looking. We know a guy who tore up his pickup truck because he forgot this. He was resting his Mini-14 on the truck's fender, taking aim at a distant coyote. The first shot missed, and it made an odd noise too. But the rifle was an autoloader and the coyote was still there, so he kept his eye glued to the scope and fired again. This time he picked up his head to check on that awful metallic noise. Turns out he'd fired two 5.56mm rounds into the hood where it rose up in front of his rifle's muzzle. But in looking through the scope, all he could see was a clear line of sight to the coyote.

A bullet doesn't travel in a straight line. It arcs downward under the pull of gravity (remember tra-

See how high that sight sits above the barrel? Until the bullet from this AR-15 is some distance downrange, its path will be as much as three or four inches below what the shooter is looking at through the scope.

jectory?). To hit a distant target, the sights of a rifle have to point the barrel upward so the bullet can rise in its arc and then drop into the target. When a bullet is 20 yards or more downrange, it has climbed far enough to clear anything that might be in front of the muzzle but not high enough for you to see it in the scope.

WHAT GOES UP MUST COME DOWN

We see it all the time on TV: Crowds, usually in the Middle East, firing guns into the air. Haven't you wondered where those bullets come down again? Harmlessly, out in some desert maybe?

Maybe not. When Saddam Hussein's sons were finally cornered and killed during the Iraq War, on July 22, 2003, more than 20 other people were reported killed by bullets fired into the air in celebration.

A bullet fired up at a very steep angle travels until its energy is gone, and then it stops moving upward and falls back to earth. On the return trip, the bullet is no longer propelled by gunpowder, it's being pulled downward by gravity. In a vacuum the bullet would hit the ground with the same energy that it left the gun, but in our atmosphere it is affected by air resistance, which slows it down considerably but not enough to be harmless.

Every falling object has a terminal velocity, the speed at which the acceleration of gravity is cancelled out by the resistance of the air. Terminal velocity depends on the size, shape and mass of the object. A human body leaving a plane without a parachute eventually hits the ground at about 120 mph, or 176 fps, no matter whether it falls 1,500 feet or 15 miles. A falling 7.62mm bullet from an AK-47 or a 9mm pistol bullet both reach a terminal velocity of around 300 fps (if they're traveling point-first and not tumbling in the air). A bullet can puncture human skin at only 150 fps, and at 200 fps it can penetrate the skull.

It probably won't surprise you to learn that three-quarters of the victims of bullets falling randomly out of the sky get hit in the head. One-third of them are killed.

Unfortunately, even a bullet fired perfectly straight up won't come down and hit the idiot who fired it. Depending on caliber and velocity, it

Firing guns into the air on special occasions isn't like setting off fireworks. Those bullets have to come down somewhere, and when they do, they can kill people. This doesn't happen only in the Middle East, either. In the words of Detroit Police Chief Ralph Godbee Jr., speaking about celebratory gunfire: "Guns don't kill people, morons do."

could travel two miles up into the sky, where wind will push it one way or another and the earth will rotate during the time it's in the air (which could be almost a minute). So if anyone gets hurt, it's always some innocent bystander who's usually far away and unaware of danger.

A bullet launched upward at a shallower angle—less than about 45 degrees above horizontal—is still carrying some of the energy with which it was fired when it reaches the ground, so it's moving faster than if it were falling only under the pull of gravity and will hit harder.

These accidents don't happen only as a result of reckless "vertical marksmanship." Just before Christmas 2011, a man in Ohio who went to clean his muzzleloading rifle accidentally fired it into the air when it turned out to be loaded. The bullet came down a mile and a half away, where it hit a 15-year-old Amish girl, returning home from a party, in the head and killed her. Her brother found her in the road after the horse brought her buggy back empty.

When movie cowboys ride into town firing their guns into the air, they're shooting blanks.

When a navy ship fires a 21-gun salute, it's shooting blanks. (But even the blast and the wad from a blank is dangerous if you're standing too close.) If you fire a gun, accidentally or on purpose, without aiming it at a target, make sure it's pointed at the ground—not up into the sky.

And if you're a squirrel hunter, think about this the next time you shoot up into a tree: If you miss the squirrel and the tree, where will your bullet go? Even a tiny 40-grain .22 can travel nearly a mile.

Accidents with Guns (and First Aid)

If you read this book carefully and stick to the rules and common sense, you won't accidentally shoot yourself or someone else. We also cover the two most common shooting-related injuries, which are hearing loss and getting things in our eyes. (Read about protecting your eyes and ears in "Armor All.") But there are other ways to get hurt with a gun.

You can, for example, pinch your thumb or fingers in the action. You'd have to be fairly clumsy to do this, but it's possible, especially if you're in a

"Watch what you're doing, Marine!" These Vietnam-era recruits handling the M1911 pistol learned, among other things, where *not* to put their fingers. The slide on any type of semi-automatic slams shut hard enough to cause injury. They're wearing ear and eye protection too.

hurry or if you're not familiar with a certain kind of gun. Normally you can feel a pinch as you begin to close the bolt or lever or whatever, and then naturally you stop. Semi-automatics, though, slam shut hard when you hit the bolt-release button, so be extra careful there—keep your fingers away from the moving parts.

You also can catch a finger under an external hammer, which you'll find on most revolvers, some pistols and some older (or old-style) rifles and shotguns. This can draw blood, especially on a long gun with a powerful mainspring or on a revolver that has its firing pin on the hammer. Be careful.

Recoil can hurt you too, if you aren't holding the gun properly or if it goes off accidentally before you're ready. This may produce a bruise or possibly a sore wrist or a split lip. A big pistol might hurt the web of your hand, between your thumb and trigger finger. If a scoped rifle slips off your shoulder as you fire, the scope may catch you above the eye. The result might be a bruise, a headache or even a cut that bleeds.

YouTube has plenty of videos of people losing their grip on hard-kicking guns and getting smacked in the face, but a lot of these seem to be unsuspecting novices who were set up by their "friends."

Severe recoil is no joke; it may not cause a direct injury, but it can shock you enough to make you flinch when you go to shoot again. Flinching is an involuntary and uncontrollable reaction that comes just as you pull the trigger—your body is saying, *No way!* This makes it impossible to hit anything, and getting rid of the habit of flinching can take a long time.

(This is one reason that new or young shooters should start out with .22 rimfires; you learn to shoot without having to worry about recoil. Then, once you've learned how to hold a gun properly, you can move up to bigger calibers. Getting a little bigger yourself helps too.)

The accidents or mistakes we've just listed usually result in bruises and swelling or also lacerations or cuts. Unless a cut bleeds heavily, these injuries are not life-threatening. Even so, if you get hurt, your concentration will be affected and you won't enjoy what you're doing as much. Stop shooting, unload, take a break and go home. Tell your parents what happened and show them the injury.

If no one's home, you may need to clean and disinfect a cut yourself and then stick a Band-Aid over it. If you have a bruise or swelling, cool it down with some ice in a plastic bag. Don't put this directly on the spot, though—wrap it in a washcloth or towel first. When a parent gets home, show and tell. He or she will decide what more needs to be done, if anything.

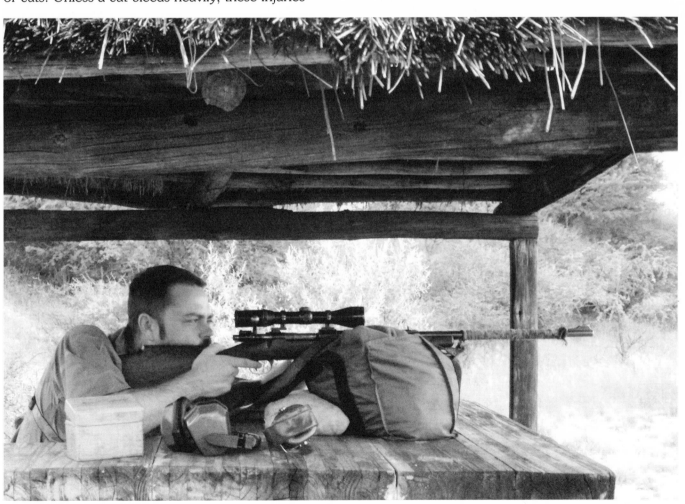

Silvio Calabi

Too much recoil can ruin your shooting and even mess up your face. If a hard-kicking rifle slips off your shoulder, you may get "scope-eye," which is a bruise or cut on your forehead. The stock has to be long enough to put some distance between your face and the scope for safety. This hunter is sighting in his scope before a safari. He should be wearing those earmuffs!

How Far & How Hard

Bullet Travel & What Happens When They Hit

BILLY DIXON'S 5.3 SECONDS

In 1872 Dodge City, Kansas, was the last stop on the Atchison, Topeka and Santa Fe Railway and the hub of professional buffalo hunting. Something like 1½ million bison hides were shipped out of Dodge between 1872 and 1878. As buffalo became scarce in that area, some hunters ventured south from there into Texas. This was dangerous; the Indians in that region—Comanche, Kiowa and Cheyenne—were angry about white intrusions, and the US Army couldn't provide much protection.

In what is now Hutchinson County, Texas, the tiny town of Adobe Walls had been set up to serve hunters. It had a hide-buyer's house, a blacksmith shop, a general store, a saloon and an outhouse. On the morning of June 27, 1874, there were 29 buffalo hunters, skinners and residents in town when at least 200 Indians attacked. Fighting lasted most of the day. Despite the Kiowa medicine man's bulletproofing spells, the attackers suffered heavy losses. Not yet ready to quit, on the second day, June 28, the Indians carried

Buffalo hunter Billy Dixon's long shot with iron sights at the Battle of Adobe Walls made him famous. A modern sniper can reach much farther, but only with a big scope and a special rifle and ammunition. This photo is from Dixon's wife Olive's book, *The Life of Billy Dixon*.

out hit-and-run skirmishes and probing actions.

On day three the town's defenders spotted a group of about 15 Indian warriors sitting on their horses in plain sight on a bluff east of Adobe Walls. Maybe they were discussing tactics. Clearly they thought they were at a safe distance. One of the hide hunters decided that they were an inviting target. His name was Billy Dixon, and he was particularly skilled in long-range shooting.

His weapon was a Sharps, the legendary single-shot rifle. To those who bragged that Winchester was the gun that won the West, Sharps men always replied that theirs was the gun that made the West safe for Winchester.

Sharps percussion breechloaders had served in the American Civil War (1861-1865), and by 1874 they were being chambered for some of the most powerful cartridges available. The rifle in Dixon's hands was probably a .50-90—that is, a .50-caliber bullet of about 475 grains in front of a charge of 90 or more grains of powder. Primitive scopes were available by then, but Billy didn't have one.

An original Sharps "Big 50"—a Model 1874 .50-90 rifle like Billy Dixon's, with an aperture rear sight for long-range shooting. This rifle fired a fingertip-size bullet meant to drop buffalo that might weigh a ton. The Sharps factory was in Connecticut, but most of the rifles went to the mountains and plains of the West.

He took careful aim at a barely visible target and fired. The heavy bullet began its leisurely journey toward the unsuspecting warriors. Its mortar-like trajectory arced it close to a hundred feet above Dixon's line of sight. It's unlikely that the Indians heard the shot or saw the puff of smoke, but suddenly one of them fell off his horse.

This was unaccountably strong medicine. The Indian leaders decided they had urgent business elsewhere, and the Battle of Adobe Walls was over.

The fate of the ineffectual Kiowa medicine man is unknown, but Billy Dixon and his Sharps passed into history. Later a group of Army surveyors determined that the distance of his shot was 1,538 yards, or seven-eighths of a mile.

Eighteen seventy-four turned out to be a good year for both Billy Dixon and Sharps. Dixon was hired as a scout for the Army and went on to earn the Medal of Honor at the Battle of Buffalo Wallow on September 12. And two weeks later, at the Creedmoor range in New York, Americans with Sharps and Remington rifles narrowly defeated Ireland's famous team of marksmen to win an international long-range shooting championship.

Dixon's fame lives on. He may have been the inspiration for Matt Quigley, Tom Selleck's Sharps-shooting cowboy character in the movie *Quigley Down Under*.

LONG-RANGE SHOOTING TESTS

A century later, in a newsletter article about Dixon, a forensic scientist questioned whether a Sharps could even send a bullet that far. He must have missed class the day that maximum range was covered.

Way back in October and November 1879, the US Army conducted long-range shooting trials on the beach at Sandy Hook, New Jersey. Two .45-caliber "trapdoor" Springfield service rifles were tested with different bullet weights and charges along with a British Army .577/.450 Martini-Henry rifle at 2,500, 3,200 and 3,500 yards. One of the Springfields with different rifling in its

barrel and the British rifle wouldn't reach 3,500 yards. The other Springfield, firing a 500-grain bullet ahead of 80 grains of powder, achieved the maximum distance: 3,680 yards, or 2.09 miles. This was more than one mile farther than Dixon's famous shot at Adobe Walls.

A stopwatch and the newly invented telephone were used to determine that the flight time of the bullet was just about 21 seconds. Perhaps even more impressive was that, at maximum range, the bullet could still penetrate a one-inch pine board.

Forensic scientists are an inquisitive bunch. In the early 1990s several of them decided to apply

20th Century technology to the Billy Dixon shot. They took a new .50-caliber Sharps, believed to be similar to what Dixon used, to the Yuma Proving Ground in Arizona. The US military tests all sorts of artillery, mortars and missiles inside Yuma's 1,300 square miles of desert.

With the barrel of the Sharps tilted upward at 32 degrees above horizontal, the best angle for maximum range, a 675-grain bullet backed by 90 grains of powder landed 3,600 yards downrange. The 450-grain bullet propelled by 100 grains of powder went 2,585 yards.

A few years later a writer named M.L. McPherson published a story in *Precision Shooting*

Magazine about his attempt to replicate the Dixon shot. He set up a single life-size horse and rider target at 1,538 yards. (Remember that Dixon was shooting at a group of riders, not just one; his overall target was larger.) McPherson fired 130 rounds at the target with a new .40-caliber Sharps and succeeded in hitting it 13 times. He calculated the flight time of the bullet at 5.3 seconds.

Bullets can travel a very long way and are still capable of causing serious damage and injury when they get there. You may have seen the warning printed on many boxes of .22 Long Rifle ammunition: "RANGE ONE MILE BE CAREFUL." Believe it.

Maximum Ranges

Cartridge	Bullet Weight	Muzzle Velocity	Maximum Range	
	(grains)	(feet per second)	(yards)	(miles)
.22 Long Rifle	40	1,350	1,600	0.90
.357 Magnum	158	1,430	2,350	1.34
.45 ACP	230	850	1,800	1.03
.223 Remington	50	3,300	3,600	2.04
.243 Winchester	100	3,070	4,000	2.27
.30-06 Springfield	152	2,800	3,500	1.99
.375 H&H Magnum	270	2,740	4,500	2.56
Shot Size	**Diameter**			
	(inches)			
12-gauge slug	0.645	1,500	1,420	0.80
.410 slug	0.380	1,600	850	0.48
0 buckshot	0.32	1,100	704	0.40
No. 2	0.15	1,100	330	0.19
No. 5	0.12	1,100	264	0.15
No. 7½	0.095	1,100	209	0.12

At the Yuma Proving Ground

One of your authors was lucky enough to be able to test-fire his own .30-caliber prairie-dog rifle at Yuma.

The particular range to which he was assigned was 30 kilometers (18.6 miles) long. The rifle was mounted in front of a control room filled with computers and other instruments and surrounded by thick armor plate. Alongside the rifle was an ultra-sensitive Doppler radar system.

The computerized Doppler tracking radar that followed the flight of the .30-caliber bullet. Normally it tracks artillery shells that weigh as much as 100 pounds or more.

A voice from the control room asked for the bullet weight (220 grains), ballistic coefficient of the bullet (0.629) and its muzzle velocity (3,020 fps). After some programming and calculating, the control room announced that maximum range would result from elevating the rifle muzzle to 32 degrees.

The staffer who was managing the operation said that they were more experienced in tracking "big bullets"—like the ones fired from tanks—and so he predicted that the radar would be able to follow the tiny projectile for about a thousand yards; beyond that, the bullet's trajectory would be calculated by computer.

With the radar elevated for tracking, the control room gave the 5-4-3-2-1 countdown, and the bullet was on its way. A blue light on the radar module flashed to indicate that something was happening, but the screen didn't move . . . and then, after what seemed like forever, it slowly began to return to horizontal as it followed the arc of the bullet downward. A few minutes of data-crunching followed, and then the control room announced that radar had been able to track the bullet fully 5,500 yards downrange, at which point it was still 900 yards above the ground. Three more rounds were fired to confirm. The final data showed a flight time of 34 to 35 seconds and a maximum range of between 6,500 and 6,600 yards. That's 3¾ miles.

The cradle holding the author's .30-8mm Remington Magnum rifle came off a 1970s Soviet tank. The apparatus is elevated for maximum range, and the rifle is ready to fire.

This is why a shooter has to be aware of what lies *behind* a target. (Number 8 of the 15 Commandments of Gun Safety: "Always remember that if the bullet misses or passes through the target, it could hit something or someone behind it." Or if it ricochets off and continues.) Think about what's *above* your target too. In this case the author's bullets arced almost *one mile up* as they traveled downrange. This is one reason why small aircraft have to detour around the Yuma Proving Ground.

RICOCHETS & BOUNCEBACKS

It's all too easy to skip or bounce a bullet off a hard surface or even off surfaces that don't seem hard at all. This is called a ricochet, and it can happen when you least expect it.

It's generally true that the shallower the angle at which the bullet hits a surface, the more likely a ricochet becomes. But this doesn't mean that if you shoot at something hard at a high angle nothing will happen. If you fired a bullet squarely into a slab of rock, for example, fragments of stone could bounce back in all sorts of unpredictable directions. A bullet that hits a mild steel plate seems to turn itself inside-out and may bounce right back toward the shooter. However, target plates of an especially hard steel called T1 make even metal-jacketed bullets blow up on impact, so they can't ricochet or bounce back.

In "You'll Put Your Eye Out!" we told you that many years ago the Daisy company replaced its lead BBs with steel. Unlike soft lead, when a steel BB hits a hard surface, it bounces off and keeps going. These ricochets are part of what makes even low-powered BB guns potentially dangerous.

If you've ever skipped flat stones across a pond, you already have a good idea of what happens when you fire a bullet—or a shotgun pellet or a BB—at water at a low angle. It bounces off and keeps going. Aim the gun at a higher angle, and the bullet is likely to just dig into the water and come to a quick stop (just as you do, when you belly-flop into a swimming pool).

It's unpredictable, though. The potential for ricochet depends on many factors beyond just the angle of the hit, including the surface itself and the speed and material of the bullet and even its shape. A bullet can ricochet off a grassy lawn if the conditions are just right.

The military sometimes puts ricochets to good use. In the days of sailing ships, gunners extended the

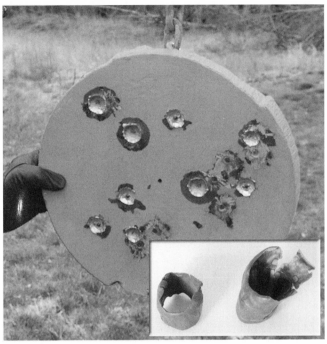

Steve Helsley

Bouncebacks and ricochets can be serious. This copper-jacketed .470 Nitro Express bullet hit the steel plate and not only turned itself inside-out, but also part of it bounced straight back to where the shooter was standing, 50 yards away. Luckily, no one was hurt. (This was the wrong kind of steel to use as a target.) BBs and air-gun pellets can do this too.

range of their cannons by skipping the balls across the water into an enemy's hull. Today it's possible to bounce a bomb into the mouth of a cave by dropping it from an airplane at a certain speed and distance above the ground. There are stories of snipers ricocheting bullets off walls or ledges into buildings.

None of this is terribly useful to us, though. For us, the possibility of ricochets and bouncebacks is just one more good reason to be aware of what lies beyond our target when we fire a gun. It is also one more really good reason to wear shooting glasses.

HOLLYWOOD AND NEWTON'S THIRD LAW

Who can forget Clint Eastwood's famous line in *Dirty Harry*? "This is a .44 Magnum, the most powerful handgun in the world, and would blow your head clean off...."

The .44 Magnum is no longer the most powerful production handgun in the world (that would be the .500 S&W Magnum), but it can generate more than a thousand foot-pounds of energy at the muzzle. A 12-gauge shotgun produces about twice that much. No wonder, then, when you see a bad dude get whacked with a sawed-off double-barrel in the movies, he's blown right off the porch or through a window. That's a ton of punch—two tons if both barrels are touched off together! Awesome power, wouldn't you say? And the mighty .45 pistol cartridge, with its hefty 230-grain bullet, will flatten a person with just a hit in the arm. The old-time cowboys' big .44 Special will knock a horse right off its feet.

Well, no, they won't. None of these things can happen.

"Knockdown power" is a widely accepted, near-sacred belief. It is also wrong. If in school you have already been introduced to Sir Isaac Newton (1642-1727), you know that this English scientist had something to say on the matter. His Third Law of Motion states: "For every action there is an equal and opposite reaction." That is, for every force there is a counterforce that is equal in size and opposite in direction. Punch your fist into the wall. Your fist exerts a force on the wall, but the wall exerts an equal force back onto your fist. Ouch!

Dirty Harry's handgun (which very few cops carried even when cops had revolvers, because it was so big and heavy and hard to shoot): a Smith & Wesson Model 29 .44 Magnum that generates more than a thousand foot-pounds of muzzle energy. More than enough to knock a bad dude off his feet, right?

When a rifle or handgun launches a bullet, the bullet exerts an equal push backward. But even the most powerful cartridges, such as the .50 BMG or a .700 Nitro Express, firing the biggest bullets don't knock the shooter down.

An inexperienced shooter or one who is caught by surprise might drop such a gun or stagger or even fall down in fright, but he won't be pushed to the ground by the recoil. Watch a real rifleman fire one of these cannons: He'll sway backward slightly and the rifle's muzzle will lift a foot or so, but that's it.

Now let's follow this bullet downrange, keeping Newton's Third Law in mind. When the bullet hits something, whether it's a tree or a target plate or a body, it meets push-back that's equal to the force of its impact. (Like the wall on your fist.)

We've already established that the first reaction, the one when the bullet was fired, wasn't enough to knock down the shooter, so how can the bullet knock down a person it hits? Much less pick him off his feet and slam him into a wall?

For a bullet's impact to knock someone over, the recoil of the shot would have to knock over the shooter. This doesn't happen even in the movies, or the good guys would go flying too. If the recoil doesn't do this to the shooter, the bullet won't have the energy to do it to someone downrange. Even worse, the recoil felt by the shooter is actually greater than the bullet impact because of the added push of the gas in the detonating cartridge.

Still don't believe it? In 1962 the editors of *American Rifleman*, the technical magazine of the National Rifle Association of America, tested this another way. In a sort of antique *Mythbusters* episode, they put the knockdown question to the test.

It turns out that when a bullet strikes an object, the force it exerts on the object lasts just slightly longer than one millisecond (one one-thousandth of a second), no matter whether the bullet penetrates or just splats on the surface. That will blow up a watermelon, but will it move an object backward?

To demonstrate, the NRA put a 175-pound wooden mannequin on a free-rolling platform as a target. The dummy moved easily with just the touch of a fingertip. Shooting it with a .22 Long Rifle moved it 1/16 of an inch. A hit from a .38 Special revolver rolled it 3/16 of an inch. A 230-grain .45 ACP (Automatic Colt Pistol) bullet moved it all of a half-inch. Finally, they got out a .30-06 rifle and fired a 150-grain bullet at it at 2,900 fps. This is far, far more powerful than Dirty Harry's .44 Magnum, and in the movies it would have blasted the victim halfway to next week. In real life it shoved the dummy backward just 2¼ inches.

BEGINNER'S DIGEST

It is occasionally stated that the impact of a bullet can knock a man or an animal down.

This idea should be distinguished from 'stopping power', which means the ability to kill or make helpless. Bullets achieve their intended effect by interfering with life functions, and a bullet has stopping power if it does this immediately so that the animal collapses or at least cannot move. 'Knockdown' implies that the animal is thrown violently to the ground.

Such an action can indeed be seen in the case of a very small animal such as a ground squirrel, or even a woodchuck weighing a few pounds. In larger animals, a semblance of this might be given by a convulsive muscular movement. Experienced hunters, however, would not credit such a real effect in an animal the size of a whitetail deer or larger, having often observed that after the first hit which makes the animal

1　175-lb. manikin was mounted on free-rolling platform to show the motion caused by the bullet impact

2　For firing, figure was placed on smooth side of Masonite sheet for easiest movement. Camera was aligned with figure and a marker (see arrow) to record displacement, which was measured

KNOCKDOWN

insensible to pain or shock, there is no visible effect of further hits. When men are hit by small arms fire in combat, they are not knocked down.

Nor would the so-called knockdown effect be given credence by any engineer acquainted with the quantities involved. There is indeed a large momentary force, at the instant of striking, which damages the target. Such damage often has been illustrated in photographs of bullets striking gelatin blocks. The bullet energy is expended in this way and not in moving the target.

The .45 ACP is a comparatively heavy pistol cartridge, firing a 230-gr. bullet at 800 feet per second (f.p.s.). When brought to rest in 6" of travel in a target, the bullet exerts an average force of about 800 lbs. The total time, however, is only slightly over .001 second, much too short to move a heavy target very much. A target weighing 175 lbs., even if it were entirely free of any frictional contact with the ground, would be given by this impact a velocity of less than 2 inches per second, which is hardly noticeable.

For comparison, this velocity also would be produced by a push of about ½ lb. lasting one second.

The 150-gr. bullet of the commercial .30-'06 hunting load has a muzzle

3　After the firings, freedom of movement was rechecked with trigger scale pulling on screw hook in figure's back. Figure required only 1 lb. pull to move. Hole indicated by arrow was made by .45 bullet which missed lead plate — this impact caused less movement and was not counted. Back sheet was loosened by bullet striking interior lead plate, showing momentary impact force

velocity of 2970 f.p.s. Striking and remaining in a target with a penetration of 6" it develops an average force of about 5800 lbs. during about .0003 second. A 175-lb. target moving with perfect freedom would be given a speed of about 4 inches per second. A push of only 2 lbs. lasting for one second would do the same.

Gun recoil, with which all shooters are familiar, provides another way of looking at this matter. The recoil impulse involved in bringing the bullet up to speed is equal to that on the target in stopping it, except that the gun recoil is always heavier by the reaction from accelerating the powder gases also.

To make the movement clearly visible, THE AMERICAN RIFLEMAN con-structed a wooden dummy of approximately the height and outline of a man. It was mounted on a platform rolling on sealed ball bearings of very good quality. Lead plates within the figure brought its weight to 175 lbs. and stopped the bullets. The figure moved freely at the push of a fingertip.

Impact of a .22 long rifle standard-velocity bullet caused the figure to roll back 1/16", an amount barely visible. The .38 Special factory bullet moved the figure 3/16"; the .45 M1911 Service bullet moved it ½"; and the .30-'06 commercial 150-gr. bullet moved it 2¼". These give a good idea of the comparative movement from impact of different bullets, and of the smallness of the movement throughout. ∎

MAY 1962　　　　　　　　　　　　　　　　　27

The *American Rifleman* story showing the 175-pound test dummy on its free-rolling platform. Even a solid hit with a .30-06 bullet, three times more powerful than a .44 Magnum, moved the dummy just 2¼ inches.

STOPPING POWER

We've been talking about "knockdown," a force that is different from "stopping power," which is how that force affects whatever has been hit.

Stopping power is a vague term too, but it has practical meaning. When a bullet hits an animal or person, it usually, as a doctor might say, "interrupts the life functions." It penetrates skin and tissue and may cut blood vessels, muscles and tendons and break bones. A bullet that snaps an animal's spine

Brad Fitzpatrick Outdoors

Stopping an animal with a bullet isn't always the same thing as killing it, and where a bullet is put is much more important than how powerful it is. To practice for hunting really big game in Africa, this hunter is firing a double-barreled rifle at a realistic elephant target at the Safari Shooting School in Texas. (Where is his eye and ear protection?)

usually drops the animal in its tracks. (It may even look like it was flipped over onto its side, but that's the effect of gravity plus where or how it was standing.) A bullet into the brain, heart or lungs will also stop an animal, either near-instantly or within some minutes, depending on a whole raft of factors. It

doesn't have to be a large bullet, either, as Karamojo Bell showed with his 1,000-plus elephants killed with .275-caliber rifles. This is stopping power, and it's the reason a relatively tiny bullet can kill so massive an animal as a rhino or an elephant.

A bullet doesn't necessarily have to go deep, either. A .600 Nitro slug might not penetrate a charging elephant's thick skull, but the impact on the animal's forehead may stun it and make it drop to its knees. It's been stopped, literally, but not killed. The hunter has to follow up with a fatal shot, or the beast will regain its senses and be a nuisance again. (This won't work with a .275, which has relatively little shocking power and has to penetrate to a critical organ to be effective.)

So stopping power is not an overwhelmingly fast or heavy bullet; it's a well-placed one.

And, no matter what, a bullet or shotgun blast can't throw its victim up against a wall or even push him to the ground.

Hollywood is never bothered by such details. Six-shot revolvers fire 20 times without reloading, cowboys shoot Indians from galloping horses, action heroes leap from one building to another while accurately firing pistols in each hand, and Dirty Harry's .44 puts bad guys into orbit. Hope we didn't ruin it for you, but now you know.

Knockdown Force

Here's another way to look at knockdown force: Imagine being charged by a big bull rhino. The beast weighs three tons. But you're facing him with a .600 Nitro Express firing a 900-grain bullet that generates 8,400 foot-pounds of energy at the muzzle. Three tons is only 6,000 pounds—you've got him covered. Hey, they don't call these things "stopping rifles" for nothing!

Well, again, no. The force required to stop the beast is equal to its own momentum, which is easy to calculate: mass (in pounds divided by 32.2) multiplied by its velocity (in feet per second). If he's coming at 15 miles per hour, that's 22 fps, so the formula is (6,000 ÷ 32.2) × 22 = 4,099 foot-pound-seconds.

Now let's figure out the momentum of the bullet, which would have to be the same or more in order to stop the rhino—that is, to completely cancel its forward rush. The 900-grain bullet has a muzzle velocity of 2,050 fps, so let's say Mr. Rhino is close enough that the bullet's velocity has dropped to a nice, round 2,000 fps by the time the two collide. Nine hundred grains equals 0.1285 pounds, so momentum becomes (0.1285 ÷ 32.2) × 2,000 = 7.9 foot-pound-seconds.

Still feeling confident about knocking the rhino on his butt?

We know that a bullet's energy comes from both its mass and its velocity, and something light and fast can make as much energy as something that's heavier but traveling more slowly. So let's see how fast your .600 bullet would have to be traveling to generate enough momentum to counteract the rhino. If we divide the bullet's mass (0.1285 pounds) into 4,099 foot-pound-seconds, the pounds cancel out and we get 31,898 fps! That's eight times faster than the hottest cartridges yet made, and they fire tiny 50-grain bullets, not fingertip-size .600 slugs.

Even if it were possible to drive a bullet that fast without destroying the rifle, the recoil would of course knock you ass over teakettle too—Newton's Third Law and all that.

Jofie Lamprecht Photography

A big bull rhino that weighs three tons and charges at 15 miles per hour has much more momentum than a bullet can generate, so the hunter has to "interrupt its life functions" with a well-placed bullet instead.

Armor All

Protecting Your Ears, Eyes & Other Body Parts

We're not telling you to wear ballistic armor whenever you go out to blow up tin cans with your .22. No, the main thing here is to protect yourself against two kinds of incidental injury—one that otherwise *will* happen every time you fire a gun (or are near someone who does) and another that *can* happen any time you're shooting or are around shooting. You can protect yourself easily in both cases; you just have to remember to do it.

EARS

A lot of shooters, particularly older ones who didn't wear hearing protection when they were kids, think everyone around them is just mumbling all the time. Many shooters also have tinnitus, a high-pitched buzzing in their ears that never goes away. We can make up for some hearing loss with hearing aids, but they're expensive and annoying. Tinnitus can't be cured or gotten rid of, and it's really unpleasant.

The best way to protect your hearing is with foam ear plugs worn in addition to earmuffs. Some people think ear defenders aren't needed while shooting smallbore guns like .22s or .17s—but you know better.

The good news is that both problems can easily be prevented by wearing some kind of hearing protection when we shoot. The goal is to prevent the sonic blast of a too-loud sound wave from reaching the sensitive micro-hairs inside our ears that we hear with. No one is immune to hearing damage, so it's not a matter of if, but when and how much. And once the damage is done, the ear can't heal itself or be repaired.

A .22 makes a sharp *crack!* when it goes off, but it's not a huge noise. No big deal, you say. True, maybe, for a few shots. But over a year, how many times do you hear it? And then we graduate to bigger guns that make more noise, and we start shooting sporting clays or combat pistol competitions, or hunting. Remember: The damage adds up. Our ears don't "rest" when we're not shooting and then start fresh again.

If you've watched shooting competitions or demonstrations, you've already noticed that almost everyone wears earmuffs. Most of them also have plugs in their ears under the muffs. This doesn't interfere with shooting; in fact, the reduction in noise helps them concentrate, for better scores, in addition to protecting their hearing.

It's hunters who really have a problem. They need to hear what's going on around them—the sounds of a bird dog's bell, a deer tiptoeing through leaves, the snort of a buffalo. Many hunters figure that they're not going to fire their guns often, so they can get by with naked ears. It's sort of true; a deer hunter might shoot just once or twice in an entire season (or not at all, if he strikes out). Again, though, the damage adds up, and just one blast from a rifle can cause damage.

The best solution for hunters is expensive: custom-fitted electronic plugs that allow normal sounds to enter the ear but that instantly shut down when they detect a noise that's too loud. (These plugs are often some hideous color like neon orange, because the owner lost his first pair when he put them down somewhere and walked off without them.)

The next-best thing is dirt-cheap: foam plugs that you squash in your fingers and stick into your ears. They expand to fill any ear canal, no matter how oddly shaped, and they block the worst of a gunshot. Some hunters put these things halfway into their ears, so they can hear, and then jam them all the way in when it's time to shoot. This is helpful—if you remember and if you have time. Every gunshop and shooting range gives away packets of these things.

Target shooters, and here we mean everyone who uses a gun in a situation where they can control when they fire, should wear foam plugs or over-the-ear muffs specifically meant for shooting, or both. (Or use a suppressor—see "Silencers: Naughty or Nice?.") Make sure the earpieces, or temples, of your shooting glasses don't ruin the seal of the muffs around your ears.

If you're standing around and watching someone shoot and you don't have your ear defenders with you, block your ears with your fingers.

It isn't just shooting, either. If you're next to someone on the bus and you can hear the music they're listening to in their earbuds, it's too loud. Even if they don't notice it yet, they're losing hearing and lowering the threshold for more damage. They are that much closer to permanent loss.

Everyone, not just shooters, is exposed to noise that's too loud. Leaf blowers, lawn mowers and chain saws will do damage; so will dance clubs and rock concerts, certain motorcycles and just about every airplane engine, if you're too close. These noises may not be as momentarily loud as a gunshot, but they go on for much longer.

Pay attention to what you're hearing. If running the power mower or the snowblower is your job, wear the ear protection you use for shooting.

EYES

Losing part of your hearing is bad enough, but an eye? It doesn't take much to injure or destroy an eye, either. Even worse, something could not only destroy your eye but also penetrate the back of your eye socket and enter your brain. (We went over this in "You'll Put Your Eye Out!")

It isn't just a ricochet, either, or a misdirected shotgun pellet. Hot combustion gasses can come back at your face. (Percussion and flintlock guns, and even modern revolvers, are prone to this.) Automatic guns eject empty cartridge cases with considerable force. People who shoot clay pigeons have shards of broken targets flying around. Hunters

Different lens colors can help you see targets better depending on light conditions, but protecting your eyes from bits of clay pigeon, twigs, brush and even shot pellets is even more important than helping you shoot well. And that means choosing the right lens material.

dodge twigs and brush. Guns can explode and fling bits of shrapnel around like grenades. Let's not even mention BBs, airgun pellets or paintballs.

And finally, like good sunglasses, shooting glasses should also filter out ultraviolet rays of sunlight. Protecting your eyes while shooting is not merely a good idea, it's essential.

Just as with ears and hearing, the solution is simple: safety glasses or goggles (or helmet visors, if you insist on Paintball or Airsoft). There are three different sets of standards for impact resistance in eyeglasses. You can find them easily on the Internet, if you like to wade through legal and technical jargon, but all you really need to know is that you should wear high-quality *shooting* glasses.

Don't rely on ordinary sunglasses or your own eyeglasses to stop a shotgun pellet or a bit of shrapnel. They may stop it, but they may not, either. And then your eye will have to deal with not only the pellet or whatever, but also shards of broken lens.

Impact-resistant glass is heavy. The best shooting lenses are plastic: CR39, Polycarbonate or Trivex. Polycarbonate was invented in the 1970s for aircraft windshields and military pilots' helmet visors. Trivex is newer, just as strong but thinner and lighter, and has better optical qualities. Both materials block ultraviolet rays too. They are softer than glass and need scratch-resistant coatings. The lenses also have to be mounted in a tough frame; impact-resistant lenses aren't much use if they pop out of their frames when they're hit.

If you wear glasses anyway, you can find shooting glasses that fit over them. Wraparound lenses offer more side protection, but the extra curvature of the lenses may cause some distortion. The parts of the frame that go back to your ears are called the temples. We like cable-style temples, the ones that wrap around your ear. They stay on better.

Once you've decided on the frames and lens material, you can pick lens colors to enhance your aim. Shooting glasses often come with several sets of interchangeable lenses. Shooters who are looking for better contrast, to make their targets stand out, use yellow, orange or reddish lenses, depending on the target and the background and whether it's sunny or cloudy. Hunters usually want no shift in how they see colors, so they choose neutral gray lenses that reduce sunlight evenly, not just part of it. (Sunglasses, in other words, but impact-resistant ones.) On a gray day, gray lenses may be too dark; in that case pop in the clear ones.

Try them all and see which ones you like. Make sure you get them mounted right in the frames, so they don't come out just when you might need them the most.

OTHER BODY PARTS

Many shooters wear thin, close-fitting gloves. They give decent trigger feel and they don't make you any more clumsy when it comes to reloading. They do, however, protect your hands from a hot barrel (somewhat). On a cold day they're warm, on a hot day they soak up some sweat, and in both cases they can improve your grip on a gun.

Hats are always good. They help protect your head and face from the flying junk that glasses are meant to ward off. Also, just keeping the sun out of your eyes improves your shooting.

You'll see a lot of shooting shirts and jackets with patches sewn onto the shoulders. These may not soak up much recoil, but they can help you bring a rifle or shotgun to your shoulder in a nice, smooth mount that won't snag on buttons, straps, seams or wrinkles in the fabric.

Bob Allen

A shock-absorbing, foam-filled recoil pad that straps over your shoulder. This can help you get used to a new, harder-recoiling shotgun or rifle.

Some companies offer recoil pads that strap onto your shoulder or fit into a pocket on a shirt. If they stay in place, they do absorb some kick. They are most useful if you get a chance to put a few rounds through an unfamiliar and hard-recoiling gun. (If we worked for a gun company as a tester and fired lots of rounds through big-bore guns, we'd wear one.)

Beretta

Shooting gloves should fit snugly so you can hold and work the gun and feel the trigger. They can also protect your hands from hot barrels.

BULLETPROOF VESTS: REALLY?

Well, maybe. You can almost answer this question yourself if you think about it: Body armor *will* resist a bullet, depending on its mass and shape and velocity and on what sort of armor we're talking about. An undershirt that will trap a blunt-nosed, 115-grain 9mm slug generating less than 400 foot-pounds of energy is no defense against a 661-grain .50-caliber bullet that's still making 10,000 foot-pounds a hundred yards downrange.

It's the same thing with vehicles. Sure, the warlord's Land Cruiser has multi-layer Lexan windows, hardened ballistic-steel body panels, anti-mine plates underneath and puncture-proof, run-flat tires, so his enemies can fire all the AK and maybe even 12.7mm they've got at him—but a hundred-pound Hellfire missile from a Reaper drone will put him and his Toyota out of business in a single awful blast of heat, smoke and flame.

Rather than bullet-*proof*, it's better to think of ballistic armor as bullet-*resistant*. Also, the bullet has to hit the armor in the first place, and no one is covered from head to toe. Military and police vests help protect the heart, lungs and torso and sometimes the crotch and back of the neck, but hands, arms, shoulders, throat, face and head, not to mention the legs and feet, are exposed.

When special squads raid a big meth lab, they wear impact-resistant goggles and helmets, gloves, knee and elbow pads, lace-up boots with steel toe caps and insoles and, over their battle dress, bulky Type III ballistic vests. They're following the basic rule of body armor: Protect yourself against the sort of weapon that you're carrying yourself or that you expect to face. In these cases the cops usually go in with 9mm submachine guns and possibly 12-gauge shotguns. There will be several marksmen waiting outside with rifles too.

Along with a couple of pit bulls or Rottweilers, the villains inside might have pistols (9mm,

No body armor provides complete protection against every threat. Look at this SWAT warrior dressed for work: Even with a helmet and the add-on panels over his crotch, shoulders, neck and throat, he's still very exposed. Add more protection and he'd lose a lot of mobility.

.40 S&W, .45 ACP), submachine guns (9mm, .45 ACP), maybe shotguns and AR (5.56mm) or AK rifles (7.62x39mm). If they have time, they might even put on the same kind of vests.

Type III is the armor of choice here because the US National Institute of Justice certifies it against the 7.62mm NATO round—a 147-grain FMJ (full metal jacket) bullet launched at 2,780 fps. In other words, something a bit hotter than whatever either side is likely to be shooting.

There are five other standard categories of body armor. Three are rated for handgun calibers: Type IIA (withstands up to .40 S&W), Type II (up to .357 Magnum) and Type IIIA (.44 Magnum). The other two, including Type III, are for rifles. Type IV is supposed to stop an armor-piercing 166-grain bullet fired at 2,880 fps—a .30-06 round. The NIJ will also test special armor meant to counter higher threat levels.

The armor may be flexible (some combination of woven fibers such as Kevlar and nylon) or hard, with plates of steel, titanium or a ceramic such as boron or silicon carbide. A Type IIA vest is light and flexible enough to be worn under a shirt, but as the level of protection increases, the garment gets heavier, thicker and more awkward until finally no one wants to wear it any more. And then it does no good at all.

Stopping a bullet is excellent, but getting hit with a round that doesn't penetrate can still hurt—a lot, sometimes. The transmitted energy creates the "backface signature," which is determined by shooting at armor mounted on modeling clay and then measuring the indent of the bullet. In its resistance ratings, the National Institute of Justice allows for up to 44mm of backface signature. That's 1¾ inches, more than enough to cause internal injuries, depending on where you're hit.

We might say, "A bulletproof vest may keep you out of the mortuary but not the hospital."

KEVLAR & RHINO HIDE

Reportedly, more than 3,000 American law-enforcement personnel have been saved by body armor since Kevlar hit the market in the early 1970s. Kevlar is a light but super-strong synthetic fiber that was invented at the Du Pont chemical company in 1965. Strands or sheets of Kevlar are now in everything from skis to tires to boats, as well as all sorts of protective helmets and clothing, even hunting vests that will stop birdshot. Before Kevlar, fiberglass, aluminum, nylon and ceramics were used in body armor.

Armor in the form of thick leather surely goes back to prehistory. The ancient Chinese used turtle shells and rhino hide and then bronze plates sewn onto leather.

Mounted knights, the heavy cavalry of medieval Europe and Britain, wore elaborate suits of steel-plate armor. Plate was far too expensive for foot soldiers; they wore mail armor, fine links of iron chain woven together. Crossbow bolts and arrows from powerful longbows could punch right through chain mail and sometimes (depending on range, the power of the bow and the type of arrowhead, its angle of impact, the thickness and quality of the steel and other things) even plate armor. Then knights began wearing mail under their plate. No matter how good the armor, though, the problem of coverage never went away; there were always gaps or weak spots where something sharp could get in.

Just like a medieval knight's warhorse, this 1920s Crossley military vehicle was outfitted with overlapping armor plates rated to stop "automatic pistol fire." But the more armor, the greater the weight and the slower the vehicle.

Steve Helsley Collection

Some knights wound up wearing close to a hundred pounds of steel and weaponry, so archers or pikemen would go after their horses—armored too but not as completely. On foot, a heavily armored man was clumsy and could be surrounded and overwhelmed, especially if his field of view was limited by a helmet meant to keep out arrows.

There's always a trade-off between coverage and mobility. The size and weight of armor has consequences too. Knights' warhorses had to be bred bigger and bigger to carry the load. In World War II, Britain's Royal Air Force stopped issuing flak jackets because they were too bulky to wear in the Avro Lancaster bomber.

Firearms arrived on the battlefield no later than 1415, but it was another 300 years before massed musket fire finally made suits of armor obsolete. To be effective after that, the steel had to be so thick that full suits were impossibly heavy. Steel vests, however, were used into the 1940s.

Hank Morgan, the hero of Mark Twain's 1889 sci-fi satire novel *A Connecticut Yankee in King Arthur's Court*, used 19th Century technology to take over 6th Century England. At the end Morgan, "the Boss," and a small band of young cadets wipe out an army of 30,000 knights with electricity and Gatling guns.

The idea that old-fashioned armor couldn't stand up against modern guns is so common that in 1961 the National Rifle Association put it to the test. The staff of *American Rifleman*, an NRA magazine, got a genuine 17th Century breastplate, a steel vest weighing about eight pounds and a little more than an eighth of an inch thick, and shot at it from a distance of 24 feet. The results surprised them.

Blackpowder musket and pistol balls (.71 and .60 caliber) couldn't punch through. Then they shifted to modern handguns. Everything from .22 rimfire up through .357 Magnum, including metal-

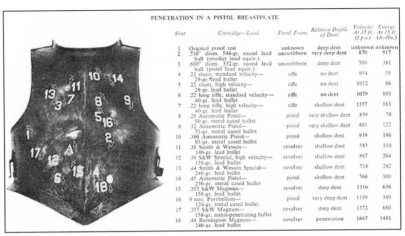

This must have been a fun test. Here is part of the *American Rifleman* magazine story from October 1961 showing the results (including dents) of shooting modern guns at a 300-year-old steel breastplate. The old armor turned out to be truly bulletproof—most of the time.

jacketed .45 ACP, at best only dented the steel. Not until they unleashed a .44 Magnum did a single round penetrate the vest.

A direct hit from a .30-caliber rifle would have wounded or killed the wearer, but this was so-called "half proof" or pistol armor. In the late 1600s, thicker musket armor was called "full proof"; had the NRA found a good example of this to test, who knows what the results would have been?

When it comes to personal combat, it's been a many-centuries-long race between offense (stones to swords and arrows to bullets) and defense (leather to bronze to iron to steel to Kevlar). Some ancient cultures went with thickness and flexibility instead of strength and rigidity: The Aztecs of Mexico used quilted cotton, while in Asia highly effective body armor was made of layers of paper or silk.

Silk is marvelous stuff. In the blackpowder era, people often put on silk when they went out to fight, because the long, strong fibers could be removed from a gunshot wound more easily than wool or cotton. Now synthetic spider silk is being tested for bullet-resistance, and at least one company offers dressy-looking clothes that will stop a pistol bullet at point-blank range. The light, flexible, silky fabric is a closely guarded secret, but it seems to be a big step forward.

Shooting at Stuff

Secrets of Becoming a Good Shot

Hey, you got a BB gun for your birthday. Great! What are you going to do with it?

If you've read "You'll Put Your Eye Out!" you know a lot about air guns already, including where to shoot them and what *not* to shoot with them. As you've seen, it's easy to set up a range for BB guns at home. You need just three things: a safe place to shoot, a backstop to trap the BBs and some targets.

Make that four things. You also need permission from your parents. Read this section and the next four (down through "The Law") carefully and completely yourself, and then show them to one or both of your parents. When they're on board with the project, you may proceed.

Assuming you're not breaking the law (see below), the best place to shoot a BB gun is usually the basement of your house. Ideally, you'll have at least 30 feet of space, although just 25 feet would be OK. If you can, set the backstop against a wall that doesn't have a window nearby. Basement walls are usually hard enough to make a BB bounce, so get someone to help you hang an old bed sheet behind the backstop to trap any stray shot.

If your house doesn't have a basement, does it have an attic with enough space? How about a room that your family will let you convert into a shooting range at least part of the time? This might work in a city apartment too. The hanging bed sheet should keep walls and windows safe.

The backstop is just a good-size cardboard box, like what a microwave oven or desktop computer comes in. (Everybody used to use TV boxes, but now TVs are flat-screens and the boxes aren't

If you can't find a big cardboard box, companies such as Beeman make pellet and BB traps that hold different targets and are safe for indoor shooting. The silhouettes spin when you hit them. If the steel deforms your BBs and pellets, you won't be able to reuse them.

fat enough.) Fill it with wadded-up newspaper and tape it closed. The cardboard won't stop your BBs, but the newspaper will. You can just put the box on the floor, or set it on top of another box or a pair of sawhorses or the like.

You can buy paper bull's-eye targets like the ones used in official competitions (like the Olympic 10-meter air-gun events) or targets with everything from squirrels to charging rhinos to terrorists on them. There are hundreds of different kinds and sizes available. There are even Websites with targets that you can download to your computer and print out.

After you've shot up some of your ammunition, open up the box and harvest the BBs. They won't be deformed, so you can use them again.

MORE TARGETS

Punching holes in paper can get boring after a while. Then you start looking around for more interesting things to shoot at. Tin cans that jump when they're hit! Save these for shooting outdoors with your .22; you don't want BBs ricocheting around the basement.

When we were younger, we had three favorite targets. One was the red cardboard tube that the BBs came in. It was about three inches long and a lot less than an inch in diameter. Hung on a string in front of the backstop, it jerked and swung around when hit. After a while, we could keep it swinging back and forth by hitting it at just the right place each time. BBs still come in tubes or small bottles; they're made of plastic, but this should still work.

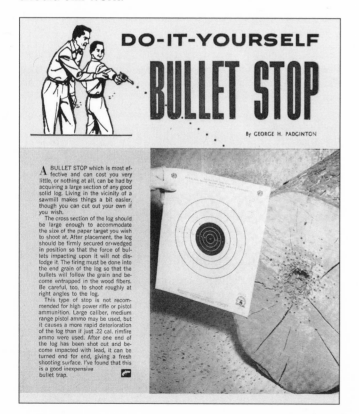

The September 1957 issue of *Guns* magazine suggested the end of a log as a cheap and easy bullet stop. It's still a good idea, at least until the wood has been shot to shreds.

Another favorite: Necco candy wafers. They're about the size of a quarter and break with a nice puff when hit by a BB—kind of like a mini-mini-clay pigeon, except obviously you can't throw them in the basement. Instead, stick them to your backstop with some folded-over Scotch Tape.

The best targets, though, were little plastic figurines, like toy soldiers. First we lined them up in front of the backstop box. Pretty soon we were hiding the "enemy soldiers" behind "barricades" and toy trucks and so on.

Some adults have gotten completely carried away with this urban-warfare game. They set up elaborate miniature street scenes, with buildings and vehicles, "innocent civilians" and hidden "enemy snipers." Instead of BB guns, they use match-quality air rifles with scopes and scale their shooting distances to the size of the figurines. Hitting a three-inch figure 75 feet away is like shooting a six-foot person at a range of 600 yards.

You can do the arithmetic yourself. Convert everything to inches first, then do a simple ratio calculation. (A six-foot human at 200 yards looks like a three-inch toy soldier at 25 feet. Your Dad probably has a 25-foot tape measure you can borrow.) Then go for it—hostage situations, counter-sniper fire, street-by-street squad actions, air extractions, whatever. You can shoot offhand or from a rest, lying down behind a barricade, against a timer, whatever. All it takes is imagination.

Whatever angles you shoot at or targets or obstacles you set up, keep the 15 Commandments (see "Safety First") in mind. Even with a BB gun, always be aware of what's behind your target and of the possibility of damage or ricochet.

NOT SHOOTING INDOORS

B y the time one of us was 15, he had an arsenal of four firearms, plus a Daisy air rifle and a Plainsman CO_2 pistol. Still too young to drive himself to a shooting range, he set up a range in the basement. He took the cardboard box a television came in, stuffed it with newspaper and taped targets to it. Then he blazed away with his single-shot Stevens Favorite and an H&R revolver, both .22s, indoors. (Not recommended. See below. He also had no eye or ear protection.)

Most kids have a friend who their parents don't like. Naturally, it was that very friend who the author invited over "to do some shooting" one day 50 years ago, when both his parents were out. Everything went fine for a while. Then the friend loaded and cocked the Stevens, pointed it straight up and *bang!*

"It was like having an ice cube pass through an artery into my heart.

"Luckily, no one was home. We ran upstairs to look. The bullet had passed through the hardwood floor and the carpet over it, just missed the dining room table and went into the plaster ceiling. Trying to flatten the bump in the floor didn't work. Covering the hole in the ceiling was out of the question. All we could do was wait.

Practice targets come in about every imaginable style. This one, from Caldwell, is life-size; the deer's vital areas are drawn in, for scoring hits, but the shooter can't see the lines at normal hunting distances. Every hunter owes it to the game to practice and practice for a clean kill.

"Dad was home for about 20 minutes before he spotted the hole in the ceiling. A full and immediate confession minimized the long-term problems. Until Dad patched the hole, though, whenever the heater came on, plaster dust floated around the room as a reminder of a very bad idea."

Firearms Indoors?

Almost always a bad idea, as you read above. Unless you live in a very unusual house, you don't have the sort of bulletproof walls and floors needed to stop a .22 bullet that's aimed the wrong way. Not to mention dealing with the noise and the powder fumes.

Also, as you know, pellet guns are generally much more powerful than BB guns, so we're including them in the category of **Do Not Use Indoors**—even in the basement.

By the way, many towns and cities have zoning regulations about building an indoor shooting range, even for private use. Even if you can follow those rules, building a safe indoor range is expensive and probably impractical. It will be easier and better to join a licensed commercial range or gun club.

THE LAW

It is illegal to discharge a firearm in many towns and cities. Furthermore, while in this book we use "firearm" to mean a gun that fires a projectile by the action of an explosive (in other words, not an air or CO_2 gun), some towns and cities define a firearm like this: "any instrument used in the propulsion of pellets, shot, shells or bullets by action of gunpowder, compressed air or gas exploded or released within it." So shooting your BB gun outdoors may be illegal.

You might even be breaking the law by firing it indoors. Really. In many places it's illegal to fire a gun within a certain distance of a house or other building—usually 100 to 500 feet. Well, shooting inside the house is within that distance, so if your BB gun is considered a "firearm," you may be out of luck. Your parents will have to figure this out for you.

Adults sometimes buy pellet guns to drive off pests like squirrels or crows that are getting into the attic or making a racket in the yard, but this may be illegal too, depending on the local definition of a firearm.

Even if the law doesn't forbid shooting an air gun in your community, going outside with a BB gun in your hands may freak out your neighbors. They may come over and ask you what you're up to or call your parents. Or they might just call the cops.

Your neighbors aren't necessarily over-reacting either. Considering the property damage and injuries to people and pets that even a BB gun can cause, they have a right to wonder whether you are a safe and responsible shooter.

'PRACTICE MAKES PERFECT'

There are a lot of other old sayings that we can quote here too. Like "It takes 20 years to become an overnight success." Or "The continuous drip polishes the stone." Or even "Stick to your guns." The point of all of them is that, whether we're talking about playing the violin or shooting baskets or shooting a gun, there is no substitute for practice.

Kim Rhode, who won her first world skeet championship when she was 13 and earned an Olympic gold medal in doubles trap five days after her 17th birthday, fires 500 to 1,000 rounds every time she goes out to practice. Which is almost every day of the week. Like all world-champion athletes, Kim has almost superhuman reflexes and hand-eye coordination. But if she didn't hone those natural abilities with constant practice, she'd be just a lucky shot, not an expert one.

Shooting practice means capping off rounds— a lot of them. But by itself, shooting doesn't do much more than give us an instinctive feel for the gun. This is very important, but if we shoot badly, doing it over and over just makes the bad habits stick harder.

Before you ask: Yes, it is possible to shoot badly and still hit the target. Just because you're crushing those Necco wafers with your Daisy doesn't necessarily mean you're an expert. If your technique is poor but you're hitting targets, just think how much better you'd be if your technique was good.

"Technique" is everything that we do in handling and firing a gun, from loading it to taking aim, the let-off (trigger squeeze) and follow-through, and reloading, plus our ingrained safety habits. Even the way we carry and hold a gun is part of our technique.

So how do you know if your technique needs work?

While you're shooting a BB gun in the basement, only two things really matter: safety and fun. Stick to the guidelines in this book and you'll be safe; if you love to shoot, you'll be having fun. When it's time to move outdoors or to a proper shooting range with a .22 rifle, your parents will have to get involved again. (We explain this in *The Gun Book for Parents*.) They will help you find a mentor: an experienced, grown-up shooter who'll help you in the next stages of shooting. Among other things, your

American shooting star Kim Rhode is an athlete blessed with awesome reflexes and skills, but she still has to hone them with constant practice.

mentor will help you develop techniques for the kinds of shooting you want to do.

Your Mentor

Mentor was a veteran warrior in *The Odyssey*, that epic story from ancient Greece. Odysseus, the hero, asked Mentor to keep an *eye* on his son Telemachus while Odysseus took off to fight in the Trojan War. With some help from the gods, Mentor did such a good job of teaching Telemachus and keeping him out of trouble that, more than 2,000 years later, we still call this kind of older, trusted counselor and teacher a mentor.

Once you have a shooting mentor, think of us, the authors of this book, as the mythological gods of shooting who are here to back him (or her) up.

Thanks to Odysseus (pictured here), we have mentors today.

Dry-Firing & the Dime/Washer Exercise

This means shooting a gun without ammunition in it—when it's "dry," or unloaded. Or, as an army gunnery instructor might say, "to simulate the firing of live rounds with an empty weapon."

Dry-firing is an important part of shooting practice, and you should build every part of shooting into it: position, aiming, breathing and trigger squeeze, as well as safety habits. Without the bang and the recoil, dry-firing even helps prevent the involuntary flinching that can come from shooting too much gun. (In fact, someone who's never fired a gun should always do some supervised dry-firing first.)

The "secret" to good shooting is endless practice—while wearing the sort of gear you'd have on in the field. Military forces usually set up very realistic practice areas that copy the sort of combat conditions their soldiers will face.

The US Army and Marine Corps can turn total newbies into marksmen in a few weeks. It requires hours of live fire on the range, and also a lot of just handling their weapons and dry-firing them in different ways. There's even something called the Weaponeer, a training device that looks, feels and "shoots" like an M16 rifle. It's linked to a computer that tells an instructor how the student is messing up and even prints out the "target" that the trainee "fired."

Here's something else the Army does that we can do too. It's called the Dime/Washer Exercise: With your rifle unloaded and cocked, and with a dime (or a washer) balanced on the receiver, aim at a target taped to the wall and *sque-e-eze* the trigger. If you can hold your aim and drop the hammer six times in a row without dropping the dime, you've mastered the smooth let-off. Do it from the standing, sitting and prone positions. Think of the trigger as the connection between your brain and your gun.

This is more difficult with guns like the Ruger 10/22, which has a rounded receiver, than it is with rifles that have flat tops, but difficult is better. (It might not even be possible with a gun that drops its hammer really hard.) The biggest drawback is that you can't do it alone; you need someone to place the dime after you've shouldered the rifle.

Ready for a real challenge? Try this with a pistol. And then with a double-action revolver, cycling it with the trigger.

Here is a critically important thing about dry-firing: The safety commandments are still in force. (Go back to "Safety First" and review.) Even though it's unloaded and you're just practicing, you must treat the gun as if it is loaded. Keep it pointed in a safe direction. Don't point it at anything you're not willing to shoot. Keep your finger outside the trigger guard until you're ready to shoot. Keep the safety on until you're ready to shoot. Be sure of your target and what's behind it. When you put the gun down or hand it to someone, open the action.

Yes, you're only dry-firing it, and, no, it's not loaded. But what if it is? As shooting instructors like to say, "Guns are sneaky. They'll reload themselves when you're not looking."

OK, so it is definitely not loaded. You've double-checked and re-checked, and anyway the ammunition is still in the safe. But dry-firing is meant to help you build your shooting technique, and safety habits are core parts of shooting technique.

If you have snap caps, add loading, ejecting and reloading to your dry-fire exercises. Most shooters seem to forget this, but good technique means more than just aim-and-squeeze. Think about facing a charging Cape buffalo with an empty rifle: You've got to grab your ammo, reload, mount, aim, fire and reload—quickly, smoothly *and* accurately. Make just one mistake and the buff wins.

SNAP CAPS

Snap caps are dummies (no powder, no primer, no projectile) shaped like the ammunition for a particular gun. They're supposed to provide something for the firing pin to hit during dry-firing, so the gun's lockwork doesn't have to absorb this impact. It's a fine idea, but not all snap caps are made right. If what the firing pin hits is too hard, the pin can deform. The best snap caps have spring-loaded disks or plastic inserts in them that give a bit when hit by the firing pin and then rebound.

One of us had an ancient British Webley .455 revolver that he dry-fired endlessly until one day the cast-metal hammer just snapped in half. Many modern guns, though, can be dry-fired thousands of times without snap caps with no damage. The real benefit of snap caps then is to practice handling "ammunition"—loading, unloading, ejecting.

(If you're dry-firing a semi-automatic of some sort, you'll have to eject the "fired" snap cap manually. Speaking of semi-autos, Ruger says that its

These are snap caps for different shotgun bores, but dummy practice cartridges come in all gauges, calibers and styles. The good ones have special inserts that absorb the impact of the firing pin without damaging it.

super-popular 10/22 rifle, our choice as one of today's top fun guns, isn't hurt by dry-firing and doesn't need snap caps.)

So have at it. Just 20 minutes of practice, especially with the Dime/Washer Exercise, three times a week can make a huge difference in your shooting.

DRY-FIRING SHOTGUNS

Shooting moving targets with a shotgun is generally harder than hitting something that's standing still with a rifle, so dry-firing can be even more helpful in wingshooting. Think about this: You have to hold, mount and fire the gun—but while everything is in motion. To hit moving targets consistently, the gun has to be moving too.

What's more, a shotgun has to *keep* moving, even after the shot has been fired. That's the follow-through, and without it you'll shoot behind the target every time.

Mount the gun to your shoulder while your body swivels toward the bird. With both eyes on the target, catch up to the bird with the gun's barrels, swing past it on the line it's flying, and pull the trigger. If everything comes together right, the gun shoots where your eyes are looking. Swinging the gun ahead of the bird creates the "lead" that's needed to intercept a moving target. (Like a quarter-

back who throws the ball to where his receiver *will* be when the ball gets there.)

You can't learn wingshooting from a book any more than you can learn how to hit a golf ball by reading about it, but dry-firing is an excellent way to practice this swing-fire-and-follow-through movement. Instead of taping a bull's-eye on the wall, as you might for rifle or handgun dry-firing, pretend the bird is at the point where two walls and the ceiling meet, in a corner of the room. Face away from that point, and then smoothly turn toward it as you raise the gun to your shoulder. Find the line where one wall meets the ceiling and follow it to the "bird." Swing to and past that point, pulling the trigger as you pass through it.

After you've made double-double sure the gun is empty, of course.

THE MAN WITH ONE GUN

Here's another old saying: "Beware the man with one gun." It refers to a dude who uses the same gun for everything. Maybe he can't afford more than one or maybe it's by choice, but the point is that he's gotten lethal with it through constant use.

Karamojo Bell, the Scottish ivory hunter who retired rich after "harvesting" close to 2,000 elephants in the early 1900s, became a crack shot partly because of his rifles. Bell used bolt-actions that weighed half as much as some of the double-barreled shoulder cannons that other elephant hunters carried. But they didn't really carry them; their gunbearers did and handed them over when it was time to shoot. Bell's rifles never left his possession,

and they were so light he didn't even have slings on them. They were always in his hands, and he dry-fired them constantly. He also used them to shoot the hundreds of zebras, buffaloes, giraffes and other game needed to feed his work crews. Bell was "the man with one gun."

He had more than one, in fact, but they were all the same. Eventually they became extensions of his hands and eyes. Where good shots killed birds with shotguns at 40 yards, Bell could shoot birds out of the sky at a hundred yards with his rifles.

When we had only our .22 rifles to shoot, we were good too.

HUNTING THE BIG MOUSE

If your grandfather is a gun buff, he probably longs for the good old days, when a kid could put his .22 rifle across the handlebars of his bicycle and ride to school to shoot at the Junior Reserve Officer Training Corps range. You could buy an army-surplus .45 revolver through the mail for $15—and, for $189.50, a 20mm anti-tank gun left over from World War II. Those were also the days when shooting rats at the dump was a cherished pastime.

After our planet's next mass-extinction event (you know, an asteroid impact followed by megatsunamis, global forest fires, toxic rains and a global ash cloud, then nuclear winter), three species will likely survive: the cockroach, the coyote and the rat. In ancient Rome the rat was *Mus maximus*, the big mouse, and people have been trying to exterminate the big mouse since cave men invented the club. There are some 64 species of rats worldwide, and they don't just

The next best thing to stalking real dump rats might be this nightmare "Darkotic" target from Birchwood Casey. The fine print says "Any resemblance to real beings, living or dead, is purely coincidental."

eat farm crops; in Europe they were blamed for spreading the plague, the Black Death of the 14th Century.

Now there's the Rat Chick Rescue and Advocacy Group, which specializes in "rat rescues" and finding them good "forever homes." From their Website: "The Rat: Always loving, always caring, always misjudged."

Cuddly furballs? Maybe to a few people, but consider the uninhabited Italian island of Montecristo (made famous in *The Count of Monte Cristo*). According to biologists, it has one rat per square yard. Since it's four square miles in area, that's 12,390,400 rats. It would take 26 tons of poison pellets to rid the island of these rats—or you, a suppressed and scoped Ruger 10/22, and a lifetime supply of Long Rifle hollowpoints.

An early (circa 1814) English shooting book was called *Hanger To All Sportsmen*, and it included "The Rat Catching Secret." During the

American Revolution the author, Maj. Gen. George Hanger, was an aide to Sir Henry Clinton, commander of British forces in New York City. Hanger wrote that the rats in Sir Henry's headquarters were so thick that "he had been forced to have the bottom of the doors lined with tin, for they had nearly eaten through the door where he kept his papers." Using obviously exceptional ratting skills, Hanger reported that in one night he caught "very near three hundred."

That was during the flintlock era, when shooting rats was completely impractical. But help was on the way.

The rimfire cartridge appeared in the 1840s. This divinely inspired combination of lead, copper and propellant became major rat medicine with the introduction of the .22 Long Rifle round in the 1880s. (In the interest of truthiness, we must note that some historians feel the .22LR was put on earth for woodchucks, not rats, while others say gophers.) At the same time, the growth of cities brought about the spread of dumps, also known as "landfills." Whatever they were called, they became rat hunters' paradises, a young lad's Serengeti plains teeming with game.

Ask your granddad about rat hunting, and he may tear up embarrassingly while recounting tales of prowling through abandoned refrigerators, bald tires and broken furniture as majestic gulls soared overhead looking for rotting fruit. It took supreme sneakiness to get within range of a feeding rat, and then keen eyes and steady hands to put a 37-grain hollowpoint into such a small target.

German and Russian snipers stalking each other through the ruins of Stalingrad in 1942, Mausers versus Mosin-Nagants, were hardly more stealthy. And what better training for hunting the wily whitetail deer in the forests of Minnesota or tracking the elusive sitatunga (marshbuck) through the remote swamps of Zambia?

Ah, nature, red in tooth and claw. And we didn't even have to clean up afterward. The carcasses were already at the dump.

Some rat hunters rose to national prominence. (Probably.) The legendary Mike "Reloading Man" Ball may have been the Jeremiah Johnson of rat hunters. At the height of his career he would slip, at night, into the rice fields around a certain major airport. The landing lights of incoming airplanes lit up the reflective pink eyeballs of rats, giving away their locations, and soon a high-velocity lead pill was en route. (Try this today and see how long it takes a police tactical team to start hunting *you*.)

For a first date, one of your authors' fathers-in-law, a hopeless romantic, took his wife-to-be to the dump with a picnic lunch to shoot rats.

Rat hunting may have been the perfect shooting sport. It was close to home, dirt cheap, offered challenging targets and caused no harm to the environment or endangered any species. And every dump was a target-rich environment. But it is now mostly a memory. Alas, the habitat is being lost. Dumps now have roofs and are called transfer stations. Do rats even live in such sterile places?

He probably wasn't a rat man, but the German philosopher Goethe said it for all of us: "There is no past that we can bring back by longing for it." So sad.

Competition

Shooting Games: Ways to Test Your Skills

Make a snowball, and what are you going to do with it? Drop it on the ground? Feed it to the dog? No, you've got to throw it at something, or someone. And what good is a basketball or a Frisbee if you can't throw it? What's a gun for other than to hit something at a distance? The enjoyment we get from throwing things and from shooting comes mostly from the satisfaction of being accurate, of hitting whatever we're aiming at. It's a skill, and skills are to be developed and then tested—which means competition.

This isn't always just fun and games, either. The peasants of medieval England were required to be skilled archers. In 1363 King Edward III declared that "every man in the country, if he be able-bodied, shall, upon holidays, make use, in his games, of bows and arrows . . . and so learn and practice archery." The point was to have expert marksmen ready whenever king and country needed soldiers.

It worked. For two centuries, until firearms took over the battlefield, the longbow kept England safe from invasion. And five centuries after Edward III's declaration, both Britain and the US created National Rifle Associations to train citizens to shoot in case the army needed them. Naturally, the training involved target shooting.

Today we call any sort of lopsided fight, where one side wipes out the other without much damage to themselves, a "turkey shoot." In colonial

Capt. Bogardus was a famous boxed-pigeon shooter. When people turned against using live birds as targets, these spring-powered glass-ball launchers were invented. To try to be more realistic, the balls were sometimes filled with feathers—but they still weren't hard to hit.

America, though, a turkey shoot was a contest. Men and boys took turns shooting at a very small target: a turkey's head. The one who killed the turkey brought it home as his prize.

Now there are more kinds of organized target shooting than ever before involving about every sort of firearm available, from the guns of the Wild West to modern submachine guns, from short-range BB guns to long-range match rifles, and shotguns of every type.

Let's start with shotguns. The first wingshooting competitions used live pigeons. Today the most popular forms of target shooting with shotguns are trap, skeet and sporting clays, with targets called clay pigeons. Just as in other sports, there are leagues and championships and professionals. Most people, however, shoot clay pigeons just for fun or to practice for hunting.

TRAP SHOOTING

A man from Boston named Charles Portluck gets the credit for inventing trap shooting around 1866. At first, this meant shooting at glass balls launched by a catapult instead of live pigeons released from a trap. For realism, the balls could be filled with feathers that flew out in a puff when the ball was hit. But then in 1880 came the clay pigeon, a small disk that shatters when struck by a shot pellet. It flew much farther and faster than a glass globe and could be made to curve in the air (like a Frisbee). It didn't leave broken glass behind, either. Rules and regulations developed, and in 1900 trapshooting joined rifle and pistol matches as an event at the Olympic Games.

In modern trap, clay pigeons are thrown from a small building, called the house, set into the ground facing away from the shooters. Five shooters stand in a row 16 yards behind the house. In turn, each one calls for a target, which the trapper launches. The clay streaks away, climbing at a shallow angle. (The trap, or launcher, swings back and forth to vary the direction.) The challenge is to break each clay before it gets out of range.

Each person takes five shots from each of five positions for a round of 25. Scorekeepers note the

The ideal shotgun target came along in 1880: the clay pigeon. Modern claybirds fly like Frisbees, shatter easily and come in different sizes and colors. They can be easy or fiendishly hard to hit, depending on how they're thrown.

hits and misses. To do well in competition, shooters usually have to break several hundred clays without a miss. It becomes a test of mental concentration and even physical stamina.

To make things interesting, there's also handicap trap, where competitors shoot from farther behind the trap house. There's doubles trap too,

The five shooting stations and the house at a trap field. The angles vary, but the clay targets are always going away from the gun. Trap, skeet and sporting clays courses typically use electric machines to throw targets, but you can get inexpensive hand throwers too.

where two clays come out of the house at the same time going in different directions. Trap shooters use 12-gauge double-barreled guns or semi-autos loaded with two shells.

The hardest is International trap. Instead of just one machine, there's a line of 15 of them in the house (here called a bunker), each set at a different angle, and the clays are thrown much faster. The shooters also stand farther back. This is trap shooting as it's done in the Olympic Games.

The American ATA (Amateur Trapshooting Association) has special classes and categories for young shooters and even gives college scholarships to certain high-school trapshooters.

SKEET SHOOTING

Skeet was meant to be like shooting upland gamebirds—grouse, woodcock and quail that flush from the ground at close range and go rocketing off into the brush. The shooting is fast and near.

The shooting positions, or stations, are in a semi-circle. At each end of this half-circle is a trap house. One is the high house and the other is the low house, and they are 42 yards apart. They throw their clays toward each other. High-house clays start at 10 feet off the ground and climb up to 15 feet; low-house clays reach the same height but are launched from three feet off the ground. Each house always throws its targets the same way and at the same speed, but as the shooter moves around the semi-circle, the angles of the clays change.

In trap shooting the birds are always going away from the gun; in skeet they cross in front of the gun.

Skeet shooters begin at station 1, at the high house. Station 7 is at the low house. The five stations in between are spaced evenly along the semi-circle. At each one the shooter gets some combination of singles and doubles that adds up to 22 targets. A double is one clay from each house thrown at the same time. This is trickier than a trap double because the birds are moving in opposite directions, so you have to swing the gun one way and then abruptly stop and go the other way to catch the second clay before it's out of range.

Station 8 is in the middle, directly between the two houses, and here the shooter takes two singles, one from each house. If he hasn't missed any so far, he shoots one more from the low house for a total of 25. Just as in trap, really good skeet shooters can shoot a few hundred birds and miss just one or two.

Skeet was invented around 1915, also in Massachusetts. At first there were 12 stations in a complete circle around one trap house, in the center, and skeet was called "shooting around the clock." But this took up too much room, so the present layout was adopted. The man who made the game famous was William Harnden Foster, a well-known bird hunter, writer and artist who was also the editor of two outdoor magazines. He wrote about the new shotgun game, and one of his readers (Gertrude Hurlbutt, of Dayton, Montana) won $100 by coming up with the winning name for it: "Skeet" (from the Scandinavian word for shoot: *skyte*).

Skeet Field Layout

A skeet field, with its half-moon layout, eight shooting stations and the high and low houses. Some shots are much harder than others, depending on where you are on the semi-circle. Station 8, on the line between the houses, takes a lot of practice, but then it's no longer so difficult.

It became tremendously popular. In World War II, American anti-aircraft gunners shot skeet as a way to learn how to hit fast-flying targets. Today there are skeet-shooting associations, tournaments and even a hall of fame. (Foster was the first member, naturally.) Serious skeet shooters use double-barreled over/ under guns in 12, 20 and 28 gauge and .410 bore. In 1968 skeet was added to the Olympic Games, where, like trap, it was made more difficult.

SPORTING CLAYS

Sporting clays is sometimes called golf with a shotgun because, just as there are different holes on a golf course, there are different stations on a sporting clays course. Each one presents clays in a way that imitates real gamebirds: "pheasants" flying fast directly away from the gun, "ducks" landing on or taking off from a pond in front of you, "quail" scattering in every direction, "doves" crossing fast, even "rabbits," which are clays rolled along the ground at high speed. There may be a dozen or more stations set in the woods or in the open, and at each one the shooter faces some combination of singles and doubles.

Clays can be thrown at all sorts of angles and speeds to all sorts of heights and distances. Clays come in different sizes and colors too. The traps, or launchers, can be on the ground or up on towers, behind bushes or on hillsides. No two stations, or even two sporting clays courses, are the same. The operator can change things around too. A trap that was throwing full-size clays could be loaded with minis, which are lighter and faster and harder to hit, and aimed in a different direction.

The British set up the first sporting clays courses long ago, but for some reason the idea didn't catch on in the US until about 1980. Today it's one of the most popular of all the shooting sports, and there are competitions at every level from local to international. Almost any kind of hunting shotgun can be used for sporting clays.

BIRDS IN BOXES

Pigeons are strong, agile, fast flyers, with big wings and strong chest muscles. Long before there were clay pigeons, shooters used real ones to test their skills.

Competitive pigeon shooting began in England in the late 1700s. If using live animals for target practice seems cruel, remember that this was in a time and place when popular entertainment included fights to the death between dogs, bulls or bears, and there was nothing that "the mob" enjoyed more than seeing criminals executed in public, usually by hanging. By comparison to these spectacles, shooting pigeons ("rats with wings") with expensive shotguns was a polite activity for gentlemen.

By 1812, when the first pigeon-shooting club, at London's Old Hats Tavern, was organized, rules regarding scoring, distances, shooting styles, guns

Ernest Hemingway, the famous writer, shooting boxed pigeons at the club he belonged to in Cuba in about 1941. The shooting stations are arranged as they are on a trap field; the bird boxes (called traps) are off to the right. Hemingway has fired his Winchester pump-action shotgun once—you can see the empty shell in the air—and he's about to shoot again, to try to "anchor" the bird before it can escape over the penalty fence.

and cartridges were being drawn up. Other clubs quickly sprang up, and the sport spread across Britain and then to Europe and America.

It became an expensive game with big prize money and big bets on the scores. Newspapers and magazines reported on the matches—and the disagreements, penalties, scandals and disgraces that went along with them—for their readers. (Baseball, football and basketball were still in the future.)

Just as racing made automobiles better, pigeon-shooting competitions advanced the design of shotguns and ammunition, and makers whose products won tournaments bragged about it in their advertising.

The shooter stood facing a row of small boxes about 30 yards away called traps. Twenty yards or so beyond the traps was a fence, inside which a pigeon had to fall in order to count.

When the shooter called for a bird, the trapper pulled a cord that opened one of the boxes. The pigeon inside would try to escape, and the gunner would try to kill it. To bring down one pigeon—launching itself off the ground at unpredictable angles, flying fast and dodging erratically—inside the fence took skill. To win a match of 10 birds in a row took skill, great concentration and some luck.

The first recorded American pigeon shoot took place in Ohio in 1831. As it had overseas, "trap shooting" spread rapidly. A famous competition in Kentucky in 1883 pitted professional sharpshooter "Doc" (William F.) Carver against Capt. A.H. (Adam Henry) Bogardus, the American and world pigeon champion. Carver outshot the captain 19 times in 25 matches. By this time, pigeon tournaments in the United States were drawing huge crowds, and the winners became celebrities.

Pigeon shooting even made a one-time appearance at the Olympics, in the Paris games of 1900. But by then the public was turning against using live targets, and the clay pigeon took over.

They may now be called boxed-bird or flyer shoots, but live-pigeon matches are still held, mostly in Spain and parts of Latin America and at some private gun clubs in America.

HELICE, OR ZZ BIRDS

Live pigeon shooting is so challenging that a humane version of it almost had to be invented. (Modern trap is the direct descendant of pigeon shooting, but it's much easier and nowhere near as exciting.) So a Belgian nobleman came up with a game called Helice (pronounced "*hell-EES*"), which is French for "propeller." The targets, called ZZs ("zee-zees"), look like orange plastic helicopter rotors 11 inches across. Each one has a white cap in the center, between the two wings. The ZZ is spun up to high RPM (revolutions per minute) by an electric motor, so when it's released by the trapper it flies off at crazy angles. The shooter has to hit it hard enough to knock the cap off before it crosses the penalty line: the fence that's 21 meters behind the traps.

A shot-up ZZ bird from the Italian World Cup. The white cap has to be knocked off the rotor to score a "kill." Doing this can be even more challenging than shooting boxed pigeons, and it is a lot more humane.

Everything is arranged just as in pigeon shooting, with five or seven traps that are released at random when the shooter calls for a bird, and the electric motor in each one constantly swings back and forth to change the launch angle. If anything, Helice is even more difficult than shooting live birds. It's as expensive to shoot too, even though the targets aren't live and can be used

over, because a human has to reload the traps by hand after every round.

Now let's leave shotguns and wingshooting and look at handgun competitions.

FAST DRAW FOR SPEED

Clyde Howell earned "the badge of the gunslinger," a limp, from shooting himself in the leg while practicing fast draw. In a magazine story in 1959, Howell, who was one of the pioneers of this sport, said he'd been working on his fast draw for more than 25 years. It didn't become a national fascination, though, until the cowboy movie *High Noon* came out in 1952. The hero, played by Gary Cooper, saved the girl, Grace

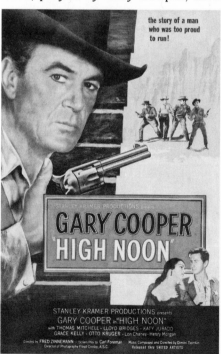

the story of a man who was too proud to run!

GARY COOPER "HIGH NOON"

STANLEY KRAMER PRODUCTIONS presents
GARY COOPER in "HIGH NOON"
with THOMAS MITCHELL · LLOYD BRIDGES · KATY JURADO
GRACE KELLY · OTTO KRUGER · Lon Chaney · Henry Morgan
Directed by FRED ZINNEMANN — Screen Play by Carl Foreman   Music Composed and Directed by Dimitri Tiomkin
Director of Photography Floyd Crosby, A.S.C.   Released thru UNITED ARTISTS

Kelley (who later became the real-life Princess of Monaco), and the entire town with his lightning-fast gunplay. Boys of all ages took note. Then, in 1955, the TV Western *Gunsmoke* started its record-setting 20-year run on CBS.

Each episode began with actor James Arness, "Marshal Matt Dillon," squaring off against a faceless outlaw on the main street of what was supposed to be Dodge City, Kansas, sometime after the Civil War. The show became a monster hit. Each week kids all over the country would test their reflexes in

that opening sequence. (We always wondered how many TV screens wound up shattered by bullets.)

Marshal Dillon's adversary was played by a stuntman named Arvo Ojala, a genuine fast-draw expert who taught two generations of movie and TV actors how to handle guns. (He also invented the steel-lined safety holster, although too late to save Clyde Howell's leg.) Marshal Dillon was the hero, so naturally he won every time. Western novels, movies and radio and TV shows had a code of unwritten rules; one of them was that the villains were always "back-shootin', no-good polecats" in black hats, and they always lost in the final dramatic showdown.

Such do-or-die confrontations with six-guns were historical nonsense, the product of Hollywood screenwriters' imaginations, but they touched something in the American soul. By the late 1950s, 200,000 people were reportedly taking part in fast-draw competitions, including stars like Clint Eastwood, Jerry Lewis and Sammy Davis Jr. (Ask your parents.) Championship matches were held in Las Vegas. A man named Dee Woolem, one of the "cowboys" who staged shoot-outs for the crowd at Knott's Berry Farm, in California, became the "top gun." He was clocked at 0.37 seconds to draw and fire his single-action revolver on a signal, and 0.12 seconds when he could draw on his own. It takes that long to blink your eye.

FAST DRAW WITH ACCURACY

Some people pooh-poohed fast draw because it was just about speed and ignored accuracy. It was getting dangerous too. In 1959, in its magazine *American Rifleman*, the National Rifle Association complained about the fast-draw "craze" and the "needless accidents" it led to: "Teen-agers and grown men, in all parts of the country, have become devotees of the fad with exaggerated zeal." The problem was that people were drilling themselves in the foot or leg while racing to "clear leather" with a loaded gun. The NRA wanted shooters to switch to blanks, wax bullets or even BB pistols.

But in a place called Big Bear, California, a group headed by Jeff Cooper, a Marine WWII veteran and gun writer, went a different way. Their "leather slap" events with live ammunition led to the formation of the South West Pistol League. The SWPL encouraged accurate fast-draw shooting by coming up with timed and scored pistol competitions that included running, climbing, crawling, quick reloading and shooting with the weak hand. Not only that, but instead of wheelguns most competitors used Colt Model 1911-type semi-auto pistols that were carried cocked and locked.

Old-school pistoleros feared bloody mayhem. Instead, SWPL competition led to dramatic advances in shooting techniques and handgun and holster design. Eventually Jeff Cooper was elected to the NRA's board of directors.

In the 1950s and '60s the firearms training of police officers varied from inadequate to non-existent. Almost every cop carried a Smith & Wesson or Colt double-action revolver, and the FBI recommended the so-called combat crouch for close-in shooting. This began to change when an early Big Bear competitor, Los Angeles County Deputy Sheriff Jack Weaver, proved that standing upright and using two hands to shoot could be deadly quick and accurate. This became known as the Weaver Stance.

Dee Woolem, the fast-draw champion, appeared on the September 1959 issue of *Guns* magazine. He's not shooting a television; that's an electric timer.

Armand Swenson, the pistolsmith to the SWPL and himself a competitor, was just as influential. Swenson customized Model 1911s to make them super-accurate and reliable. He added thumb safeties that worked for either the right or left hand, beveled the magazine wells for faster reloading, checkered the front straps for better grip, and came up with other features that are now standard on combat and self-defense pistols.

All these advancements had a huge impact on police training and equipment. Today the revolver and the combat crouch are barely a memory.

Interest in combat pistol shooting spread beyond the United States. In 1976, in Columbia, Mis-

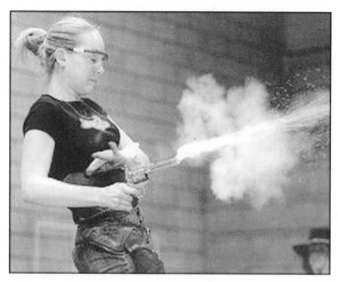

A fast-draw competitor lets it rip. Her right hand snatches the gun from the holster while her left slams across to fan back the hammer for the shot. A sound-activated timer measures her speed. Notice her eyes are closed and the shot doesn't seem to be aimed. She's firing special blank cartridges like movie rounds.

souri, representatives from the SWPL and the Missouri Practical Pistol League sat down with shooters from Asia, Europe, Africa and New Zealand. The result was the International Practical Shooting Confederation, IPSC. The new group elected Jeff Cooper as its first president and adopted the SWPL motto: *Diligentia, Vis, Celeritas* (Accuracy, Power, Speed). The word "pistol" doesn't appear in their

name because they anticipated that rifles and shotguns would someday be included in IPSC matches.

As competition heated up, IPSC guns and holsters got more and more specialized. The sights, extended magazines and compensators developed for these heavily modified "race guns" finally made them impractical for law-enforcement or normal self-defense use, so, in 1996, yet another group formed: IDPA, the International Defense Pistol Association. Later that group too added long-gun matches, but IDPA emphasizes "practical" guns and "real-life self-defense scenarios."

There are other organizations and matches that focus on "three gun" (pistol, rifle, shotgun) competition and even four-gun events that include submachine guns. You can watch many of the top competitors—such as Jerry Miculek, who once fired eight shots from a revolver on four targets, hitting each one twice, in 1.06 seconds—on YouTube.

Law-enforcement agencies and the NRA were slow to accept these new shooting sports, styles

A hardcore Bianchi Cup competitor working her tuned and tweaked "race gun," complete with some sort of optical sight, in a two-handed grip. The Bianchi Cup is the annual National Action Pistol Championship, the biggest handgun competition in the world, with $500,000 in prize money at stake. (Notice the empty shell in the air and the eye and ear protection.)

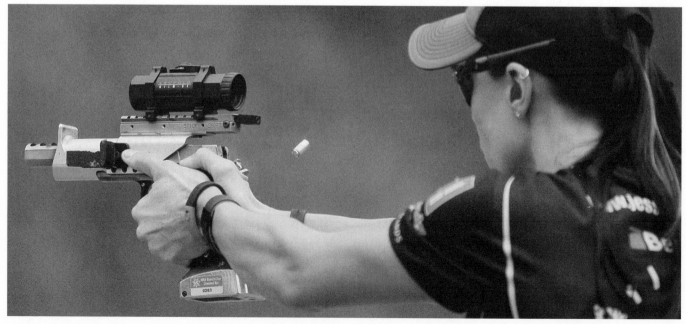

Daniel Brenner

and gear. That changed in 1984 when the NRA became the sponsor of the Bianchi Cup, which is the National Action Pistol Championship. Today it's co-sponsored by MidwayUSA, the giant shooting-products supplier, and the Bianchi Cup calls itself the "most prestigious and richest shooting tournament in the world." It is held in Columbia, Missouri, where the IPSC was born.

COWBOY ACTION SHOOTING

Meanwhile, the first fast-draw shooters, the ones interested in the Old West (or at least Hollywood's notion of the Old West) didn't die out. In 1981, in California, some of them started what they called Cowboy Action Shooting. This led, a few years later, to the formation of SASS, the Single Action Shooting Society, which has grown

Cowboy Action "shootists" have fun. They give themselves Old West nicknames like Pistol Pete and Calamity Jane; compete with old (or old-style) rifles, shotguns and revolvers; and dress in costumes. This Winchester Model 1897 pumpgun fan is looking good—notice the protective Oakleys and earplugs, and the empty shell in the air.

tremendously. Entire families take part. Members call themselves "shootists" and dress in Old West costumes, compete under Old West nicknames like Six-Gun Sam, Calamity Jane and (of course) Marshal Dillon, and use the sorts of rifles, revolvers and shotguns that were around in the 1800s. Some of the competitions involve shooting from horseback or even stagecoaches.

SASS chapters around the country get quite imaginative with their events. Here's a scenario created by the Rivanna Rangers (who are based in Virginia) that's supposed to be set near Roswell, New Mexico, where aliens allegedly crash-land their UFOs:

COWBOYS & ALIENS

Apache Country, New Mexico Territory:
A passel o' alien critters has appeared from th' sky with flyin' machines. They're eatin' the livestock and kidnappin' an' killin' folk. Th' aliens is big an' tough.

The Rivanna Rangers have moved in a wagon full of guns and ammo to deal with the scourge. Buffalo rifles, 10-gauge shotguns with buck and ball, and heavy-loaded Colt .45s.

Original fast draw is still around too, with dozens, or hundreds, of local, state and regional groups all over the globe and a few rule changes for safety. The World Fast Draw Association now limits competitors to wax bullets propelled by .22 blanks or shotshell primers; live ammunition is not allowed. Speed is still key, but competitors also have to put their (wax) bullets on a target, either a man-size silhouette or a balloon.

One of Jeff Cooper's students in the early days at Big Bear was a man named Bob Munden. As a kid, he practiced shooting in a dump near his home. He competed in his first match with live ammunition when he was 11 years old. He went on to set 18 fast-draw records, including the fastest time for a self-start shot: .0175 seconds, or 17.5 milliseconds. You literally cannot see his hand move. That's much *faster* than a blink of the eye.

LONG-RANGE MATCHES

The National Rifle Association of America was founded in 1871 by a group of military men who were disgusted by the poor marksmanship of soldiers during the Civil War (1861-1865). Their goal was to promote target shooting—to get civilians interested in it and to teach them how to do it. The thinking was that this would make the army much more effective the next time America went to war and had to enlist new soldiers. One of the first things the NRA did was ask Congress for $25,000 to buy 70 acres of moorland on Long Island, near New York City, from a family named Creed and turn it into a shooting range. The American NRA's first Annual Matches were held at the new Creedmoor Range on October 8, 1873.

The British already had set up a National Rifle Association in 1859 for the same reason. Their soldiers had shot poorly in the Crimean War (1853-1856). Britain's NRA held its national matches at a place called Wimbledon Common, outside London. Rifle shooting became very popular. By the late 1870s, 2,500 shooters were gathering at Wimbledon for two weeks each year, and teams from Ireland, Scotland and England competed for trophies.

In 1873 Ireland won the team championship. Their captain, Arthur B. Leech, wrote a letter to the editor of the largest newspaper in the US, the *New York Herald*: "At the great meeting held annually at Wimbledon, a team of eight Irishmen, shooting with Irish-made rifles, this year beat the picked eights of England and Scotland. As the great American nation has long enjoyed a world-wide reputation for skill in rifle shooting, it occurs to me that the enclosed challenge from Irish riflemen, now the champions of Great Britain, might be accepted, and if so, a team would be organized to visit the United States in the summer of 1874."

The American NRA accepted the challenge. The match would be at Creedmoor. Each competitor would get 15 shots at 800, 900 and 1,000 yards. The Irish would use Rigby muzzleloading rifles, while Remington and Sharps would build breechloaders for the home team.

On September 26, the day of the event, a crowd of 8,000 people gathered to watch. At 800 yards, the American team posted a score of 326 points to the Irish team's 317. The *New York Herald* and other newspapers telegraphed the scores to their offices in the city, where they were posted on public bulletin boards, and from there they were relayed to Britain by cable.

Then it was time for lunch and speeches. Arthur Leech announced that he would like to leave a souvenir of his team's visit, a large and ornate silver tankard in the shape of an old Irish tower. It was inscribed: "Presented for Competition to the riflemen of America, by Arthur Blennerhassett Leech, Captain of the International Team of Riflemen, on the occasion of their visit to New York."

Competition resumed. At 900 yards, after each man's 15 shots the score was Ireland 312, America 310. The Irish lead would have been greater, but one of their members blew it. J.K. Millner bull's-eyed his first shot at 900 yards—but on the wrong target, thus earning a zero! Total scores now were 636 for America, 629 for Ireland.

At a thousand yards the Irish caught and then passed the Americans. The match came down to the last shot, by Col. Bodine of the United States. Bodine was about to sip a fizzy drink when the glass bottle exploded in his hand. In spite of the bleeding he got into position and fired: bull's-eye! The Irish had won at that distance, 302 to 298, but they lost the overall match by just three points—931 to 934. America had won the Leech Cup.

Today at Wimbledon rifle shooting has been replaced by tennis. In America the Creedmoor Range is gone too, swallowed up by New York

City. The NRA's National Matches are now shot at Camp Perry, in Ohio. (The British shoot at a place called Bisley.)

The Leech Cup, the oldest target-shooting trophy in the United States, is still hotly contested every year. The match is fired at 1,000 yards, prone and unsupported, with open sights, but now it's 20 shots with bolt-action rifles and the 800- and 900-yard stages are gone. The biggest change, though, is in the competitors. As it did in 1874, victory in the 2011 Leech Cup hung on the last shot. But the Irish and Americans of more than a century ago would have been shocked to hear that the winner was a woman. Nancy Tompkins, of Prescott, Arizona, edged out the second-place finisher by one point. Since 1995 Tompkins has won the Leech Cup six times—and lost it once to her daughter Michelle.

As we said at the beginning of this section, shooting is a skill, and skills are to be developed and then tested—which means competition. In King Edward III's day in England, shooting meant bows and arrows. Today, think of a kind of firearm or air gun, and chances are that there is an organized form of target shooting for it, complete with official targets, trophies, sponsors and a rulebook. Want to shoot military rifles at a thousand yards? Air pistols at 10 meters? Rimfire .22s while you're skiing? (That's called biathlon—very interesting!) Pre-1896 blackpowder rifles at silhouettes of pigs, turkeys and rams? It's out there, along with much, much more, at every level from local clubs to college teams to national and international competition and the Olympic Games.

The Leech Cup—two feet tall and made of silver—was presented to "the riflemen of America" by Ireland's shooting team in 1874 at the Creedmoor range near New York City. Target shooting was very popular then, and the match drew tremendous public attention in the US and Britain. The American team won by just three points. Shooters still compete for the Leech Cup every year.

One of the 1874 Irish team's Rigby long-range match rifles. These were still muzzle-loaders, but they were famous for their accuracy and consistency. John Rigby, whose company made the rifles, was the best shot in the tournament.

The Yankee team that won the Leech Cup used breechloading cartridge rifles specially made by Sharps and Remington. This is a No. 1 Creedmoor model, one of the finest rifles Remington ever made.

Game: Animals & Birds

Taking Guns Afield for Hunting

A game animal is one that's hunted, either for its meat or as some kind of trophy. It's a wild animal, not a domesticated one we'd find in a pet store or on a farm. A cow is not a game animal; a Cape buffalo definitely is. A chicken

One of Africa's "Big Five," the Cape buffalo. *Not* a domestic animal; bad-tempered when disturbed, very dangerous when wounded. As Robert Ruark wrote in one of his hunting books, a Cape buffalo glares at you like you owe him money.

pecking in a barnyard is not fair game, but a ruffed grouse or a pheasant rocketing out of a thicket is. A hamster, no; a squirrel, yes.

There is small-game hunting and big-game hunting, and then there is BIG-game hunting. In North America "big game" usually means deer. It's true that North America has much larger game animals than deer—elk and moose and the big northern bears, for example—but for most of us who hunt near home in the US and Canada, the whitetail or mule deer are our big game. (Along with wild pigs, which are spreading across America like a bad cold.) Traditionally, though,

a big-game hunter is one who travels to Africa to hunt the great variety of animals there, from kudu, eland and other antelopes to leopard, lion and Cape buffalo and even the biggest game of all: elephant. An African hunt is a safari, which is Swahili for "journey."

Theodore Roosevelt, our 26th president and an enthusiastic outdoorsman, was one of the first Americans to go on safari. Just 18 days after his term of office ended, early in 1909, he boarded a ship in Hoboken, New Jersey, en route to Mombasa, in what was then called British East Africa.

Kermit Roosevelt, age 19, with a lion he shot in East Africa with his famous father. Their expedition lasted 15 months and got Kermit out of his first year of college. His rifle is a lever-action Winchester Model 95 in .405 Winchester.

(Kenya and Uganda today; the continent of Africa has, by one count, 56 different countries.) With him was his son Kermit, who'd gotten a break from his freshman year at Harvard to go with his father, and four naturalists. This was the beginning of a fantastic adventure that lasted 15 months, with nearly a full year in the field. On the march across the savannah (the African plains), the Roosevelt party's column of hunters, naturalists, trackers, gun-bearers, skinners, guards, grooms, horses, mules, wagons, camp staff and 200-plus porters stretched for more than a mile. Their camps spread over acres. Roosevelt's tent flew the Stars & Stripes overhead. Eventually, he and Kermit shot 17 lions, 11 elephants, 20 rhinos, 10 Cape buffaloes, 10 eland, nine giraffes, eight hippos and so on, down to four each of crocodile and python. In all, the party collected more than 3,000 animals, even insects. There was some complaining in American and British newspapers about the huge bag, but this was a scientific expedition charged by the Smithsonian Institution and the American Museum of Natural History with obtaining specimens for their collections. (Some of these animals are on display in Washington, DC, and New York City to this day.)

Theodore Roosevelt was famous everywhere, so the world eagerly read the news reports of the expedition and his own stories, which he sent to the nearest telegraph office by messenger for publication at home in *Scribner's Magazine*. Roosevelt's book of his journey, *African Game Trails*, is still a terrific read today; back then it was a best-seller. Young and not-so-young boys everywhere promised themselves that they too would someday explore exotic lands and face wild beasts.

This was the beginning of what's now called the safari business, where sportsmen and women hire guides to take them hunting somewhere in southern Africa. From Roosevelt's day up into the 1970s, these guides were called white hunters. Then, as more and more African colonies broke away from their European masters and became independent countries, people began to get touchy about anything "white" as implying racism. Today, even though most of them are still white, they're known as PHs, or Professional Hunters. In all the countries of Africa that allow hunting, they must pass tough exams in order to become licensed. By the way, they're not all men any more.

HUNTING FOR IVORY

Big-game hunting in Africa is now mostly for the adventure of being in the bush and facing challenges that most people can only read about. There was a time, though, when it was possible to make a living by shooting elephants for their tusks. Before plastics were invented, ivory was used for a lot of things: buttons, hair pins and combs, drawer pulls and door knobs, billiard balls and piano keys, jewelry, trinkets and decorative items such as fancy pistol grips. Ivory includes teeth from whales, walruses, wild pigs and a few other animals, but elephants were the prime source. A very big bull might carry 200 pounds or more of it. In the early years of the 20th Century a handful of

white men spent months and even years at a time in the African bush hunting these tuskers. It was grueling, dirty, dangerous work, but it could make a man rich. And for a certain kind of man, it sure beat sitting at a desk.

One of them was Walter Dalrymple Maitland Bell, born in Scotland in 1880. From the moment he could read adventure novels he yearned to hunt elephants. At about the age of 10, he tried to sell a pocket watch for a steamship ticket to East Africa, but the shopkeeper called the police, who returned him home. As generations of "problem" children have been, Bell was sent to boarding school. He got himself out by cracking a senior boy over the head

Walter Dalrymple Maitland Bell, nicknamed Karamojo Bell, took a break from chasing elephants to be a British fighter pilot in WWI. His harvest of ivory made him a rich man, and his unusual life made him well-known.

(and adventures in the Yukon Gold Rush, in Canada, and the Boer War, in South Africa) to become an ivory hunter. He was still only 22 then, so he had plenty of time.

This determination, not to mention unusual toughness and intelligence, and a sense of humor finally made him "Bell of Africa" (as one of his books was called, years later), the most famous and successful ivory hunter of all.

He sawed his first elephant skull in half to see exactly where, and how big, was its brain and how to slip a bullet past the bone that protected it. He peered into the gut cavity of a dead elephant while his trackers pushed spears in from the outside, to learn the angles to the vital organs. He realized that a small bullet could kill an elephant just as easily as a big one, if it was put in just the right spot, and much better than a big one put in the wrong spot.

with a cricket bat. His family went to Plan B: They packed him off to sea as a cabin boy. Bell jumped ship in New Zealand and then worked his way home. He was still only 14, so his family sent him back to school, this time in Germany. Not for long, though. He escaped in an Eskimo kayak he built after reading a book about exploring the Arctic.

Bell was 16 by now. His family caved in and bought him a single-shot rifle and some ammunition and a ticket on a ship to East Africa. He got a job hunting for meat to feed the work gangs that were building the railroad inland from the coast, through the wilds of Kenya and on into Uganda. No elephants, though. It took Bell six more years

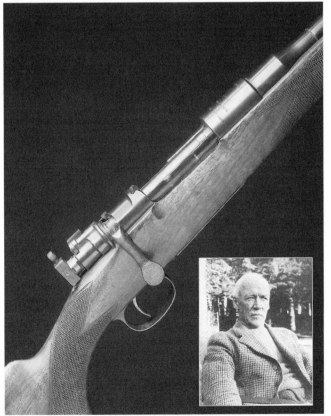

Holt's Auctioneers

Karamojo Bell became famous partly because he hunted the largest land animals, elephants, with light rifles other people used for deer. This is one of his guns: a Rigby .275 bolt-action. Bell is shown here in his 60s.

The largest pair of elephant tusks on record: 236 and 228 pounds. (Any tusks that weigh more than 100 pounds are rare.) The bull was shot in 1898 by an African slave with a blackpowder musket. An American ivory dealer paid about $5,000 for the tusks, equivalent to $120,000 today. They were never cut up for billiard balls or piano keys; these tusks are now in the Natural History Museum in London.

Bolt-action .275-caliber rifles made on German Mauser actions by John Rigby & Co. in London became his favorites. These were half the weight and one-third the price of the double-barreled rifles that other elephant hunters used, and the ammunition was much cheaper too. (This was business. Costs had to be kept down!)

Bell became a crack shot, cool and quick under pressure. Like the professional buffalo hunters of the old American West, he also learned how to approach a herd and which elephants to kill first and how in order to drop as many big tuskers as possible before spooking and scattering the others.

One day on a bend in the Nile River in northeastern Uganda, shooting in a cold, hard rain and grass taller than he was—with a young native boy at his side with a backup rifle—Bell dropped 19 elephants in a row. Eleven lay so close to each other that he could jump from one to the next without touching the ground.

This remote part of Africa was the home of the Karamojong tribe. Bell spent so much time there that he became known as Karamojo Bell. He hunted from 1902 until about 1920, with time out for trips back to civilization to sell ivory and buy supplies and occasional visits back to Scotland. He also served as a fighter pilot in the British Royal Air Force in World War I (1914-1918).

Bell killed somewhere between 1,700 and 2,000 elephants. This amounted to at least 145,000 pounds of ivory—almost 73 tons, which made him a millionaire. He was able to retire to an estate in Scotland, where his wife, Katie, was waiting, when he was only in his 40s.

Even before World War II (1939-1945), shooting elephants for ivory was becoming more and more restricted, but the commercial sale of ivory was banned worldwide only in 1990. This was meant to halt elephant poaching, which was turning into an epidemic. It worked, more or less, and today the greatest threat to elephants is not hunting, illegal or licensed, but loss of habitat. Human populations across southern Africa are exploding, and each new farm chips away at game country. When elephants find a new crop of maize where before there was forest or savannah, they gratefully wade in and eat. The farmer, naturally, objects and runs them off by banging pots and pans together to make a racket. After this happens a few times, elephants lose their fear and may turn on the farmer. Then they're called "problem" animals and often are shot by game wardens. It's a lose-lose situation.

MAN-EATERS OF INDIA

A few hunters made a specialty of wiping out genuine problem animals, especially the big cats that became man-eaters. The most famous of these men was Jim Corbett, who was born in northern India in 1875. Between 1907 and 1940 he tracked down and killed something like 19 tigers and 14 leopards that likely had accounted for around 2,000 people.

Corbett was the son of a postmaster who had gone to India from Ireland. Until it became independent, in 1947, India was the largest colony in the British Empire (25 times bigger than England itself), and hundreds of thousands of people from England, Scotland, Ireland and Wales went to India to work. Many of them settled there and raised families.

Corbett grew up in a small town called Nainital, in the foothills of the Himalaya Range. He attended a local British school with other white children but had just as many native Indian friends, and he could speak Hindi as easily as English. From the beginning he was interested in hunting and fishing, learning to identify bird calls and to track animals, and all the thousand details of wildlife. He learned to shoot the old-fashioned way, first with a ratty old muzzleloader and then, one cartridge at a time, with rifles and shotguns whose recoil belted him black-and-blue.

When he was 18, Corbett went to work for the Bengal and North Western Railway as a shipping manager. On his vacations he went back to Nainital, where he was making a name for himself as a hunter. In 1907 a government agent asked him to try to hunt down a man-eater, a tigress so notorious that the peasants thought she was a *shaitan*, an incarnation of the devil.

This particular devil came to India in 1902 when she was driven out of Nepal, where she'd already eaten some 200 people. Civilian and government hunters and even a unit of Gurkha troops went after her with no success. By the time Corbett was called in, she was taking a fresh victim *every* three to five days. When Corbett arrived in a tiny village called Pali, 30 miles from his hometown, he found it in a state of terror. No one dared step outside.

That evening Corbett sat under a tree, hoping the moon was bright enough to show him the tiger over his sights if it approached. With "teeth chattering, as much from fear as from cold," he sat out the long night and finally at dawn fell asleep with his head on his knees. Nothing. After a cup of tea and resolving never to do such a stupid thing again, Corbett told the headman that he would shoot some meat for the village. Three locals offered to guide him for *ghooral*, small mountain goats. With a single-shot, blackpowder Martini-Henry army rifle, Corbett killed three *ghooral* with three cartridges, shooting steeply uphill at 200 yards. Back at the village, Corbett's guides swore the range had been more than a mile; and, since the goats had rolled downhill almost into their laps, the *Sahib*'s magic bullets even brought the animals to his feet! The Corbett legend was beginning to build.

Man-eating tigers are especially challenging to hunt because they have learned human behavior. Corbett tracked this one for hours one day by following the trail of blood and body parts of a girl the tiger was carrying. Finally he decided to use hundreds of men, marching abreast with noisemakers through the forest, to drive the tiger off the steep ridge where she lived.

The district *tahsildar*, an Indian official, insisted on backing him up with an ancient shotgun loaded with slugs. When the tiger appeared, Corbett fired his .500-caliber double-barreled rifle at her three times, at ranges from 300 to 30 yards. And then, with a wounded tiger just steps away, he was out of ammunition. He'd been overconfident; the third round had been his reserve.

Jim Corbett with a huge tiger known as the Bachelor of Powalgarh. India's peasants worshipped Corbett for saving them from deadly man-eating cats.

Corbett grabbed the official's shotgun and turned to where the tiger crouched on a rock. He aimed at the animal's open mouth, 20 feet away, and fired. The tiger collapsed.

Corbett found the slug not in the cat's head but in its right paw; he could pluck it out with his fingers. Two bullets from his .500 were what had finally killed her. The jubilant natives lashed the carcass to stout poles and, forming a long line, passed the tiger hand-over-hand a thousand feet up the steep ridge to where their village was.

In thanks, the lieutenant governor of the province presented Corbett with a new rifle. By coincidence, it was the same type of modern, lightweight rifle that Karamojo Bell used for his ivory hunting: a Rigby .275, built on a German bolt action.

Also like Bell, Corbett became a legend in his own time and wrote a series of books about his adventures. They are still in print in India, where Corbett is regarded almost as a saint. His home, near Jim Corbett National Park, India's oldest wildlife reserve, is preserved as a memorial.

India's government once encouraged tiger hunting "to protect Indian men, women, and children from the savage creature" and even offered a bounty of 50 rupees for an adult tiger, with bonuses for certain man-eaters. The government kept detailed records. For example, in 1877-'78, 1,635 people were listed as killed by tigers in India—along with 1,409 by wolves, 500 by leopards, 179 by bears, 79 by elephants, 57 by hyenas and 2,503 by "other," for a total of 6,362. Poisonous snakes reportedly killed 33,951 more people.

On the other hand, the total recorded bag by hunters in 1877-'78 was even bigger: 45,335 animals, from elephants to hyenas, plus almost a quarter of a million snakes. Hunters killed 3,072 tigers in that period.

India banned tiger hunting entirely in 1972 but, as with Africa's elephants (and so many other species), habitat loss due to human population growth has taken a terrible toll. The tiger suffers from poaching too; its organs are in high demand for bogus folk-medicine "cures." There were 60,000 tigers in India when Corbett was young; today the number is below 2,000.

WILD ANIMALS VS. HUMANS

Wild animals still kill humans in fairly large numbers, especially in the African and Indian countryside. Total numbers are hard to pin down, but it seems certain that more than 2,000 people are drowned or fatally trampled, gored, clawed or bitten every year in Africa and India by hippos, crocodiles, lions, leopards, tigers, rhinos, buffaloes, elephants, bears, hyenas, wolves and so on. (Snakes account for many thousands more people all by themselves, but by far the most deadly "animal" of them all is the mosquito, carrier of malaria, yellow fever and dengue fever.) Except for crocodiles and sometimes a big cat, which grab humans to eat them, most of these attacks amount to an animal defending itself from what it sees as some kind of intrusion.

True cases of man-eating lions, leopards, tigers and even bears have always been rare, but they still occur. In India man-eaters are often cats that have been crippled somehow, maybe by porcupine quills, which limits them to feeding on slower, weaker prey, such as people tending their farm fields. In southern Africa, however, the most famous man-eaters, such as the lions of Tsavo, were healthy specimens. The theory is that they learned to eat human flesh because they lived near the routes of the Arab slave caravans, which left a trail of dead and dying "merchandise" by the wayside for them to sample.

(In southern Africa slaves were known as "black ivory" because the slavers forced their captives to carry elephant tusks to the trading posts where they would all be sold, a uniquely efficient if

One of the notorious pair of mane-less lions that killed dozens of railroad workers at Tsavo, in Kenya, in 1898. The construction boss, Lieut. Col. John H. Patterson (shown here), finally hunted them down. The story became a movie, *The Ghost and the Darkness*, which was released in 1996. The mounted lions are now in the Field Museum in Chicago.

unusually cruel method of asset management. Mass slavery was not eradicated in Africa until the 1920s.)

HUNTING FOR MEAT & SPORT

Commercial hunting for ivory, skins, meat, feathers or some other part of a wild animal to sell is generally illegal everywhere. (Illegal hunting of any kind is called poaching.) Hunting animals that hunt us or our livestock is rare but it still occurs. And many people around the world still hunt to put meat on their own table. Few of us would starve without it, though, so it's probably better to say that many hunters make a point of eating what they kill, and they use this as one of their reasons for hunting.

All around us, even in city parks, the struggle for life and death goes on forever: Spiders trap and eat flies, songbirds pluck spiders from their webs, hawks swoop down on songbirds, and so on. Within a few miles of downtown New York, Chicago and Los Angeles, coyotes kill and eat deer. The predator-prey relationship means survival. One of the benefits of civilization is that we no longer need to kill and butcher our own meat; a vast industry has

Steve Helsley

This Colorado elk was hunted for meat. Now the work begins; it has to be field-dressed, gotten out of the woods, skinned, and then butchered. Do this just once and you'll gain new respect for a hamburger—and for hunters.

been created to do it for us. Because of this, some people now think hunting is cruel and should be banned. Most people who oppose hunting buy meat from a market and wear leather shoes and belts and carry leather handbags, all products of this industry. Few of them, however, give a thought to how cattle, pigs and sheep are "processed" for market. They don't understand ethical hunting either, or the relationship between hunting and conservation, or the fact that most hunters don't really like the act of killing—but if they don't do it, they're not hunters.

Which is more natural: stalking and killing a deer in its environment with a well-placed bullet and then butchering it yourself? Or buying a steak from a cow that was raised in a pen on chemically enhanced feed and then trucked to a factory that cut it up on an assembly line?

There are now too many people in the world for everyone to hunt their own meat, and slaughterhouses treat animals more humanely than they once did. But many hunters regard what they do as the most honest form of "shopping" for meat, just as many people grow their own vegetables in a garden. And just as gardeners take care of their fields and plants, hunters watch over their natural resources. The sale of hunting licenses and the taxes on guns and ammunition raise many millions of dollars each year in the US alone, and much of this money goes to wildlife management and conservation.

Hunting also helps keep game populations in balance, since four-legged predators such as wolves and mountain lions were wiped out long ago in much of the US. (Which was done mostly for the benefit of people who raise cattle, pigs and sheep for market.)

HUNTING FOR TROPHIES

Trophy hunting has an especially bad reputation among people who believe that Modern Man should no longer kill wild animals, especially for sport. Trophy hunting means finding and killing the best-possible example of some kind of game animal as an example of the hunter's skill. (Hunting demands physical fitness and woodcraft, a certain steadiness under pressure, and skill with a gun or bow.) Although trophy hunting isn't hunting for food, the meat is never wasted. It is given to a nearby village, eaten by the hunter or camp staff, or taken to a butcher shop to be sold.

The trophy itself—the horns or antlers, skull or skin—is part of the hunter's reward. Keeping a trophy is as natural as hunting itself, and it should be a sign of our respect for the animal. A trophy is also a remembrance of days in the field and the rare experience, awe and excitement of being a natural predator once again.

After he killed a trophy lion, Robert Ruark (read "Using Enough Gun," below) wrote: "He was the handsomest lion I had ever seen, in or out of a zoo, and I was not sorry about the collection of him. Already I was beginning to fall into the African way of thinking: that if you properly respect what you are after, and shoot it cleanly and on the animal's terrain, if you imprison in your mind all the wonder of the day from sky to smell to breeze to flowers—then you have not merely killed an animal. You have lent immortality to a beast you have killed because you loved him and wanted him forever so that you could always recapture the day . . . . This is better than letting him grow a few years older, to be killed or crippled by a son and eaten, still alive, by hyenas. Death is not a dreadful thing in Africa—not if you respect the thing you kill, not if you kill to feed your people or your memory."

However, man is not only a predator, he is also a competitor. (The two are almost, but not quite, the same thing.) The larger a rack of antlers or the heavier a pair of tusks or the bigger a bearskin, the more we value them. "Mine is bigger than yours"—so I am a better hunter and provider than you. But this isn't necessarily so; outstanding trophies have been taken easily, by sheer luck, sometimes within steps of camp. And sometimes trophies can be bought with money. A worthwhile trophy, though, usually calls for many days in the field, with hard work and sweat, frustration and disappointment before final success.

Jofie Lamprecht Photography

Days of stalking in the Kalahari region of southern Africa resulted in this grand trophy. The kudu bull had spectacular horns that measured nearly five feet along their spirals.

In Africa the trophies most in demand are called the "Big Five": leopard, lion, Cape buffalo, rhinoceros and elephant. They're impressive, sometimes dangerous animals that are challenging to hunt. (The leopard isn't big—rarely more than 200 pounds—but it is very wary and unearthly quick. A wounded leopard defending itself with fangs and claws has been compared to a chain saw with its throttle stuck wide open.) Hunting them is expensive, too, and often the bigger the trophy, the bigger its price tag.

Unfortunately, when money is on the line, people sometimes take shortcuts. They buy or breed animals with bigger horns or longer manes or whatever, and then they pen them up so that their clients can find and shoot them more easily. The hunting company makes money, and the hunter comes away with a trophy that he or she hasn't really earned.

This gives trophy hunting a bad name even among hunters. It is the very opposite of stalking a truly wild animal on foot and then killing it cleanly, with a gun or bow: fair-chase hunting for free-range game.

One of the most famous of the old-time white hunters of East Africa, Philip Percival, used to say, "If you want to have a nice hunt, leave the tape measure at home." (Some hunters even had special measuring tapes that "improved" clients' trophies.) In other words, forget sheer size and your name in the record books and concentrate on the quality of the experience instead: the wonders of scenery and wildlife; being in the bush, with its evenings around the campfire with new and old friends; and finding, tracking, outwitting and at last taking a fine trophy. That is, an impressive old animal that has made its contribution to the gene pool (left behind many offspring) and is nearing the end of its natural life.

It may not make sense at first, but this kind of trophy hunting is also the surest way to protect wild game. In Africa, for example, tribal people who live in the bush generally regard wild animals as a nuisance. Lions and leopards prey on their goats and cattle (and threaten them and their families), while other game, from elephants to warthogs, raid their crops. Given the chance, they kill these animals any way they can, often with traps or poison, even if it's illegal. But if they get a share of the money that visitors pay for the privilege of hunting there, wild animals become a resource to be protected. The local people get not only some of the cash, but also the game meat. So "if it pays, it stays."

Trophy hunting helps prevent poaching too. Game rangers and their scouts, no matter how well trained or equipped, can't patrol everywhere at once. In Africa and elsewhere, trophy hunters and their guides and trackers are out on the land, paying attention to what's going on, and often they are the first to discover any signs of illegal killing of game.

Hunting is no longer for everyone, but for people who accept that man is a natural predator and who have the desire and the skills, it can be both thrilling and deeply satisfying.

HUNTING GAMEBIRDS

Big-game hunting usually requires a rifle, or possibly a high-powered revolver. (Or a bow and arrows, but this book is about guns.) We say "usually" because some places limit deer hunters to shotguns loaded with slugs or buckshot. Many people hunt small game—squirrels, rabbits, even foxes—with shotguns because they're hard to hit with a single bullet. And at least as many people hunt gamebirds, like pheasants, grouse, quail, ducks and geese, and this absolutely requires a shotgun.

So other than for small game and deer in those restricted areas, hunting with a shotgun is called wingshooting. That is, shooting things while they're on the wing, flying.

Oops, one more exception: Turkeys, although they are technically gamebirds and hunted with shotguns, are shot while they're on the ground, so turkey hunting is not wingshooting.

(We've always wondered about this. A wild turkey on the wing is an impressive sight and a challenging target, so why not hunt them with dogs and flush them into the air before we shoot, the way we do other upland birds?)

It isn't that we can't shoot pheasants or grouse or ducks on the ground—or in a tree or while they're swimming on a pond—it's that we shouldn't. It isn't sporting, which is what modern hunting is all about. When hunters have to put food on the table or else starve, any method of harvesting game is acceptable. Today, though, for almost all of us, putting food on the table means going to the market, and hunting has become a sport (although a sport that connects us with our roots as predators). Therefore we try, sort of, to make every kind of hunting more challenging. Hunting isn't meant to be slaughter any more; it means fitting ourselves back into the basic predator–prey relationship, which improves our most ancient human skills and gets us more attuned to the natural environment.

Hitting a strong, fast-moving wild bird while it's in the air is usually much harder than shooting a big animal with a rifle. But when we were kids and found out that shotguns fire pellets that spread out in flight, we were horrified. That sounded too easy, like cheating! Then we tried it, and we have spent most of the years since trying to become decent wingshots.

Terry Allen

Happy hunter with a Texas pheasant. Bird hunting means walking the uplands with a keen-nosed dog and then being able to hit a fast-flying target when it flushes into the air.

Waterfowl—ducks and geese—live on the water. Upland gamebirds live on dry ground. "Uplands" are hillsides, meadows, woodlands and so on, any natural area that's drier than a marsh. In North America upland gamebirds include pheasants, ruffed and prairie grouse (sharp-tailed and sage grouse as well as prairie chickens), chukar and Hungarian partridge, doves, woodcock, several kinds of quail and a few other similar species. Most upland gamebirds live in flocks or coveys. Upland hunters walk the woods and fields with dogs trained to find birds, by scent, so they can be flushed into the air for a shot. A wild bird rocketing out of its hiding place can be noisy and startling. Some gamebirds can hit 50 or 60 miles per hour. All have different flight patterns. A great big pheasant flushing out of a cornfield and flying away in the open can be a fairly easy target; a ruffed grouse exploding from a hawthorn thicket and dodging away through thick pines is a very difficult target.

Upland birds have learned to be wary for a simple reason: They taste good, and about every predator, from foxes to hawks to man, likes to eat them.

Just as with big game, it's possible to hunt gamebirds that have been specially raised and put out for the gun (or to train bird dogs). This is usually more sporting than it is for four-legged animals; birds can't be fenced in, at least not if they're going to fly. They're bred in pens, but then they're released. You'll find a lot of difference between pen-raised birds, though. If they're released to fend for themselves when they're young, they learn to behave and fly much more like wild birds than if they're let out the day before the hunters arrive.

WATERFOWL

Hunting for waterfowl, sometimes called wildfowling, usually involves ducks and geese. In a few places hunters may take swans or cranes. There are many huntable ducks—mallards, wigeon, teal, canvasbacks, black ducks, sea ducks and more—and several species of geese. Naturally, they spend much of their time on rivers, lakes, ponds or salt water.

Waterfowlers usually hide themselves in blinds to wait for birds to fly by or to land nearby, either on water or in fields. They put out decoys to try to lure the birds out of the sky and use duck and goose calls to get their attention.

Gamebird and waterfowl species (and hunting seasons) are different in different parts of the US. A deer is a deer, and the males have antlers, but it

Steve Helsley

A day's bag of Canada geese shot over the grainfields where the birds go to feed. Waterfowlers often use decoys and calls to lure the birds out of the sky and into shooting range.

isn't always so easy in bird hunting and waterfowling, where you have to be able to identify the species and often tell male from female before you pull the trigger. Depending on where you live, you may be limited to just one deer per year, but you might be allowed up to three woodcock, for example, or one black duck each day. Exceed the legal limit on any species and you're a poacher and now fair game yourself—for game wardens.

The Bird Hunter's Blue Sky Rule

Muzzle control is one of the absolute, never-forget-it rules. An AD, or accidental discharge, is just a scary moment if the gun is pointed in a harmless direction. For bird hunters, muzzle control means following the Blue Sky Rule: Don't shoot at a bird unless you can see sky around it. That means the bird is high enough in the air that your shot won't hit another hunter (or a dog) on the ground. The pheasant hunter who accidentally shot one of us forgot the Blue Sky Rule.

BIRD DOGS

One of best things about hunting upland birds or waterfowl is having a dog to hunt with you. Dogs are not only great companions but also have keen senses of smell, hearing and eyesight, which all help the hunter find and then retrieve the game. A dog that's one of the pointing breeds (English setter, German shorthair, Brittany and others) sniffs out a gamebird's hiding place and then stands and points to it with

Bird dogs (like this springer spaniel) not only point and sometimes flush the game, but they also retrieve the dead birds and find wounded ones.

Terry Allen

its nose until the hunter has caught up. Then the hunter or the dog moves in to flush the bird into the air for a shot.

Labrador retrievers, golden retrievers, cocker spaniels and other breeds are flushing dogs. They smell a hidden bird and then flush it by themselves, so the hunter has to keep up and be ready.

Dogs also find the downed birds. Because of their coloring, which camouflages them in their habitat, dead birds can be difficult to find without a dog's sharp nose. A dog can also track and grab a wounded bird that's trying to get away.

In waterfowling, dogs aren't used to point. The dog sits by the hunter till it's time to fetch a duck or goose that has fallen out in the water or in a field. Labrador and Chesapeake Bay retrievers and other dogs that don't mind cold water were bred especially for swimming to downed birds and bringing them back in their mouths.

TURKEYS

Wild turkeys look nothing like the fat white birds we see on TV every Thanksgiving. Instead they're wild animals, beautifully camouflaged to fit into their habitat, and much stronger and warier than farm birds. Benjamin Franklin thought the wild turkey, not the bald eagle, should be the symbol of America. Weighing up to 25 pounds or more, the turkey is the largest of North America's gamebirds, and it is a native species, not an exotic brought in from Europe or Asia. (Pheasants originally came from China, Hungarian partridge from—well, you can guess.) In the 1970s state fish and game departments across America set out to reestablish the turkey, which had disappeared from much of its original range because of over-hunting. These programs succeeded beyond anyone's expectations, and now wild turkeys can be found again in about every state except Alaska.

As pointed out earlier, turkeys are the only birds that hunters kill on the ground. In order not to destroy the meat, hunters try to shoot them in the head; the head is a very small target, so the firearm of choice is a shotgun that delivers a tight cluster of shot big and heavy enough to be lethal out to 50 yards or so. Turkeys are wary, and it can be difficult to get much closer than that to them.

Keen-eyed and wary, wild turkeys are a challenge for hunters, who have to lure them into range with calls and decoys. Benjamin Franklin thought the turkey, not the bald eagle, should be the symbol of America.

National Wild Turkey Federation

Turkeys have very sharp eyesight, so hunters camouflage themselves from head to toe. They sit in a likely spot and use a call to try to lure the male turkeys, the toms, into range.

SHOTGUNS FOR BIRDS

Different game-birds call for different shot-guns and ammunition. You can't count on bringing down a goose or pheasant—flying maybe 60 yards away and armored with thick feathers—with the same gun and load that's best for quail or woodcock that flush at 10 yards.

Shotgun pellets spread out in flight, and the farther they go, the more open the shot pattern becomes. Waterfowl and some-times pheasants are of-ten shot at near maxi-mum range, which is 50 to 65 yards for most shotgunners. At that distance, the spread of pellets from a light shotshell might not be enough; usually you need to put at least three or four pellets into a big bird to bring it down. So, to keep their shot patterns dense enough to be ef-fective, many wildfowlers and pheasant hunters use guns with tighter chokes and shells that pack a lot of big pellets.

This might be a 12-gauge Magnum or even a 10-gauge firing up to 1¾ ounces of large pellets in a cartridge that's 3½ inches long. The recoil from these can be pretty nasty, so hunters usually shoot them in semi-automatic guns whose mechanism absorbs some of the punch.

A bird gun—light, quick-handling, often custom-fitted. This is an English double-barreled 12-gauge with a brace (pair) of British red grouse, maybe the speediest gamebird of all.

Old-time market hunters sometimes used 8-gauge and even 4-gauge guns, or small cannons called punt guns, to kill as many birds as possible, but today the 10-gauge is the largest shotgun legal for hunting.

At the other end of the bird-hunting spectrum are the people who hike the uplands all day for small, lightly feathered birds that flush at close range and dodge away through the brush. These hunters want light, easy-handling shot-guns with cartridges that carry enough shot to do the job but don't tear the birds to pieces (or knock the hunters silly with recoil). More and more upland hunters now carry 28-gauge guns that weigh a lot less than big goose guns and that fire only three-quarters of an ounce of small shot pellets.

Most shotgun pellets are lead, because it's very dense and heavy and hits hard. But lead is a poison, so for some uses lead shot is banned. (For water-fowl hunting, for example. Water birds may eat fallen lead pellets by accident when they feed in the marshes, and this can kill them.) Then nontoxic shot made of steel or alloys of molybdenum, tungsten or other metals has to be used instead.

PUNT GUNS & MARKET HUNTING

Back in the days when ships were made of wood and driven by sails, one of the most common naval weapons was the swivel gun: a light cannon, four or five feet long and with a bore diameter of 1½ inches or so. Early on it was loaded with a ramrod from the muzzle; later versions were breechloaders. Swivel guns were mounted on a ship's rail or even up in the fighting tops, the platforms on the masts where Marines were stationed to shoot down onto the enemy's quarterdeck. Swivel guns were smoothbores and usually loaded with clusters of large shot, to cut down gangs of sailors at close range when the ships had battered each other with their heavy cannons and were now alongside. Giant shotguns, in other words.

A swivel gun also could be put in the bow of a ship's boat that was manned by a crew of oarsmen under the command of a lieutenant or midshipman. It was just the thing for holding off hostile natives when landing on a South Seas island to top up the ship's supply of fresh water.

It didn't take long for hunters to realize that a gun like this also could be deadly on flocks of ducks and geese sitting on the water.

Notions of fair chase or sportsmanship didn't enter into it; this was business, pure and simple. Market hunting in great-great-granddad's day didn't mean going to the mall and hanging out at the food court. Into the early 1900s market hunting in America meant harvesting game, birds mostly, to sell to butcher shops and restaurants. In 1860 a pair of mallard ducks, plucked and cleaned, might bring as much as $1.25, not counting the value of the feathers. That's about $35 in today's money. (The feathers went to clothing, bedding and furniture makers. Everything from ladies' hats to overstuffed chairs and bed quilts required feathers.)

Market hunters came up with something similar to a naval swivel gun called a punt gun. A

punt is a light, shallow boat with a flat bottom and a squared-off bow. Hunters also called them sneak boats, particularly in America. Instead of oars or paddles, a punt has a push pole.

A punt gun is a huge shotgun, or a small cannon, that's aimed out over the front of the boat. Punt guns have a bore diameter of 1½ to 2 inches and can weigh a hundred pounds or more. Big ones can fire two pounds of lead pellets or just scrap metal at a time. A lucky shot can kill dozens of waterfowl at once. The recoil is ferocious, so big punt guns are mounted on the boat with springs or rubber straps to absorb the shock.

A modern-day punt-gunner fires a blackpowder cartridge. In Britain it is still legal to hunt waterfowl with these cannons, which have to be maneuvered very carefully into range; decoys, however, are considered unsporting.

Punt guns are still legal in Britain, where they're heavily regulated and a handful of die-hard traditionalists still use them.

Standard operating procedure is for a punt gunner to pole or sail his boat out to where flocks of birds have gathered on the water to sleep for the night. As the sun comes up, he maneuvers quietly into position and then, before the birds fly away to their daytime feeding grounds, fires his one shot. There's rarely any chance for another one; whatever birds aren't down are gone for good. However, in

Market hunting wasn't just for birds. Bison (American buffalo) were almost exterminated by commercial hunters. They were shot mostly for their hides, but this is a pile of skulls that were collected to be ground up for fertilizer. Before the Civil War, there were millions of buffalo on the plains. By 1890 only about 2,000 were left. Today American bison numbers have grown back to about a half-million, and limited hunting is allowed.

the old days groups of punt gunners working together could easily kill more than 500 ducks in one massed volley. Then the gunner stands up and poles over to pick up his bag. Usually there are cripples to finish off with a shotgun.

Market hunting of any sort, with guns or nets or by using bait, began to be banned across the United States in 1900, as waterfowl populations were being hit hard. The largest bag recorded in the US is said to be 3,008 ducks taken over eight days in Bath, Illinois, by three hunters in 1901. But it wasn't just ducks and geese that were being slaughtered. In 1909 President Theodore Roosevelt created the first of what would become the US Forest Service's National Wildlife Refuges. This was Pelican Island, in Florida, where millions of herons and egrets were being killed to provide feathers for ladies' hats.

In 1897 an English sportsman by the name of Sir Ralph Payne-Gallwey tested punt guns. He found that a 175-pound muzzleloading punt gun with a two-inch bore and firing six to seven ounces of blackpowder and two pounds of lead BB shot (about 2,560 pellets) would put two-thirds of its pellets into a 12-foot-square target at 70 yards.

By comparison, a 12-gauge Magnum, the shotgun of choice for many duck hunters today, fires just 75 lead BB shot. From a tightly choked gun barrel, at 70 yards they will spread out to a ragged circle perhaps four feet across.

USING ENOUGH GUN

A punt gun is too much gun. Back in 1966 a book called *Use Enough Gun: On Hunting Big Game* was published in America. The author, Robert Ruark, had died the year before. Although he wasn't around for very long, Ruark became wealthy and famous thanks to a string of very popular books and magazine stories, many of which had something to do with hunting.

Use Enough Gun was based on Ruark's experiences as a shooter and a hunter, which began when he was 8 years old. By 1951 he'd made enough money to be able to hunt in Africa and India. By the time he finished *Use Enough Gun*, he had been on safari many times. He wrote, "I have shot three elephant of over a hundred pounds per

tusk, killed a couple of lion . . . I have lost count on leopard, maybe 20—and have no idea about buffalo; maybe a hundred . . . wildebeest, gerenuk, oryx, duiker—in general, camp meat must run into a thousand. I have shot three tigers, been severely mauled by a leopard . . . ."

When it came to hunting and guns, Ruark knew what he was talking about, and he had a lot of valuable things to say about proper hunting manners. Furthermore, he had an enormous following. At least two of his hunting sayings are still widely remembered today. One of them is that a Cape buffalo "looks like you owe him money." This is the exact quote; it means, of course, that he's looking at 'you.'

(We hope that someday you too will be able to go to Africa and see Cape buffalo in the wilds. Even if he's feeding peacefully, when a Cape buffalo bull spots you, he picks up his head—with those curving, wicked horns—and stares balefully into your eyes, seemingly wondering whether he should come over and flatten you now or finish eating first.)

Ruark's other famous phrase is "Use enough gun." He meant enough to do the job, to kill quickly and cleanly. Not only the rifle and caliber, but also the bullet has to be right for the type of game you'll hunt.

Ruark once shot a hyena with a .220 Swift. Hyenas are not large animals, but the Swift fired a tiny (48-grain) bullet at more than 4,000 feet per second. It was the hottest, fastest commercial load of the day, meant for nothing bigger than groundhogs at long range. The bullet, too small to have much mass or to hold together at that speed, just blew apart into fragments on the hyena's hide instead of penetrating and killing. After shooting the hyena nine times with the .220, Ruark went to the other extreme and reached for his .470 Nitro Express to finish the job. He never fired the Swift again.

Use enough gun.

Too much gun, on the other hand, is punishing to carry because it's heavy, and to shoot because of its recoil and even the price of the ammunition. There's no need to shoot deer with a heavy Magnum or Nitro Express cartridge; they just aren't that big, tough, difficult to kill or potentially dangerous.

Hunting magazines and books have been around for centuries, and for centuries they have published articles about the advantages or disadvantages of one gun or cartridge versus another. This may make good reading, but the basics never change: smaller calibers for small game, bigger ones for medium game, Magnums or Nitros for the big stuff; solid or metal-jacketed bullets for thick-skinned, tough animals, expanding bullets for everything else.

Tactical marksmen and snipers follow this rule too. Using a .50-caliber long-range rifle to wipe out a hostage-taker at 75 yards may cause serious damage farther downrange as the bullet keeps going. (Remember Number 8 in the 15 Commandments.) On the other hand, shooting at an insurgent 1,500 yards away with a 5.56mm is a waste of ammo. Pick the proper tools for the job.

Don't think that hunting big game with small calibers is somehow more "sporting," either. This was a fad among certain hunters back in the 1960s who believed that a high-velocity small bullet was as effective as a bigger, slower one. The bullet's energy may calculate out to be the same, but the bullet needs a certain amount of mass to be effective (as Ruark found out on the hyena). A lightly wounded animal may go for miles, in pain and fear, or get away to die days later of slow blood loss or in the jaws of predators. A hunter owes his game a quick, clean death, and a larger, slower bullet usually outperforms a lighter, faster one. Karamojo Bell and Jim Corbett had their own reasons for using light rifles on big game and were able to get away with it by being ultra-accurate and careful (a little luck helped too), but, kids, don't try this at home.

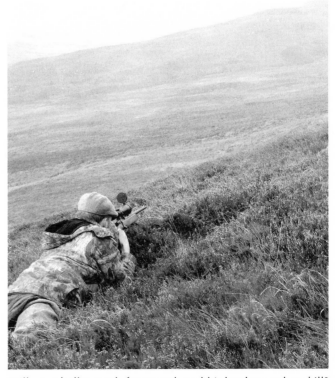

Will your bullet reach far enough and hit hard enough to kill? Can you hit what you're aiming at? This hunter has gotten as close as he can, but the camera can't even see the stag he's after.

Keeping Guns Clean & Safe

How NOT to Destroy a Gun & Where to Put Them

The easiest way to blow up a gun is to fire it while the barrel is plugged. Even if the obstruction seems minor, under the huge blast of pressure created by burning gunpowder in such a confined space, a bullet hitting even just a bit of dirt can become the irresistible force meeting the immovable object. If something's got to give, it's the gun barrel. Can you imagine the energy needed to burst a thick steel tube?

It's all too easy to get "foreign objects" into a gun barrel. One of the authors once filled a double-barreled shotgun's muzzles with snow just by walking through a prairie in the winter. The gun was hanging over his arm, barrels down. The muzzles brushed the tall grass as he moved along, picking up snow. Luckily he has the habit of looking through his gun barrels before dropping a pair of cartridges into them, so he discovered that the muzzles were blocked before it was too late. The snow was powdery-light and probably would not have resisted the shot charge—but, then again, maybe it would have.

A rifle barrel split like a banana peel. The shooter forgot to remove the bore sighter (a device that goes into the muzzle to help align the scope) before firing a round. When an irresistible force (the bullet) met an unmovable object (the bore sighter), something had to give.

Bad ammunition can leave barrels plugged too, if there isn't enough oomph to push the bullet out. With shotguns, even if the pellets come out, the big plastic shot-cup wad that holds them may stay behind, stuck somewhere near the muzzle.

Either way, if the shooter doesn't realize what's happened and fires again, the barrel is likely to burst or at least bulge. If it ruptures out near the muzzle, maybe he won't get hurt; farther back, his forward hand is in danger, and shrapnel or hot gasses could blow back into his face. (Wear those shooting glasses.)

Pay attention, be observant, think about what's happening—especially if you're out in bad weather or moving through thick brush while hunting. It isn't just the barrel, either. Dirt, snow, twigs or leaves, even grains of unburned powder can get into the action and keep it from closing. And for heaven's sake, if you slip and fall with a gun in your hands, make sure it's OK before continuing on. (If you were holding the gun pointed in a safe direction and if the safety was on and your finger was

A deluxe, all-in-one maintenance kit made by Outers, with solvents, lubricants, brushes and tools for about every caliber and gauge, plus a convenient stand for the gun while you're working on it. You don't need this much gear to clean your guns, though—just a rag, some gun oil, bore-cleaning fluid, cloth patches and a rod and brush that will fit the barrel.

This sort of on-the-spot care is just common sense. Cleaning a gun at home after using it and before putting it away is important too. This can be as much work as you want it to be—some people just love to disassemble their guns and inspect every part, cleaning and wiping and oiling and reassembling. If this pushes your buttons and you know how to do it, go right ahead. But unless you dropped the gun into the lake or were out in heavy rain or a sandstorm, or you have a gas-operated semi-auto that collects gunpowder residue in its action, it isn't necessary. Just run a cleaning rod through the bore (see below) and wipe down the outside to remove any fingerprints or sweat and other gunk.

outside the trigger guard when you fell, you and anyone around you should be OK too.) Inspect the gun closely, especially if it hit the ground. Open the action, look through the bore, and check the sights and the magazine. Brush off any dirt.

CLEANING GUNS: HOW & HOW OFTEN

Maybe you'll go on to shoot blackpowder guns or become a serious match competitor, or you'll hunt ducks and geese on salt water or fire 500 rounds a week at sporting clays— these and other specialized kinds of shooting require different methods of gun cleaning. As you progress to that sort of shooting, you'll learn (from your mentor and more-experienced shooters) how to take care of your guns.

Meanwhile, if you have a new gun (BB, pellet, .22) read the care-and-use manual that came with it. If you're shooting a gun that didn't come with any instructions, here's what you should know about basic care and maintenance.

First, every shooter should have these items in a gun-cleaning kit:

1. A cleaning rod skinny enough and long enough to go all the way down the barrel. Shotgun or rifle cleaning rods are usually in three sections that screw together; one section has a handle. For short barrels, just use the section with the handle.

2. A brass bristle brush and a tip (maybe with a slot in it), which both screw into the end of the rod and are the right size for the bore of your gun.

3. Cotton cleaning patches. These are also sized for gauge or caliber.

4. A bottle of solvent to remove powder residue and traces of bullet metal or plastic wadding that builds up in the bore while shooting.

5. A small bottle or spray can of gun oil to lubricate moving parts.

6. A silicone-impregnated cloth to wipe fingerprints, skin oil, sweat, water or whatever from the gun. (Because they're salty, sweat and blood make a gun break out in rust like pimples.) You can use a soft cotton rag instead with a few drops of gun oil on it, but run this through the laundry every now and then. Oily rags can cause fires.

7. An old toothbrush and some cotton swabs (Q-tips) to get solvent and oil into hard-to-reach places. A spray can of pressurized air can be very useful too, to blow dirt away.

Here's what you do with these items:

1. Find a table that you can use, and spread newspaper on it. (This'll get dirty.)

2. Make absolutely sure the gun is unloaded: nothing in the chamber, nothing in the magazine or cylinder. If the gun has a detachable magazine, pull it out. (If there are still cartridges in the gun when it's time to clean it, you've screwed up big-time.)

3. Partly disassemble the gun, if possible. If you can, take the barrel off. If it's a bolt-action, pull out the bolt.

4. This is where it gets dirty: Attach the bristle brush to the cleaning rod, dunk it in the solvent and scrub out the barrel. (Push and pull the brush all the way through several times.) Do it from the breech end if possible. If you have to do it from the front, don't let the rod scrape the edge of the muzzle. (This can hurt a gun's accuracy.) You can put the newspaper on the floor and rest the end of the gun barrel on it or on an old towel on the newspaper, and work the brush up and down like that.

5. Now attach the other tip and push/pull cotton patches up and down the barrel, changing them each time. (They're disposable, so throw them away.) Look through the barrel every now and then at a strong light; the bore should become shiny-bright. If it's a rifle or handgun, you'll see the spiral lines of the rifling. If you can't see down the barrel because the action blocks the light, you can get a little angled flashlight to stick in the ejection port while you look down the muzzle. When a patch finally comes out clean, put a few drops of oil on it and run that down the bore. Now the barrel is clean and has a light film of oil to protect against rust.

6. Certain parts of the action need a drop of oil to prevent friction and rust. A *drop* of oil—too much attracts dirt and can build up and get gummy.

7. Thoroughly wipe the outside of the gun, both the metal parts and the stock, with the silicone cloth or the slightly oily rag.

8. Put the gun back together. Make sure it's uncocked, and put it away properly. Gunmakers often recommend storing long guns muzzle-down, to keep oil from slowly oozing into a wooden stock or pooling in the action.

All guns need occasional cleaning to prevent rust, to keep the bore unobstructed and to make sure the action works smoothly. This helps ensure that a gun is safe to use and accurate to shoot, and it protects the value of a gun too. Besides, dirt and rust are just plain nasty, and they send the message: *I don't deserve to own a gun!*

If you get into the habit of inspecting a gun before you put it away and at least wiping it down, you'll know that the next time you take it out it'll be good to go.

The Right Ammunition

Bad ammunition can instantly mess up a gun. We told you what a bullet or a wad, left in the barrel, can do. The next best way to damage a gun (other than neglect) is to fire a round that's too powerful in it. This usually doesn't hurt the barrel, because it's extra-thick at the chamber, where the bang takes place, but if the action can't withstand the extra pressure, something's going to fail there. A well-made action usually won't burst, but it may jam, and then you can't open it.

Factory-made ammunition is extremely reliable, at least in America and Europe, so bad cartridges are generally the fault of shooters who load their own. It's easy to put too little or too much or the wrong kind of powder into a shell, and the results are rarely good.

You're not loading your own ammunition, at least so far, so this isn't a concern yet. But you do need to pay attention to what sort of ammo you feed your guns. For example: More than a dozen different .22 rimfire cartridges have been produced over the years. There are a half-dozen .300 Magnums out there under various makers' names, and at least four different 9mm pistol cartridges. Twelve-gauge shotgun shells may be 2, 2½, 2¾, 3 or 3½ inches long. No matter what you've heard, the .223 Remington is not the same as the 5.56mm NATO round. Nor are the 7.62 NATO and the .308 Winchester completely interchangeable. There are plenty more such opportunities for confusion too.

Modern guns are clearly stamped with their specific caliber and ammunition. Make sure that's exactly what you shoot out of them. The weight of the bullet or shot charge may vary, depending on what it's meant to be used for, but every box of ammunition will indicate caliber, make and whatever other information you need to figure out whether you can shoot it in your gun.

Older guns and older ammunition may not be so well identified. When in doubt, don't shoot. If you can't close the action on a cartridge, there's a problem. Again, stop. Your mentor or an experienced gunsmith needs to check this out.

These are all 12-gauge shotshells, but obviously they don't all go in the same gun. You have to know exactly what ammunition fits your gun's chamber(s) and is safe to shoot.

Steve Helsley

Storing Your Guns

Where you keep your guns is important for two reasons: First, when they're not in use they should be where other people (like your little brother or sister) can't get at them. The best place is a steel vault or safe specially built for guns, with a secure lock on the door. Only you and your parents should have the key or the combination.

Your parents may decide that only they will have the key or combination so you can't take out a gun without their permission. Don't complain. When you get your driver's license, you'll go through the same process with the car—but if you've already showed them that you can handle guns well, your parents likely will be more generous with the car.

Guns should never be stored loaded. If we have to explain why, go back to the beginning and re-read this book.

Accidental shootings are very rare in the United States, but when they do happen, they're extra sad because they almost always happen to friends or family members. This is why some people also put locks on the triggers or block the

A GunVault storage box programmed to open only when it recognizes a combination code or even the owner's fingerprints. The box itself should be fastened to something so that it can't be stolen. You are responsible for keeping your guns not only clean and safe, but also out of other people's hands.

actions when they put their guns away and keep the ammunition in a completely different place. People who have break-action guns usually store them disassembled in their leather cases. Gun manufacturers have now come up with personalized locks that let only an "authorized user" fire the weapon.

Accidental shootings are about impossible if someone has to a) get at the gun, b) unpack it and put it together, and then c) find the ammunition and load it.

By the way, if you store a gun "negligently" (in an unlocked place or without disabling it with a trigger lock or something similar) and an unauthorized user causes harm with it, in many places you could be charged with a crime.

The other reason for securely storing guns is to keep them clean and protected from moisture,

This Sentry steel locker holds five long guns and has a shelf for ammunition. Some gun safes have combination locks; this inexpensive one has a key. Safes come in all sizes, and some are fireproof. Some even have dehumidifiers to prevent rust. These are expensive, but the guns they're meant for are worth much more. And how do you put a price on safety?

fire and even damage by insects or small animals. We've seen a wooden gunstock that was chewed by something toothy and heard of gun barrels plugged up by insect nests. Some gun safes have built-in dehumidifiers to remove any dampness from the air. Ammunition has to be kept dry too.

Depending on your home situation, it might be best to store your guns (and ammunition) at a shooting club or target range that has proper lockers.

There are always exceptions: Plenty of people, even in modern-day America, live in places where dangerous wild animals are common enough that guns are kept out in the open and even loaded. They might be where small children can't reach them, but everyone in the family knows better than to mess with them.

Ordinary household locks can keep guns from being used by the wrong people at the wrong time. This revolver (left) has a padlock around its top strap. The M1911 pistol has a bicycle cable threaded through its slide and grip that can also be looped around something unmovable like a beam.

TRAVELING WITH GUNS

Even if you live in an area where a gun rack in the back window of a pickup truck is still a common sight, always put a gun in a case when it's time to transport it somewhere. If the gun has a trigger lock or some other safety device on it, leave it in place. Naturally, the gun should be unloaded too. A carrying case protects a gun (and its sights) from scrapes and dirt and also hides it. Even if it's perfectly OK to leave a gun in view—in a locked car, say—it still freaks out some people, who may call the cops. Needless hassle. Also, leaving a gun in plain sight might encourage a thief to break in and grab it.

There is no federal law against carrying firearms

A felt-lined, leather-and-wood case custom-made for a matched set of fine double-barreled shotguns, along with their special tools and cleaning gear. The case alone is worth more than an ordinary shotgun, and a pair of guns like this may cost more than a high-end car.

for "lawful purposes." But besides the safety rules, there are usually state and sometimes local laws to follow. In general, you may transport a gun and ammunition in a car if it's unloaded and locked in the trunk in a case. No trunk? Then it has to be in some other locked container outside the passenger compartment, like a toolbox in a pickup truck bed or a camper trailer.

Licensed hunters can usually carry their guns in the car—but often not at night, since hunting after dark is illegal. Carrying guns on boats, ATVs or snow machines may be regulated too.

Traveling with guns on commercial airliners, trains, buses and ships is strictly controlled.

School zones, national parks, military bases and properties that belong to the federal government usually have their own firearms rules.

Wearing a loaded handgun openly in a holster is legal in some places and not in others. Some states require a permit to carry concealed firearms; a few do not.

What we've written here is very general, and laws change all the time. You—and your parents and your shooting mentor—have to know the rules for where you live and shoot. This is easy now, since you can find the information on the Internet—on Websites created by your state fish and game department, your town or city, and/or your police department.

By the way, if you're caught violating these laws, no matter what else happens to you (a fine or worse), your gun will probably be confiscated. You might even be banned from possessing a gun for some time.

Flying with guns requires a rugged travel case that is lockable and padded to protect a rifle and scope from airline baggage handlers. This one is aluminum, but some are made of heavy plastic. Traveling overseas with firearms generally isn't difficult, provided you follow the rules.

Silvio Calabi

Reloading Ammunition

Gunpowder + Bullet + Primer = *BOOM!*

Sooner or later, serious shooters usually learn to load their own ammunition. People who shoot a lot of trap, skeet or sporting clays may reload their empty shells as a way to save money, but handgun and rifle shooters often do it because they're looking for some performance edge: a special round that prints extra-tight groups on a target, or a superhot varmint-buster that gives great results out to a thousand yards. Maybe they're working up a modern load for a century-old double rifle, carefully substituting modern powder for the old Cordite that the original loading used and tuning it to hit hard and accurately at Cape-buffalo distances.

Reloading ammunition doesn't necessarily require a lot of equipment, although it can, but obviously it does require explosive materials. Working with and storing powders and primers is perfectly safe, if you know what you're doing and develop good procedures and habits.

If you don't know what you're doing, it's an invitation to possibly serious trouble. At best, ammunition that's loaded incorrectly just won't function; at worst, it can destroy a gun and take you with it.

For now at least, stick with factory-made ammunition. And read on about gunpowder, Atomic Pearls and exploding bullets.

BLACK POWDER

Some scientists believe that life on earth arose from a sort of primordial soup, a perfect combination of chemicals and energy. Before there were AR-15s and red-dot sights, before there were Mausers and metallic cartridges, even before there were muskets and lead balls, there was the "primordial soup" of firearms—their DNA, if you will: charcoal, sulphur and saltpeter, or potassium nitrate.

Whoever first combined these ingredients into something that went bang has been lost to history. Where it happened has been variously identified as China, India and England. Exactly when isn't known either, but it's certain that by the 13th Century gunpowder was being used in firearms. (The Chinese were putting it into rockets—fireworks, that is—long

before then. They may have invented firearms too.) With some refinement, this material would remain the standard propellant for handguns, rifles, shotguns and artillery until the 1880s.

That was when a Frenchman named Paul Vieille came up with something called *poudre B* (*poudre* meaning powder, and B standing for *blanche*, or white), or smokeless gunpowder. After that, the predecessor became known, naturally, as black powder. Smokeless powder was so much better in so many ways that it made the black stuff obsolete overnight. More than 125 years later, though, black powder is still with us.

The proportion of the ingredients in black powder has varied through the centuries, but it is

Steve Helsley

Pyrodex is a substitute for black powder, used in modern muzzleloading and blackpowder cartridge guns. Like smokeless powder, it's highly flammable but not explosive and therefore safer. This canister of Semi-Smokeless, still sealed, dates from about 1900; Semi-Smokeless burned cleaner than black powder.

ing them takes some doing. Black powder, on the other hand, can be set off just by a buildup of static electricity. In spite of strict safety precautions, the factories that produce it still blow up periodically.

Black powder is made by thoroughly pulverizing and mixing the ingredients, adding water, pressing the mixture into a cake, and then breaking that into granules. Black powder for shooting comes in a variety of grain sizes ranging from very fine, for priming flintlocks, to coarse, for cannons. State and federal laws regulate how much of it we can have in our possession.

Until dynamite and other high-order explosives like trinitrotoluene (TNT) were discovered, late in the 19th Century, black powder was a critical tool in mining, tunneling, canal building and other big construction projects. Those uses no longer apply, but black powder is still popular for Cowboy Action Shooting and several kinds of target shooting. (Handled properly, black powder can produce very consistent velocities and excellent accuracy.) It's also used by people who hunt with old-style guns or take part in reenacting Civil War or Revolutionary War battles. Blackpowder shooters joke about having to "run around the smoke" to see whether they've hit anything, and they like to refer to smokeless powder as a passing fad.

Black powder will likely be with us for a long time to come for another reason as well: It's one of the key ingredients in fireworks.

generally about 75 percent saltpeter, 15 percent charcoal and 10 percent sulphur. When black powder burns, it throws off clouds of whitish smoke. It also smells bad (like rotten eggs, from the sulphur) and leaves behind a nasty residue that makes gun barrels begin to rust almost immediately. And finally, although it is what's called a low-order explosive, black powder is dangerously unstable.

Many modern explosives (and smokeless powder) are surprisingly easy to handle, and detonat-

BROWN AND THEN SMOKELESS POWDERS

For centuries, what we now call black powder was simply gunpowder; there wasn't any other color or kind. Whether you were shooting a flintlock pistol across the field of honor or an 18-pounder from the gun deck of a navy frigate, it did the job. But when rapid-firing, breechloading repeating rifles arrived, in the 1860s, the limitations

of this powder became obvious. It left a gun barrel dirty enough to affect its accuracy, and the residue was highly corrosive. Plus there was a limit to how fast it could drive a bullet.

Black powder suited the old muzzleloading, single-shot era. Modern guns, especially machine guns, needed a propellant that burned cleaner and didn't gum up the works; and if it pushed a bullet to greater velocities, so much the better. This would make a bullet more powerful and reduce how much it dropped on the way to the target too.

By the mid-1800s an improved powder had arrived, primarily for artillery. This was known as brown, or prismatic, powder. It used the same basic ingredients as black powder—saltpeter (potassium nitrate), charcoal and sulphur—but in different proportions and with some added moisture in a special form of charcoal. It did perform better, but it was soon overtaken by other developments.

In 1846 two scientists, a German and a Swiss, independently discovered nitrocellulose, also known as nitrocotton or guncotton. The following year an Italian chemist discovered nitroglycerin, the first explosive that was more powerful than gunpowder.

And then, in the early 1880s, while others were still refining prismatic powder, Paul Vieille, the French chemist, altered nitrocellulose to create his *poudre blanche*, or white powder. (The name was meant to confuse German spies.) This was the first smokeless gunpowder, and it was immediately put to use in a new French military cartridge and rifle. For its weight, *poudre B* produced three times the energy of black powder, so it could launch bullets at much higher velocities. It also burned cleanly, with no more barrel fouling or clouds of dirty white smoke.

European countries went to war with each other every few years, so this was important. (In 1858 a metallurgist named John Scoffren wrote that gunpowder "not only materially affected the art

An 1890s English advertisement for different grades of the new smokeless gunpowder. Shooters and gunmakers spent a lot of time working up equivalent loads that would let them keep using their old guns with the new powder—without blowing them up.

of war, but exercised most important influences on the fate of empires and the progress of civilization.") The Germans bribed a French soldier to bring them a sample of his country's new rifle and its ammunition, which they then copied. Meanwhile, the British combined nitrocellulose with mineral jelly and nitro-

Steve Helsley

Powder cans dating from 1924 to today, with an old muzzle-loading powder horn and a percussion-cap dispenser. The science of propellants has changed tremendously.

Steve Helsley

You can see why blackpowder shooters joke about having to "run around the smoke" to see if they've hit what they were aiming at. This could be a serious problem if the target was a charging elephant or lion.

glycerin to create their first smokeless powder, called Cordite. By 1900, all the major armies of Europe had new rifles that fired smokeless powder.

Target shooters, police officers and hunters benefited from smokeless powder too. In 1915 in the United States, the .250-3000 Savage was the first cartridge to drive a bullet (just 87 grains) faster than 3,000 feet per second. Twenty years later the .220 Swift hit 4,100 fps with a 48-grain bullet.

Since then, smokeless powders have been highly refined for specific applications, to improve accuracy, diminish muzzle flash and reduce barrel wear. Velocities, however, have not increased significantly. Most modern rifle bullets still leave the barrel at between 2,500 and 3,500 fps.

Both black and smokeless powders can be dangerous, but particular care must be taken with

black powder. (It is a genuine explosive set off even by just a buildup of static electricity.) Smokeless powder is much more stable, so it isn't considered an explosive, and it has to be burned in a confined space to produce maximum pressure. Putting a match to smokeless powder produces a bright flame but no bang.

Used incorrectly, though, black and smokeless powders both can reduce a gun to jagged pieces of wood and metal.

BULLETS THAT GO *BOOM!*

I f you were 12 years old in the late 1950s, odds are that you were the proud owner of a Daisy BB gun. A fortunate few of us also had a supply of tiny firecrackers called Atomic Pearls. If you stomped on one of these beauties or threw it hard against the sidewalk—*bang!* They were round and about the diameter of a BB, but size varied. A clever operator would sort through his stash of

Atomic Pearls to find the ones that fit the Daisy. Exploding bullets!

These had a variety of uses, none of which was to be shared with Mom or Dad, that appealed strongly to a young lad.

Atomic Pearls disappeared long ago, so don't get your hopes up. But exploding projectiles are still around. Cast-iron cannon balls were hollowed out and filled with gunpowder as early as the 15th Century. Getting them to blow up on impact instead of in the cannon required another three centuries of trial and error, but eventually exploding artillery shells became standard. Along the way, it occurred to someone to try to put explosives into something much smaller: a bullet.

Originally, bullets were round balls. But around 1850 another Frenchman, Claude-Étienne Minié, perfected a longer, cone-shaped projectile. At about the same time, the first rimfire .22 cartridges appeared. Then someone figured out how to combine these two advancements: Drill a hole in the nose of the bullet and fill it with powder; then plug the hole with a rimfire blank, reversed so it faced forward. When this loaded-up round hit something hard, *boom!*

Actually, more like *bang!* You can't pack much explosive into such a small space, which has been the problem with exploding bullets all along.

These were used in muzzleloaders, so it was very important not to pound such a bullet down the barrel of the gun with the usual ramrod, or you'd risk setting off the rimfire cap and exploding the bullet. The tip of the ramrod had to be shaped so that it pressed against the body of the bullet, not its sensitive tip.

SIR SAMUEL BAKER

Sir Samuel Baker was a 19th Century English explorer, big-game hunter and author who spent many years in Africa. Baker's adventures with guns and exploding bullets are worthy of investigation by the *MythBusters* team. In one of his books, he wrote:

"Among other weapons, I had an extraordinary rifle that carried a half-pound percussion shell—this instrument of torture to the hunter was not sufficiently heavy for the weight of the projectile; it only weighed twenty pounds: thus, with a charge of ten drachms of powder, behind a HALF-POUND shell, the recoil was so terrific, that I was spun round like a weathercock in a hurricane. I really dreaded my own rifle, although I had been accustomed to heavy charges of powder and severe recoil for many years.

One of Sir Samuel Baker's rifles and a bullet. England's Royal Geographical Society, which owns the rifle, says it's a 4-bore (1-inch caliber); that isn't big enough to fire the sort of bullets Baker wrote about, so this may not be "Baby." It's wrapped with hide, probably from an elephant's ear. Hunters who were in the wilds for months at a time sometimes did this to fix gunstocks that broke or to reinforce them against breaking.

"None of my men could fire it, and it was looked upon with a species of awe, and was named 'Jenna el Mootfah' (child of a cannon) by the Arabs, which being far too long a name for practice, I christened it the 'Baby;' and the scream of this 'Baby,' loaded with a half-pound shell, was always fatal. It was far too severe, and I very seldom fired it, but it is a curious fact, that I never fired a shot with that rifle without bagging [something]: the entire practice, during several years, was confined to about twenty shots. I was afraid to use it; but now and then it was absolutely necessary that it should be cleaned, after lying for months loaded. On such occasions my men had the gratification of firing it, and the explosion was always accompanied by two men falling on their backs (one having propped up the shooter), and the 'Baby' flying some yards behind them. This rifle was made by Holland, of Bond Street, and I could highly recommend it for Goliath of Gath, but not for men of A.D. 1866."

Baker added that he had designed special ammunition, made for him by a certain Mr. Reilly, for this gun: "an iron lead-coated explosive shell, containing a bursting charge of half an ounce of fine grain powder."

"Baby" must have been a 2-bore, or 1.32-caliber, rifle. But packing a half-ounce of gunpowder into even a bullet that big is not easy. (Half an ounce of powder takes up as much room as 2,000 grains of lead, and a half-pound bullet weighs 3,500 grains in total.) The "iron shell" might have held the powder, while the lead coating added mass and a softer surface for the rifling to grip. But this was no easy thing to make, and as a "percussion shell" it still needed a detonator in the nose to set it off when it struck something. These bullets must have been unusually long.

Furthermore, 10 drams (0.62 ounces—not much more than Baker claimed was in the bullet itself) of powder is a light charge for a rifle firing a half-pound projectile. The bullet might penetrate very little, if at all, and just blow up on the skin of the elephant or rhino. This wouldn't do much more than cause a superficial burn and maybe scare the beast to death. It might have worked to drive off hostile natives if it was fired against their canoes.

So there are questions about Baker's bullets. But explosive ammunition did exist, at least for a while. Baker wrote about "Baby" in 1866; at that time the Bavarian Army in Germany had a 14.5mm (.570-caliber) explosive bullet for its single-shot Lindner rifle. Three years later, for their 11.5x50R Werder rifle, the Germans loaded up another one. This *Zundegeschoss*, or "primed bullet," had a hollow copper tube filled with priming powder set into its nose. Both of these rifles were breechloaders, which avoided the problem of seating these bullets from the muzzle without setting them off. We don't know how effective they were.

Twenty years later, the introduction of smokeless powder led to smaller bullets, with even less room for explosives. During World War I (1914-1918) the French tried to make an exploding rifle round to shoot at airplanes and observation balloons. They used an obsolete 11mm (.43-caliber) cartridge that fired a bigger slug than their normal 8mm (.32) service round, but it never became practical.

The Germans experimented with new explosive bullets too, also with poor results. Manfred von Richthofen, the legendary Red Baron fighter-plane ace, almost shot himself down with them. His bullets accidentally detonated just after clearing the muzzles of his Spandau machine guns, and the fragments went through the cowling over his airplane engine.

World War II (1939-1945) inspired Germany and maybe other countries to give exploding bullets another try. The German *B-Patrone* bullet produced a puff of smoke when it struck something, but that was all. It wound up being used as a spotter round, to see where bullets were hitting.

Testing in the United States led to the official conclusion that "the explosive effect of a bullet of this size was not sufficiently great to justify the difficulty of its construction."

Military rifle bullets are generally much smaller now than they were in WWI and WWII (which in turn were much smaller than the bullets of Sir Samuel Baker's day). The 5.56mm bullet for the M16 and M4 rifles and the Russian 5.45mm bullet for the AK-74 are both less than .23-caliber—not even a quarter-inch in diameter. Put explosives in them, and they won't go *bang!*; they'll barely go *poof*.

Bullets for hunting are often much bigger, but even if they could be made to explode, they prob-ably would be illegal in most places and frowned upon as unsporting everywhere. Whalers sometimes attach explosive heads to their harpoons, but that's another story.

German Army 8mm *B-Patrone* from WWII, shown more than twice actual size. Each bullet has its own internal primer that detonated the small charge of white phospho-rous in the nose. But with such a small amount of explosive, these were only useful as spotter rounds; the puff of smoke would show the shooter where he was hitting.

White Phosphorous

Primer

Striker

Killer Apps

The Stories Behind Famous Guns

WERE ARROWS BETTER THAN BALLS?

Gun writers and historians love to quote a letter written by Benjamin Franklin in February 1776. This was just six months before the American colonies declared their independence from the British Empire and the Revolution broke out for real. Franklin was writing to an officer of the Continental Army named Charles Lee about the prospects for war with England, and he included this:

"But I still wish, with you, that Pikes [*long spears*] could be introduced and I would add Bows and Arrows. These were good Weapons, not wisely laid aside;

"1st, because a Man may shoot as truly with a Bow as with a common Musket.

"2ndly. He can discharge 4 Arrows in the time of charging and discharging one Bullet.

"3dly. His Object [*target*] is not taken from his View by the Smoke of his own Side.

"4thly. A Flight of Arrows, seen coming upon them, terrifies and disturbs the Enemy's Attention to his Business.

"5thly. An Arrow striking in any Part of a Man puts him *hors du Combat* [*out of action*] till 'tis extracted.

"6thly. Bows and Arrows are more easily provided everywhere than Muskets and Ammunition."

The official seal of Britain's National Rifle Association, founded in 1859, has two soldiers, one armed with a longbow, the other with a musket. The argument over which weapon was better for infantry—faster, more accurate or more effective—went on for a couple of centuries.

Benjamin Franklin was a wise man, but he misunderstood a couple of points about muskets and bows. The English longbow was a superb weapon, but it had been "wisely laid aside" long before 1776 because no one could still "shoot as truly" with it as with a musket, especially in America.

A longbow was very powerful—five to six feet long, with a draw weight that was probably far more than a hundred pounds—and it fired a heavy, man- and horse-killing arrow almost three feet long with an effective range of more than 300 yards. The English and Welsh archers who made life so difficult for French knights in the Hundred Years War (1337-1453) grew up with bows in their hands. Over years of practice they developed the technique and tremendous strength to draw their bows and shoot them accurately. They could, as Franklin wrote, discharge four arrows in the time it took to fire and reload a musket once, and they could do this more or less continuously 30 or 40 times before their strength gave out. But in England these skills had been lost a hundred years before our Revolution, and the longbow had never come to America at all.

To Ben Franklin's other points: Number 3 was correct. So was Number 4, except that it's fairly easy to see an arrow coming and step out of its way, at least if you know it's coming. (It's hard to dodge a thousand arrows raining down all at once. But that's what shields were for.) Number 5 is true. Number 6 was false, at least in America, where no one knew how to make longbows and the Native American bows were much-less-powerful, short-range weapons.

A thunderous volley of musket fire, belching smoke and (if the sun wasn't bright) flame, was probably just as terrifying as a hail of arrows. A ball, even one fired from a crude musket at a pokey 1,200 feet per second, is invisible and can't be avoided (if it doesn't miss entirely). Finally, it is far, far easier to teach someone to load and fire a musket than to shoot a war bow.

The argument over bows versus guns was likely centuries old by 1776. It probably didn't go away completely until breechloading repeating rifles were perfected, almost a century later.

Paul Revere & the 2nd Amendment

Near midnight on April 18, 1775, a silversmith named Paul Revere—one of the radical patriots who called themselves the Sons of Liberty and who had carried out the infamous Tea Party in Boston Harbor—rowed himself across the Charles River from Boston to Charlestown. There he mounted a horse and galloped inland, warning villages that King George's troops were headed their way. He didn't shout, "The British are coming!" This would have been meaningless, since the people of the Royal Province of Massachusetts Bay were British themselves. His message was more specific and ominous: "The regulars are coming out!"

Soldiers of the British Army—the feared "redcoats," the best infantry on earth—were marching westward in force that night.

England had been sending more and more troops to Boston, whose citizens were angry about taxes and regulations that the Crown had put on them. Paul Revere was part of a spy network that had been set up to watch these troops and to quickly spread the word if they left the city in strength. Alerted by Revere and William Dawes, another courier, several dozen more riders fanned out across the countryside. Their job was to rouse the Minutemen, special colonial militiamen who could report armed and ready for duty "at a minute's notice." This rapid-reaction force had been in existence for more than a hundred years already, since the days of Indian attacks on settlers, and the Minutemen had been active in the French and Indian War of the 1750s too.

At first the fear was that the army had been sent to Lexington, about 15 miles by road from Boston, to seize the patriot leaders Samuel Adams and John Hancock. But when Revere and Dawes reached Adams and Hancock, well ahead of the soldiers, they realized that the British would not have sent 700 men under a lieutenant colonel just to arrest them. The goal had to be the stockpile of colonial military supplies in nearby Concord, where the Massachusetts Provincial Congress met. Revere set off again, but he was captured by a British patrol before he got to Concord. He'd done his job, though, and across the region church bells were ringing the alarm.

Just before dawn on April 19, redcoats and militiamen met on the town common in Lexington. A wild and disorganized skirmish followed. A colonist probably fired first, the famous "shot heard 'round the world," and then the British returned fire and launched a bayonet charge. Eight militia were killed; the rest scattered. The British then pushed into Concord unopposed. They split up into search parties and found the hidden arsenal, including three cannons that had been buried. Meanwhile, though, Minutemen were pouring in from neighboring villages.

A rear guard of two British infantry companies (about 90 men) took up a defensive position on the far side of the North Bridge, between Concord and Lexington, and found themselves facing 400 or more militia. This time the redcoats—exhausted from marching all night, led by an inexperienced young captain and possibly beginning to panic—fired first. Then, badly outnumbered and taking casualties, they did something almost unheard of: They broke and ran, fortunately (for them) right into the arms of a full British brigade (a thousand troops) that had been sent from Boston as reinforcements.

A long night became a very long day as the British soldiers retreated back to the city. They were attacked along the way at least eight times by the militia.

Both sides were stunned and shaken. Neither believed that the other would really shoot or that the patriot movement, having been simmering for years,

One of the most famous landmarks in Boston is this statue of Paul Revere. On his midnight ride, Revere didn't shout, "The British are coming!" That would have made no sense, as everyone in the American colony was British. But the redcoats were coming to seize the colonists' arms.

would explode into open rebellion against the lawful King. This was the start of the Revolutionary War and the birth of the United States of America—and the spark that lit the flame was the government's attempt to seize the colonists' arms and ammunition.

After the Revolution, deciding how the new nation would be governed was a long and difficult process. To gain enough support for the Constitution, the document that established the basic laws and organization of the new United States, the authors added a list of 10 amendments, or explanations, that became known as the Bill of Rights. These include freedom of speech, freedom of the press, freedom of religion and so on.

The Second Amendment reads: "A well-regulated militia being necessary to the security of a free state, the right of the people to keep and bear arms shall not be infringed."

"Stand your ground!" Colonists and redcoats face each other on the town common in Lexington on April 19, 1776. The "shot heard 'round the world" has just been fired, and the world will never be the same again.

Considering how the United States became an independent country, it's not hard to see why the Bill of Rights gave this particular privilege so much importance. Richard Henry Lee of Virginia, one of the first statesmen to propose that the American colonies break away from England, wrote: "To preserve liberty, it is essential that the whole body of people always possess arms and be taught alike, especially when young, how to use them."

Firearms (and other weapons) had arrived in what became Massachusetts with the first Pilgrims, in 1620. Guns put meat on the table and defended against Indians and helped the colony survive. For the next couple of centuries, as the new nation spread across the North American wilderness, the notion of taking guns away from law-abiding citizens was simply unthinkable.

The Constitution was adopted in 1787. As each new state joined the union during the next 160-plus years, 45 of them adopted similar "right to keep and bear arms" provisions in their own constitutions.

It wasn't until the second half of the 20th Century that the meaning of the Second Amendment began to be debated in public. The argument focused on whether the right to keep and bear arms was an individual right or a collective right.

In other words, does the Second Amendment apply to individual gun owners or only to those in a government militia?

The Constitution also established the three branches of American government: legislative, executive and judicial. The legislative branch (Congress) passes our laws, the executive (the President) enforces them and the judicial (the courts) interprets them. And so, to a large degree, the courts determine the ultimate meaning of the Constitution, its Bill of Rights and all other laws. In 1868, after the Civil War, the Fourteenth Amendment was added. Its "due process" clause has become the legal vehicle for determining if a right included in the Constitution applies (is "incorporated") to individuals in a case before a state court.

As some states have no "right to keep and bear arms" provision in their constitutions, this too would be clarified by the courts.

After a number of legal challenges to the Second Amendment at state and federal levels, the United States Supreme Court took up these matters.

In 2008 the Supreme Court ruled in *District of Columbia v. Heller* that the "right to keep and bear arms" is an individual right. Two years later the Supreme Court ruled in *McDonald v. Chicago* that the federal right was incorporated under the Fourteenth Amendment and so applied to all 50 states.

It is important to understand that no right is absolute. The most common example of this involves the First Amendment: The right to free speech does not allow someone to yell, "Fire!" in a crowded theater if there is no fire. Firearms rights are subject to restrictions too, including many related to age, mental health and criminal convictions. Our constitutional rights evolve as the legislative branch of government passes new laws and as the courts provide new rulings on those laws.

Pistols at Dawn: The Duel

For centuries a dispute between gentlemen that went beyond some mild name-calling could turn into a formal fight to the death. Being accused of cheating at cards, for example, or of cowardice was often enough to spark a challenge. So was paying too much attention to another man's wife or even just a strong difference of political opinion. Personal honor was at stake.

The man who felt himself insulted would "demand satisfaction." The point was not necessarily to kill his adversary but to show a willingness to put his life on the line to stand up for his honor or beliefs. To decline a challenge meant that the man didn't truly believe in the rightness of his position—or at least didn't feel that it was worth risking his life to defend it.

(This had its roots in the ancient custom of trial by ordeal. If someone accused of a crime could survive a fight or being dunked in a pond, God was obviously on his/her side and he/she was innocent. This was before everyone had a lawyer.)

In Britain and America the era of the pistol duel was about 1770 to 1870. Gentlemen owned pairs of special pistols that were beautifully made and balanced and perfectly matched. When it was time to fight, the duelists' supporters, or seconds, carefully supervised the loading of the pistols and then offered them to the combatants to choose. Everything was supposed to be equal.

Holding the pistols down by their legs or up in the air, the duelists stood back to back and then, at a signal, walked away from each other an agreed-upon distance. This was usually 12 paces or to a mark on the ground, but it might be less if the insult was especially grave. Then they turned and fired. A confident shot might wait for his trembling opponent to fire first and miss, and then take aim . . . and after he'd made him wait long seconds, deliberately kill him. A good shot might go for the

Eugene Onegin and Vladimir Lensky's duel in the snow, painted by Ilya Repin. This is a famous scene from Alexander Pushkin's classic Russian novel *Eugene Onegin,* published in the 1820s. Duelists continued to meet on "the field of honor" for almost another century.

stomach, to cause a wound that led to a slow and painful death, or he'd just wing his opponent in the shoulder or leg to make a point without killing him. A doctor was often standing by.

If both men missed, accidentally or on purpose, the seconds would ask if they wished to reload and continue. Often the answer was no; just by showing up both had proved their courage, and "honor was satisfied." (Duelists sometimes just "deloped," or fired their pistols into the ground.) Or they might in fact have another round. If it went as far as three sets of misses, though, the seconds would call off the contest. This was getting ridiculous!

The seconds—each duelist usually had two—didn't simply stand by idly. They often were armed too, and part of their job was to see that no one cheated and even to get involved if necessary. A duelist might turn and fire before reaching the agreed-upon distance. If so, one of the seconds might shout a warning or even shoot the cheater. There are sto-

Thomas Hager

Many gentlemen owned pairs of perfectly matched dueling pistols like these, made by William & John Rigby in Dublin, Ireland, in 1828. The bores were supposed to be smooth, but some gunmakers hid rifling in them in order to make the pistols more accurate—and deadly.

ries of rigged duels where one side had a man with a rifle hidden in the bushes nearby to fire at the same instant as his duelist, and of seconds who opened fire on each other too.

Dueling pistols were single-barreled muzzle-loaders with flint or, later, percussion locks. Since the owner's life might depend on every shot fired, they were made with the greatest care. The powder and ball were critical too. No detail was too small to overlook. Calibers were usually 32 or 36 bore (.526" or .506"), and the barrels were typically eight to 10 inches long.

The code of honor required dueling pistols to be smoothbores, but the benefits of rifling to accuracy were too real to be ignored, especially when lives were on the line. Some gunmakers offered "scratch rifling"—spiral grooves in the bore that were so faint that they could have been caused by over-eager cleaning. This might be missed by the duelists' seconds, who inspected and loaded the pistols in the field, often under dawn light. Other makers hid their rifling deep in the bores so the muzzles remained smooth. Secret rifling in both pistols may have been winked at because it benefited both parties equally.

Many famous politicians, military officers, authors, painters, musicians, businessmen and titled aristocrats got involved in duels, some many times. In fact, the more prominent you were, the more likely it was that someone would "call you out." The

most famous duel in American history took place on July 11, 1804, in New Jersey, between Gen. Alexander Hamilton and Col. Aaron Burr. Burr challenged Hamilton because of years of severe political disagreements that finally became personal.

As you may know, Burr fatally wounded Hamilton. What you may have forgotten is that Burr was then the Vice-President of the United States and later started the company that became the Chase Manhattan Bank. Hamilton had been the first Secretary of the US Treasury.

Dueling took place all over the world and often with weapons other than pistols—mostly swords. It was usually illegal, but the law rarely was enforced until the 20th Century. Still, duels often took place in some out-of-the-way place and at dawn, for secrecy. Islands in rivers between states or countries were popular dueling sites, because they were difficult to get to and there might be confusion over which law applied.

Dueling died out late in the 19th Century, but our fascination with it did not. The "sport" even made an appearance at the Olympics in Athens in 1906. The competitors shot at dummies dressed like gentlemen with targets on their chests, not at each other. Before that there was a school in Paris that taught dueling skills by dressing its students in heavy coats and wire-mesh or glass masks and letting them shoot wax bullets at each other. "Bloodless dueling" spread as far as New York City, but it died out quickly.

Some might say that Paintball is just a modern form of this. The temptation to attack an enemy is sometimes overwhelming. Kids in schoolyards do it. Gang members do it. Nations do it. And to this day Her Majesty Queen Elizabeth II, Monarch of the United Kingdom, has an official champion to stand up for her should she ever be challenged on the field of honor. He is Lt. Col. John Lindley Marmion Dymoke, Lord of the Manor of Scrivelsby, in Lincolnshire, England. He has never been put to the test. Not yet, anyway . . . .

COLT: TWO FAMOUS .45S

THE SINGLE ACTION ARMY

To non-shooters it's almost one word: "Coltfortyfive." But shooters know better. The Colt company has been making handguns for almost 200 years, and the guns certainly have not all been .45 caliber. In fact, there are two famous .45-caliber Colts, one a revolver and the other a semi-auto pistol. They're both .45s, but they take different cartridges. They're both more than a hundred years old, and they're both still being made by Colt and many other companies.

In 1872 Colt's Patent Firearms Manufacturing Company won a competition to supply the US Government with a new revolver called the Single Action Army. The SAA was a breechloading six-shooter with a cartridge that was also new: the .45 Colt. At the time, this was the most powerful handgun round yet invented. The Army was so pleased with the SAA that it called it "the best weapon to carry on the person that has ever been produced" and ordered thousands of them.

Samuel Colt had died 10 years earlier, when he was only 47, but he had become rich on an idea that he'd had when he was a teenager. Colt had always been interested in guns, explosives and machinery. When he was 16, sailing as a cabin boy on a ship to India, he carved a wooden model of a revolver, a pistol that could fire six times before it had to be reloaded. This was in 1831, when most guns were muzzleloaders that fired just one shot at a time.

FIG. 1.   FIG. 2.

NOMENCLATURE.

A. Barrel.	G. Hammer.	N. Trigger and screw.	T. Short-guard screw.
B. Frame.	H. Main-spring.	O. Hammer-notches.	U. Sear and bolt (combined)
B'. Recoil-plate.	I. Hammer-roll and rivet.	P. Firing-pin and rivet.	spring and screw.
C. Cylinder.	J. Hammer-screw.	Q. Ejector-rod and spring.	V. Back-strap screw.
D. Base-pin.	K. Hammer-cam.	Q'. Ejector-tube.	W. Main-spring-screw.
E. Guard.	L. Hand and spring.	R. Ejector-head.	X. Front sight.
F. Back-strap.	M. Bolt and screw.	S. Ejector-tube screw.	Y. Base-pin catch-screw.

This is how *Farrow's Military Encyclopedia* of 1895 showed the US Army's new Colt SAA revolver. It recommended using only "the best sperm oil" (whale oil, that is) to lubricate the revolver's moving parts.

Revolving guns weren't new. Most of them had a cluster of barrels, which the shooter turned by hand to bring each barrel under the hammer so it could be fired. Colt's model had just one barrel, but behind it was a cylinder that turned, with chambers for six shots.

This was very clever, but it wasn't new, either. Many gunmakers had experimented with revolving cylinders, and by 1818 a man from Boston named Elisha Collier had produced a flintlock gun with one barrel and seven chambers in a cylinder. After each shot the cylinder had to be turned by hand. These Collier guns were used by British troops in India, and Colt probably saw one there or aboard the ship. Colt got the rest of his idea from the ship's steering wheel, which always locked into position after it had been turned.

Able to fire six powerful .45-caliber cartridges in a few seconds and then be reloaded almost as quickly, Colt's Single Action Army model of 1873 was called "the Peacemaker." It may be the best-known gun of all time—along with the AK-47. This is an SAA revolver from Colt's current catalog.

Colt's revolver was like Collier's but with two improvements: First, it wasn't a flintlock; it used the new percussion caps. And second, pulling the hammer back with the thumb to cock it also mechanically rotated the cylinder to line up the next chamber with the barrel and then lock it there. The shooter could fire the gun six times with just one hand.

Colt made his first real revolver three years later, and after that it took almost 40 years of improvements and different models (and a patent problem) to get to the Single Action Army. What really made the SAA possible, however, was metallic cartridges.

Before these came along, each chamber had to be loaded from the front with a paper cartridge: Tear the paper, pour the powder into the chamber, then ram the rest of the paper and the ball down after it. Or you had to pour powder from a dispenser into the chamber and follow that with a ball. The ramrod was built into the gun under the barrel. Then a percussion cap had to be put on the nipple behind each chamber. But the SAA fired factory-made cartridges that just dropped into each chamber from the back.

Colts were already well known before the Single Action Army. They were used in the Civil War, and then were carried by the soldiers, miners, lawmen, traders, farmers, ranchers and cowboys who settled the West and fought the Indians. Samuel Colt was called "the Peacemaker," because people could settle arguments just by pulling out one of his revolvers. His guns were known as "equalizers," from the saying "God made men. Sam Colt made men equal." As good as the SAA was, though, it might have disappeared but for an accident of timing and history. By the late 1800s people all over the world had become fascinated with tales of the Wild West, and the hero of these stories always relied on his trusty Colt. Buffalo Bill's Wild West Show (and others) traveled the eastern US and Europe staging "Indian battles" and other entertainments, and Colts were used often. Newspaper reporters and dime novelists gave the Peacemaker nickname to the Single Action Army itself and made it famous. Then came the movies. The first feature film ever made in Hollywood, in 1914, was a western called *The Squaw Man*. Since then the Colt SAA has had a supporting role in thousands more books, stories, movies and TV shows. Today gun collectors pay huge amounts of money for Colt six-shooters that belonged to famous people.

The SAA could be ordered with different barrel lengths, grips, sights, finishes and engraving, and even with detachable shoulder stocks. Every legendary sheriff and outlaw seemed to have his own favorite style. Peacemakers weren't all .45s, either. Colt eventually made them in calibers from .22 to .476 Eley (a British military round of the 1880s) and sold them all over the world. The SAA and the .45 Colt cartridge made the transition from black to smokeless gunpowder too. Colt stopped making the SAA for a while, but demand was so great that the company had to bring it back. Today a lot of companies produce their own versions of this classic; Colt still offers it in .45 and .357 Magnum.

THE MODEL 1911

The only problem with the Single Action Army was just that: It was a single-action. It had to be cocked by thumb before it could be fired. Colt followed the SAA with its double-action New Army Model 1892. No thumb required.

Double-action, however, wasn't ideal either. Cocking the hammer with the trigger takes a long finger pull against a lot of resistance, which makes the gun wobble. It can be done fast, but to be accurate takes lots of practice and skill.

There was another way. The first true machine gun, the Maxim, in the 1880s operated by recoil energy. The recoil slammed back the bolt, which kicked out the empty shell and re-cocked the hammer, and then a spring closed the bolt again. On its way forward, the bolt picked up a fresh round from the magazine and shoved it into the chamber. All the shooter had to do was squeeze the trigger. Why not use this system on rifles, pistols and shotguns too?

European gun companies came out with the first recoil-operated pistols, but the best one turned out to be another Colt, the Model 1911, and it too was a .45.

A gunmaking genius named John Moses Browning created the M1911 and its new cartridge. Browning was born in 1855 in Utah. He had 21 brothers and sisters, and his father was a gunsmith. By the time he died, in 1926, he held 128 firearms patents and his name was on the Browning Arms Company. But he was more interested in inventing guns than in managing a factory, so mostly he sold his gun designs to other manufacturers.

Designed by John Browning and made by Colt, the Model 1911 became a worldwide success. It was carried by American soldiers and many others through both world wars, Korea and Vietnam. It's still the most popular combat and self-defense pistol ever made.

These designs included more than a dozen rifles and shotguns, a dozen pistols and five automatic weapons. One of the latter was the awesome M2 heavy machine gun, which fires the .50 BMG round. BMG stands for Browning Machine Gun. The M2 has now been on duty with American forces continually since 1921! (Generations of soldiers have called the M2 "Ma Deuce.")

Browning began work on the Model 1911 pistol around 1895. It was called the 1911 because that was the year the US Army selected it as its sidearm.

Always looking for superior firepower, American forces had gone from Colt's SAA to its New Army Model in 1892. Not only was the New Army Model a double-action revolver, but it also fired a different cartridge: the .38 Long Colt. It was easier to shoot than the .45 because it recoiled less, but it was also less powerful. No big deal—until 1899, when American troops were sent to put down the Moro Rebellion in the Philippine Islands. The Moros were Muslim warriors fighting for their independence; as we would say today, they were highly motivated. Soldiers said that even multiple hits from a .38 sometimes didn't discourage a Moro swinging his bolo knife. The Army shipped some .45 Colt single-actions to the Philippines, and supposedly the heavier, harder-hitting bullets did the trick.

And then along came auto pistols, which were easier to shoot and faster to reload than re-volvers (with pre-loaded magazines). The US Ord-nance Department invited manufacturers to send their pistols to be tried out. Meanwhile, Col. John T. Thompson (who later invented the Tommy gun) and a major from the Medical Corps named Louis LaGarde test-fired all sorts of handguns at human cadavers and even live cows, and then announced that the Army's new pistol should not be less than .45 caliber. The Colt company and John Browning were listening.

In 1904 Browning created a new cartridge that fired a .45-caliber bullet weighing 230 grains at 850 feet per second. It was slightly less powerful than the .45 Colt SAA round, but it was a lot more compact. It was named the .45 ACP, for Automatic Colt Pistol. Then Browning set about perfecting the gun itself.

After years of testing and development, the .45 Automatic Colt Pistol beat out all other competi-tors. John Browning himself attended the last big trial, where one of his guns fired 6,000 rounds in two days without a problem. Whenever the pistol got too hot, it was dunked in a tank of water. On March 29, 1911, it was declared the winner.

John Browning's 1911 pistol was a success all over the world. (Did you notice the one fired at Leonardo DiCaprio in *Titanic*, a movie that was set in 1912?) It was carried by American soldiers and many others through the two world wars, Korea and Vietnam. In WWII Colt couldn't keep up with the orders, so other companies were licensed to produce it too. It is still the most popular combat and self-defense pistol ever made, exactly the sort of "man-stopper" that Thompson and LaGarde and every trooper wanted.

British and American lieutenants aboard the SS *Mongolia* in April 1917, possibly in a combined training exercise on deck. The American holds an early model 1911. *Mongolia* carried troops to Europe in the early days of WWI. The US Navy equipped the ship with six-inch guns, with which she fired on, and may have sunk, a German submarine in the English Channel. This was the first American naval action of that war.

In 1985, though, after more tests, it was replaced as the official US sidearm by the Beretta M9. This caused a tremendous uproar. Not only was the beloved .45 ACP giving way to a less-powerful round—the 9x19mm cartridge, originally made for the Luger semi-automatic pistol—the Beretta wasn't even an American pistol; it was Italian!

The selection committee pointed to the advantages of the new pistol. Its magazine held 15 cartridges compared to the M1911's seven. It was double-action, meaning that once the slide had been worked to chamber a round, the hammer could be lowered (for safety) and then fired with the trigger finger. (If it's down, the M1911's hammer has to be thumbed back, single-action, for the first shot.) The 9mm round was used by all other NATO armies, and the US should use the same ammunition as its allies. Even though it was less powerful, a metal-jacketed 9mm bullet could penetrate certain kinds of body armor of the day that would stop the fatter .45 round. And finally, the Army's old M1911s were worn out and had to be replaced anyway.

Furthermore, except for the Ingram MAC-10, no one was making .45-caliber submachine guns any more either. The Thompson, the M3 "Grease Gun" and the Reising of World War II and Korea were long gone, replaced by lighter, handier submachine guns that fired the 9mm round.

The grumbling hasn't completely stopped yet. Some American troops have quietly gone back to the M1911 and the .45 ACP for the same reason that it replaced the .38 Long Colt more than a century ago. They say the 9mm isn't stopping those highly motivated Muslim warriors, this time in Iraq and Afghanistan.

Well, OK. But here's an interesting thing: The Thompson-LaGarde tests, which in 1904 selected .45-caliber bullets for their "stopping effect at short ranges," also recommended that "soldiers armed with pistols or revolvers should be drilled unremittingly in the accuracy of fire" as there was "no hope of stopping an adversary by shock or other immediate results." In other words, where a bullet is put is always more important than how big or powerful it is. (Read "Stopping Power" and "Knockdown Force.")

Back when he was an undercover cop, one of the authors had a bad day at work. He was hit by two .38 bullets and two .45s. He couldn't feel any difference between them.

The Vietnam War: With just a flashlight and a .45 pistol and probably thinking about booby traps and snakes, an American soldier prepares to enter a Viet Cong supply tunnel.

It's hard to find anything that has lasted for a century or more without enormous changes. Your family car doesn't look or drive anything like the first practical automobile, built in 1885. All that a Boeing 787 Dreamliner has in common with the Wright Brothers' biplane of 1903 is that they both can fly under their own power. ENIAC, the first fully functional digital computer, was the size of a house, weighed 50 tons and cost a half-million dollars when your grandparents were your age. Compare that to the computer on your desk now.

But imagine a Texas Ranger who traveled through time from John Wesley Hardin's day to appear at your shooting range today. You could hand him a Single Action Army made last week and he'd know exactly what to do with it. (He'd be surprised, though, that firing it didn't make a cloud of white smoke.) He probably would be carrying one himself. Same goes for a Doughboy—as American troops were called in World War I—if you handed him a Model 1911.

WINCHESTER: THE 'COWBOY' GUNS

In 1950 Universal Pictures released a block-buster movie called *Winchester '73*. The cast included some big names but, as you may have guessed, the real star of the movie was a Model 1873 Winchester. The story line was the adventures that the rifle had as it passed through different characters' hands.

The original 1950 movie poster for *Winchester '73*. Actor James Stewart got top billing, but the real star was his rifle. It was called "the gun that won the West," and it was the first of many Winchester lever guns. Like with the Colt SAA, Hollywood helped make it popular.

(It seems like ancient history now, but the fighting between the US Army and the Indians ended only in 1890, in South Dakota. That was just 60 years before *Winchester '73* came out and well within the lifetime of many people who saw it.)

Sam Colt might have objected, but Winchester's Model 1873 rifle was called "the gun that won the West." Back in 1950 some moviegoers perhaps could tell the difference between a Model 73 and, say, a Model 94, but today most people see a lever-action rifle and just think *Winchester!* Other American gun companies, especially Marlin and Savage, made superb lever-actions too, but Winchester gets most of the credit. There have been 16 different lever-action Winchesters: 14 rifles and two shotguns. John Browning, the genius who invented the Colt Model 1911 and so many other great firearms, designed five of them. (He even based his first machine gun on one of them, but that's another story.)

Browning and most other important American gun designers—Eli Whitney, Sam Colt, Eliphalet Remington, John Garand, Gene Stoner, Bill Ruger and so on—were engineers and machinists. Oliver Winchester, however, was a businessman. He knew about advertising, managing money and how to choose employees and products. Winchester was born in Massachusetts in 1810. He became a carpenter's apprentice and then a house builder. Then he switched careers and started a clothing company in New York City that made a fortune in men's shirts. In 1855 he bought the Volcanic Arms Company, in Connecticut, which had been started by Horace Smith and Daniel Wesson, who later became famous for Smith & Wesson handguns. Winchester renamed it the New Haven Arms Company.

When the Civil War started, in 1861, New Haven Arms was making a 16-shot lever-operated rifle called the .44 Henry (named for Benjamin Tyler Henry, the man who designed it). At a time when single-shot muzzleloaders were common, this was radical. At first, though, the Union Army didn't want it. Too fragile, they said, and besides, it needed special ammunition, not just powder and ball. But many soldiers bought Henry rifles and ammunition for themselves. The South called it "that Yankee rifle they load on Sunday and shoot all week!" By 1863 the Union and some European governments were buying Henrys, and New Haven Arms began making money.

After the war, in 1866, Oliver Winchester sold his shirt business, and New Haven Arms became the Winchester Repeating Arms Company. The first rifle with the Winchester name on it came out that year:

A Winchester Model 1886. This one has a full-length magazine tube under the barrel. With almost every new lever-action model, Winchester also brought out more-powerful ammunition.

The Model 1866 was an improved version of the Henry, and the Henry was based on a gun made by Volcanic Arms.

Like the Henry and the Volcanic, the Model 66 was operated by a finger lever under the stock grip. The lever could be worked very quickly with the rifle at the shoulder and even on a moving horse. Other benefits of the lever-action were that the shooter could uncock the rifle just by lowering the hammer with his thumb, and (as the Confederate Army found out) the magazine tube under the barrel could hold a lot of ammo. They weren't precision target rifles, but Winchesters were accurate enough out to 150 yards or more, depending on the cartridge.

The Henry and the Model 66 both fired the .44 Henry, a stubby little rimfire round. The Model 73 got a slightly bigger centerfire version called the .44-40 Winchester. Colt and Remington and other companies made revolvers for both of these rounds, which made it easier to pack ammunition. But with each new Winchester model after that—1876, 1886, 1892, 1894, 1895—came more-powerful cartridges (except for the 92, which was only for handgun ammunition, from the .25-20 Winchester to the .44-40). Still, the US Cavalry kept its Springfield breechloading carbine through the Indian Wars, which ended in 1890. Even though it was only a single-shot, the Springfield was more powerful and accurate than most Winchesters. It was harder to reload on horseback, but the troopers normally used their horses only as transportation; they dismounted to fight. (Never mind what you see in the movies.)

The late-model 1895 lever-action could fire the .405 Winchester, which was introduced in 1904 as a big-game cartridge. Theodore Roosevelt and his son Kermit both brought Model 95 .405s to Africa on their year-long safari in 1910, and they reported that the rifles "did admirably with lions, giraffes, elands and . . . hippos."

It turned out the M95 could even handle the modern, high-pressure .30-06 Springfield round, which came along in 1906. This was partly because of its five-round box magazine, which stacked the ammunition vertically. You can't put cartridges with spitzer (pointed) bullets into a tube magazine because of the risk of setting off a primer with the point of the bullet behind it. However, the box magazine makes the 95 uncomfortable to carry in one hand.

Otherwise, lever-actions generally balance and handle very well, more like a good shotgun than a rifle. They're outstanding for quick shooting at close range, and they're also quite flat, so they fit neatly into a saddle scabbard. This is why a lot

The Winchester Model 95 lever-action rifle had a box magazine, which could safely hold cartridges with high-performance spitzer (pointed) bullets. In Africa, both Kermit Roosevelt and his father used .405-caliber M95s for big game.

of ranchers still carry them as everyday working rifles. For some reason, though, while lever-actions were popular in the US, Canada and Mexico and down into Central and South America and even Cuba, they never caught on anywhere else. With one exception, sort of: Russia.

When World War I began, in 1914, the Russians had an excellent bolt-action military rifle called the Model 91 Mosin. But they couldn't make the rifles fast enough for their huge army. Russia ordered more Mosins from Remington and Westinghouse plus another 300,000 lever-actions: Winchester Model 95 military muskets with bayonet mounts. The caliber was 7.62x54R Russian. The rifles were delivered in 1915 and 1916, but most were never used because Russia withdrew from the war. Fifty years later, thousands of them wound up back in the US and were sold on the open market at cheap prices.

In 1955 Winchester came out with its most unusual lever-action, the Model 88, the only lever gun that didn't have an exposed hammer. It had a different bolt, too, that was strong enough for any high-pressure ammunition. The M88 sold well, but it was discontinued in 1973.

Winchester has made all sorts of rifles with all sorts of actions, but the most popular has been the Model 1894, especially in .30-30 Winchester caliber. It was the first lever-action Winchester specifically designed (by John Browning) for smokeless powder. For many years the 94 was America's traditional "deer rifle," and by 2006 more than 7½ million had been made. For a while it was even available as a .410 shotgun.

In 1938 Daisy copied the M94 with the Red Ryder, and that became the best-selling BB gun. Marlin set some production records with lever guns too. One of Annie Oakley's favorite rifles was Marlin's Model 1891, a lever-action .22. This became the Model 1897, and then the Model 39, and finally the Model 39A, and it's been in continuous production longer than any other gun in America.

Winchester produced lever-action .22s also. Now the company is again offering versions of the Models 86, 92, 94 and 95 in calibers that range from .357 Magnum to .405 Winchester. Lever-actions still rule!

When Oliver Winchester died, in 1880, his company passed to his son William, but he died just three months later. William's widow, Sarah, inherited half of the company and an income of $1,000 a day. (That's like $22,000 per day today.) Sarah and William's only child had died when she was a baby, and Sarah came to believe that the Winchester family was cursed because of all the deaths caused by their rifles. A psychic told her to build a house for all of those spirits and that if construction ever stopped, she herself would die. In 1884 in California she started adding rooms to an old farmhouse. Construction continued around the clock, seven days a week, 365 days a year for the next 38 years. When Sarah died, in 1922, the house had 160 rooms. It's now a National Historic Landmark known as the Winchester Mystery House.

DR. GATLING'S RAPID-FIRE GUN

The taming of horses, swords made of bronze, the longbow and the crossbow, gunpowder—these advancements all led to tremendous changes in combat. However, it's likely that the machine gun has had a greater effect on warfare than anything else. At least so far.

Once guns arrived on the battlefield, probably in China in the 12th Century, inventors immediately began trying to increase their firepower. Early firearms were not only horribly inaccurate but also very slow to load and incapable of sustained fire. Around 1481 Leonardo da Vinci, in Italy, designed one of the earliest guns that could, at least in theory, produce a high rate of fire. It had three rows of multiple barrels so that when one row was being fired the others could be reloaded.

For the next four centuries all manner of firearms were introduced. One of the most interesting was Englishman James Puckle's repeating gun of 1718. It had a single barrel and a revolving cylinder with six chambers. A hand crank turned the cylinder, and the gun fired whenever a chamber lined up with the barrel. Puckle even came up with interchangeable cylinders that could be pre-loaded for faster firing. To make his gun appeal to King George I, who was a Protestant, Puckle proposed two kinds of cylinders: one that fired round bullets for use against Christians, the other square bullets for "slaying heathen Turks."

Almost 150 years later in Indiana it was an American medical-school graduate and farm-equipment inventor named Richard Gatling who created the first practical machine gun. He began work on it in 1861 as the Civil War began and earned a patent on it the next year. His design reversed Puckle's gun. Instead of six revolving chambers, Gatling used six revolving barrels, also turned by a crank. Each barrel fired once per revolution. The ammunition was fed by gravity from a magazine that sat on top of the gun. The story goes that Dr. Gatling took the

A 10-barrel Gatling gun on a tripod with its gravity-fed, rotating magazine. In its first 50 years, the Gatling gun fired paper, rimfire and centerfire cartridges in calibers that ranged from .30 to 1 inch. On a windless day, blackpowder Gatlings must have made an impressive smoke cloud during rapid fire.

idea from the planting machine he'd invented for farmers, where a cylinder dropped a seed into a furrow with each turn of a handle. The rate of fire was determined by how fast a team of gunners could turn the crank to revolve the barrels and reload or replace the magazine.

In spite of Gatling's best efforts to sell it, his gun didn't see much use in the Civil War. (In 1864 he wrote a letter to President Lincoln calling his invention "just the thing needed to aid in crushing the present rebellion.") But early versions of his gun were unreliable, and many army officers regarded the guns as either wasteful of ammunition or "ungentlemanly."

The Confederacy surrendered in 1865. By 1876 the US military was reduced from more than 1 million troops to about 26,000 and its funding shrank even more. The Army eventually did buy some improved Gatling guns but still had no plan for how to use them. Lt. Col. George Custer could have brought Gatling guns to the Little Big Horn but chose not to. Would a couple of them have changed the outcome?

A modern, electrically powered, seven-barreled Gatling gun—the 30mm Avenger, mounted under the nose of an A-10 Warthog ground-attack jet. The recoil is so severe that the gun has to be mounted where it doesn't throw the plane off course.

US Air Force

Meanwhile, both the British (in Africa) and the Russians (in Central Asia) and then other countries found uses for Gatling's invention. In 1898 US forces used Gatlings to great effect in Cuba during the Spanish-American War.

The Gatling gun was officially declared obsolete in 1911. Single-barreled, truly automatic machine guns by Maxim, Hotchkiss and Colt—smaller, lighter, faster, more portable and less expensive—ruled the battlefields of the First World War (1914-1918). But this wasn't the end of Dr. Gatling's gun.

Already in 1893 Gatling had been granted a patent for an improvement to his gun that used an electric motor to turn the barrels. Correspondence from the War Department in 1914 indicated that this motorized Gatling had achieved "a rate of fire of 3,000 rounds per minute from its ten barrels."

Impressive as this was, it didn't seem terribly useful at the time, and the electric Gatling gun would have to wait another half-century to be rediscovered.

Putting "more lead in the air" became increasingly important during World War II (1939-1945) for all sorts of reasons, such as shooting down bigger and faster airplanes, like the first jet, the German Me 262. But the rate of fire of single-barreled machine guns is limited by how fast their actions can cycle (eject-reload-cock-fire). In 1946 a 10-barreled .45-70-caliber Gatling (that had been made in 1903) was connected to an electric motor and managed *5,000 shots per minute*—about four times as many as any single-barreled machine gun could achieve.

The electric Gatling was adaptable to cartridges of almost any size, including those that could destroy armored vehicles, so designers first built a 20mm (.84-caliber) model. Then they went in the other direction and downsized the Gatling for the army's 7.62x51mm M14 rifle round. The result was the "Minigun," which has been installed in airplanes, helicopters, boats and all sorts of vehicles, even sport-utilities. Arnold Schwarzenegger used a Minigun in his *Terminator* and *Predator* movies. Its ability to fire up to 6,000 rounds per minute—100 per second—is impressive, but since it weighs more than 65 pounds and 1,000 rounds of ammo weighs another 55 pounds, it's not a gun you walk around with (unless, of course, you're the Terminator).

The saying "Everything old is new again" applies neatly to Dr. Gatling's gun. His design of 150 years ago is now being used to shoot down rockets: The Phalanx Close-In Weapon System is the US Navy's last line of defense against anti-ship missiles, and it is a very bad boy indeed.

To the ancient Greeks, a phalanx was a tight formation of heavily armed infantry. The automated, radar-controlled Navy Phalanx looks like R2-D2, but its 10 electrically driven barrels can launch 4,500 20mm tungsten or depleted-uranium projectiles per minute. It simply chews incoming missiles or artillery rounds to shreds. And then there's the Avenger, a 30mm Gatling with seven barrels spun by hydraulic pressure. Also known as the GAU-8/A, this is what makes the US Air Force A-10 Thunderbolt ground-attack jet a devastating tank-buster. The recoil of sustained firing at 4,200 RPM is enough to throw the "Warthog" off course, so the cannon is mounted off-axis in the plane's belly to compensate.

When asked why he had invented his gun, Dr. Gatling replied, "It occurred to me that if I could invent a machine—a gun—that would by its rapidity of fire enable one man to do as much battle duty as a hundred, that it would to a great extent supersede the necessity for large armies, and consequently exposure to battle and disease would be greatly diminished." He was, of course, entirely wrong. It only made battle more deadly.

GEN. THOMPSON'S TRENCH BROOM

Indiana's Richard Gatling and Maine's Hiram Maxim brought the world the rapid-firing machine gun. Then an American army officer from Kentucky made the machine gun portable.

The Thompson Sub-Machine Gun, as it was officially called, was the invention of Brig. Gen. John T. Thompson, West Point class of 1882. Thompson wasn't a combat commander; he was an ordnance officer, a weapons specialist. During the Spanish-American War of 1898, he shipped Gatling guns to American troops in Cuba. Afterward he supervised the development of the famous Model 1903 Springfield army rifle. He and a medical-corps officer created the tests that decided that the army's pistol should be no less than .45 caliber. And then Thompson was appointed chairman of the committee that chose the Colt Model 1911 to be the official sidearm of the US military.

Gen. John T. Thompson, US Army, retired, shows off a version of his gun without a shoulder stock. At first he called it the "Annihilator."

Then came the Great War, which began in Europe in 1914. (For reasons that should be obvious, it wasn't called World War I until after World War II.) Thompson wanted to serve, but America did not enter the war right away, so he left the army and became chief engineer at Remington Arms. The company built a huge factory to make rifles for the British and Russian armies, which were allied with the French and the Italians against the Germans. Thompson re-enlisted in 1917, when the US finally got into the war, and was put in charge of all of the army's arsenals and production of small arms (firearms that can be carried).

The Great War proved that old-fashioned military tactics didn't work against modern weapons such as submarines, fighter planes and bombers, tanks, breechloading artillery, flamethrowers, poison gas and even radios, barbed wire and buried mines.

British officers, for example, thought the newfangled machine gun was ungentlemanly and only to be used against native tribesmen in places like Africa and India. They were still in love with the horse and sent cavalry charges against the Germans. The Germans, however, had no problem with machine guns, and they slaughtered the British and their allies.

Both sides took cover in trenches dug across the battlefields of France and Belgium, and there the troops stayed while the generals tried to figure out what to do next.

Magazine called it "the most efficient man killer of any firearm yet produced," but the military wasn't interested.

The Great War was supposed to be the war that ended all wars, so afterward America again drastically cut the size of its military. Many high-ranking officers thought they'd never need Thompson's gun. Some of the older officers still thought of machine guns as "cheating" too. The Marines in particular saw

themselves as precision riflemen not given to "spray and pray" shooting.

Gen. Thompson's company, the Auto-Ordnance Corporation, turned instead to police departments and the general public. (Until the National Firearms Act of 1934 there were no restrictions on the sale of machine guns in America.) To Thompson's dismay, one market did immediately adopt his product: criminals! The first recorded use of a Thompson in gang warfare was in Chicago on September 25, 1925. Because of its impressive *rat-a-tat-tat* noise, it was nicknamed the "Chicago typewriter." Pretty soon every bootlegger and bank robber wanted a Thompson. In response the FBI started buying them too.

A Model 1928 Thompson Submachine Gun with a 50-round drum magazine. It was meant for the close-quarters trench warfare of WWI, but the military didn't buy it until WWII. Meanwhile, though, crooks and then cops made it famous.

Gen. Thompson thought that what American soldiers needed was not their long-range bolt-action Springfield rifles but handy, fast-firing weapons for combat at arm's length—"trench brooms" for cleaning the Germans out of their ditches. To keep things simple, it had to use standard military ammunition. The .30-06 Springfield round was too powerful, so Thompson went with the .45 ACP (Automatic Colt Pistol) cartridge from the Model 1911. He called his invention a submachine gun, and the word stuck. A submachine gun is lighter and smaller than a machine gun and fires pistol ammunition.

The war ended before he finished his new gun, but he stayed with it. The US Army and Marines tested it in 1920 and '21. *Scientific American*

True success, however, had to wait until the next world war, which started in 1939. American soldiers and their allies loved the Thompson. They called it the Tommy gun, and it was ideal for house-to-house combat in Europe and against Japanese troops dug into the Pacific Islands. The Tommy gun was still on duty with the American military as late as the Vietnam War, which ended in 1975.

Ten years later US forces switched from the Model 1911 .45 pistol to the Beretta M9, which fired the 9mm round. The Thompson could be made to fire the same cartridge, but by then it was obsolete for other reasons. Compared to an Uzi, a Heckler & Koch or other more modern submachine gun, the Thompson is big and heavy.

In 1921 Auto-Ordnance had slowed the gun's rate of fire to about 800 rounds per minute and settled its weight at around 12 pounds, nicely balanced. This helped tame the recoil of the big .45 ACP cartridge, and keeping the muzzle on target was much easier than legend has it.

Fired from the shoulder, it was reasonably accurate out to a hundred yards in full-auto or single-shot mode. Fired from the hip, it really could sweep out a trench, as Gen. Thompson had wanted. The gun was also well made and simple, with few moving parts. Without tools, it could be disassembled for cleaning in less than two minutes.

Different models used straight 20- and 30-round stick magazines or round drum magazines that held 50 or 100 cartridges. The hundred-round drum was not only heavy (and took forever to load) but also so wide that the gunner couldn't fire from the shoulder because he couldn't get his arm around the magazine to hold the front grip.

"Tommy gun" is still a household word, and

Some kids have all the luck. Mike Helsley, age 12, firing a Model 1928 Thompson with a 100-round drum magazine. (The weight helps keep the muzzle down.) Note the ear and eye protection. And the grin.

it still refers to what may be the most recognizable gun ever made. Auto-Ordnance is still in business, too, producing semi-automatic Thompsons for people who want a piece of history that still shoots up a storm.

RUSSIA'S AK-47 ASSAULT RIFLE

Chances are that no matter where you live or what language you speak, you know what an "AK" is, or at least you think you do. AK-47 stands for "Automatic by Kalashnikov of 1947," and it is the most famous and widely used of all assault rifles. The AK seems to be everywhere—on TV, in movies, and in newspapers and magazines. It is estimated that *100 million* AK-47 rifles have been made. So far, anyway. That's one for every 70 people on earth.

(The runner-up as the world's most popular assault rifle is the American M16, but it's far back in second place. Over 50 years only about 8 million M16s have been built.)

The AK's inventor, a Russian soldier named Mikhail Kalashnikov, didn't set out to be a gun designer. When he was drafted into the Soviet army in 1938, just before World War II, he was a clerk for the Turkestan-Siberian Railway Department. During his training to be a tank driver, he designed a number of devices to improve the tank's operation. His officers remembered this, so after he recovered from injuries received in 1941 during the 19-day Battle of Bryansk, he was reassigned to work on creating new weapons.

The Union of Soviet Socialist Republics (the USSR, now Russia) was pushing hard to develop an assault rifle. This became known as "Stalin's contest,"

Andrey Ugarov

One of the world's most famous gun designers, Maj. Gen. Mikhail Kalashnikov, being declared a Hero of the Russian Federation at his 90th birthday celebration in Moscow.

and Senior Sergeant Kalashnikov wound up winning it. (Joseph Stalin was the Premier of the Soviet Union during World War II. If there were an award for the Worst Leader of All Time, he'd be a top contender.) No one could imagine just how significant Kalashnikov's accomplishment would turn out to be.

Generally, armies have two small-arms cartridges: one for handguns and submachine guns, the other for rifles and light machine guns. For the Soviet Red Army, these were the 7.62x25mm and the 7.62x54mm. The smaller one often didn't penetrate well, while the other was too big and powerful for close combat in cities. When Kalashnikov began his design work, the Battle of Stalingrad had just ended. During that bloody six-month horror, which was one of the turning points of the war, the fighting often had been not just house-to-house but

room-to-room in bombed-out buildings. The attacking Germans eventually were captured or killed, and the Russians had seen the need for a new, lightweight, fast-firing rifle.

The ordnance department designed the cartridge first. It wanted a medium-power round that didn't create too much recoil in automatic fire and was compact enough that a soldier could carry a lot of them. The department's pistol and submachine-gun round launched an 86-grain bullet at 1,390 feet per second, and the rifle cartridge produced 2,880 feet per second with a 147-grain bullet. The new 7.62x39mm split the difference: a 122-grain bullet at 2,320 feet per second. Soviet forces adopted it in 1943.

The first rifle to use it was the SKS-45, which is short for "Semiautomatic Carbine by Simonov of 1945." The SKS had a fixed 10-round magazine. (It was used by China, East Germany and many other Communist countries also.) Meanwhile, Kalashnikov and his team were finalizing the AK design. It would have a detachable magazine, usually for 30 rounds, and be capable of semi-automatic or automatic fire. It was approved in 1947 and went into full production in 1949.

The AK-47 arrived too late for the big war, so it was fired in anger first in East Berlin in 1953, when Soviet troops were ordered to put down an uprising of their dissatisfied German "comrades." Three years later the Red Army used tanks and AK-47s to smash a revolt in Hungary, another country that had been trapped inside the USSR ("behind the Iron Curtain," as it was said) when World War II ended.

Since then AKs have played major roles in scores of revolutions, wars, terrorist attacks and political assassinations, not to mention thousands of crimes. Because so many of them have been made and they're so easy to buy, the AK-47 is the weapon of choice for villains everywhere, from drug cartels in Central America to warlords and poachers across Africa. It is so well known that in some places boys are named "Kalash." The rifle even appears on the national flag of Mozambique!

For his work, Kalashnikov received the Stalin Prize First Class in 1949. Many more awards followed. In 1994, on his 75th birthday, Kalashnikov was promoted to Major General by Russian President Boris Yeltsin. On his 90th birthday, Kalashnikov was declared a Hero of the Russian Federation by President Medvedev for creating "the brand every Russian is proud of."

While Russian politicians want the world to believe that Kalashnikov alone invented the AK,

The basic military-grade AK-47, with wooden stock and bayonet. Since 1947, about 100 million of these rifles have been manufactured. Because they're so common and easy to use, AK-47s became the weapons of choice for bad guys everywhere.

in 2009 Kalashnikov admitted that Hugo Schmeisser, a German engineer who was captured at the end of the war, had a lot to do with it too. Schmeisser had led the design team that created the German StG 44, the first modern assault rifle. StG stands for *Sturmgewehr*, which is German for "assault rifle."

The basic AK-47 isn't very accurate, but it is famous for being a tough, reliable, low-maintenance weapon that uneducated fighters can quickly learn to use. It can be buried under an anthill in Uganda for years and then dug up, wiped off, oiled, loaded and fired. Rain, snow, mud, dust, heat or freezing cold doesn't faze the AK. Kalashnikov once said, "Anything that is complex is not useful, and anything that is useful is simple."

(This is classic Russian thinking. Here's another good example of Russia's basic approach to engineering: In the early days of the Space Race, when the US and the USSR were competing to see who could land a man on the moon first, NASA announced that it had spent a million dollars to create

a pen that could write upside-down and in zero gravity. The Russians said, "Hey, that's great. We use a pencil." The story isn't true, but it's accurate, if you see the difference.)

The AK has been manufactured in countries from Finland to Yugoslavia to Ethiopia. Through more than 60 years, many variations of it have appeared, including the AKM, the RPK and the AK-74. The latter was the Soviet answer to the American M16, a lighter assault rifle that fires a smaller, roughly .22-caliber bullet: the new 5.45x39mm Soviet. This "Automatic by Kalashnikov of 1974" became the standard-issue Soviet military rifle and, as usual, there are different versions for different uses and add-ons like grenade launchers and night sights. Now the Russians are changing over again, this time to the AK-100 series of rifles. A lot of these (the AK-101, AK-102, AK-103, AK-104, AK-108) are meant to be sold to other countries, so they're chambered for the NATO 5.56x45mm and 7.62x51mm rounds. The Russians are keeping the AK-105 and AK-107, which shoot the 5.45x39mm round, for themselves.

Today there's a newer version called the AK-12. The point is that Mikhail Kalashnikov's famous rifle of 1947 became a "system" and inspired a lot of other guns. (Just like the American ArmaLite AR-15/M16.) There's even a semi-auto version called the Saiga that's popular with Russian hunters.

In the late 1980s semi-automatic versions of the AK began to arrive in the US, mostly from China. Efforts to ban them began almost immediately, which likely just got more people interested. Now AKs are made in the US, too—and, like Daisy BB guns, they're available with pink stocks.

The machine gun's effect on the early 20th Century was profound. The impact of the AK-47 on the second half of the 20th Century was equally significant. As the gun's production continues, although more slowly than before, generations of people yet unborn will come to know what "AK" means. In his book *The Gun,* C.J. Chivers reflects on when the "AK era" might end: "This will not be a short time. It will not even be decades. But in another half-century, or century, the rifles will have broken, one by one, and the chance exists that they will no longer be a significant factor in war, terror, atrocity, and crime."

ROCKET GUNS: STILL SCI-FI

For the past 50 years rockets have been propelling all sorts of things into space, including monkeys, people, moon and Mars rovers, satellites and reusable shuttles. Before that, during World War II (1939-1945), the Germans fired rockets loaded with explosives against England. And more than a century before that, the Sultan of Mysore, in India, had a rocket artillery corps that fired self-propelled shells.

Daisy's Buck Rogers-inspired toy ray guns. The XZ-31 (bottom), an XZ-35 (right) and the wooden prototype. No inventor has yet been able to make rocket guns work well.

Smithsonian Institution

You may wonder whether the rocket principle has ever been adapted to firearms. Why not a bullet that's a self-propelled mini-missile?

In 1929 readers of comic books first met Buck Rogers, the action hero of the 25th Century. He had a pistol that fired exploding rockets instead of bullets, so it wasn't long before a rocket pistol hit the market. But the Model XZ-31 was a toy—a popgun made by Daisy, the BB gun company. (It was followed by the XZ-38 Disintegrator Pistol and then the U-235 Atomic Pistol, also from Daisy.)

Science fiction can become science fact pretty quickly. By the early 1960s a real version of the XZ-31 had been invented: the Gyrojet, a futuristic-looking semi-automatic pistol with a new kind of ammunition made by a company in California called MBAssociates.

The Gyrojet was tested by the National Rifle Association in October 1965. The Mark I model fired 13mm (.51-caliber, or just more than a half-inch in diameter) solid-fuel rockets that were 1.4 inches long and looked like .45 ACP cartridges. Each rocket weighed 240 grains before firing and 188 grains after, when the fuel had been used up.

The gases from the propellant escaped through four holes in the rocket's base, which was angled to make the rocket spin for stabilization. (There was no rifling in the barrel.) The rocket's burn time was 0.12 second, by which time it was 45 feet downrange and had reached a maximum velocity of 1,250 feet per second. Then it began to slow down.

At 10 feet, the rocket could penetrate a one-inch pine board; at 45 feet, and maximum energy, it could punch through seven boards. At 100 yards the Gyrojet had about the same energy as a 158-grain .357 Magnum bullet at the same distance: 440 foot-pounds.

The real thing. MBAssociates Gyrojet guns, including a Mark I and the underwater harpoon model. A Gyrojet appeared in a James Bond movie, and the guns were even field-tested in combat in the Vietnam War, but they were inaccurate and unreliable.

The Mark I pistol held six rounds. When the trigger was pulled, the hammer struck the front of the rocket, which pushed it back onto a firing pin that touched off the primer. As the rocket moved forward, it re-cocked the hammer for the next shot . . . or launch.

The pistol was light—just 1 pound 12 ounces, or about a pound less than a Colt Model 1911 .45—and firing it produced almost no recoil. But there were major problems. Accuracy was awful. The best 10-shot group the NRA was able to obtain was 15 inches across, and this was from a rest at 25 yards. (A Colt 1911 would keep its bullets within about three inches under those conditions.) At close range, before the rocket achieved full velocity, penetration was poor. Firing the rocket produced a huge muzzle flash. Finally, humidity in the air could get in through the vent holes and dampen the fuel, turning a rocket into a dud.

MBA had grand plans for its Gyrojet. The company imagined rocket-firing machine guns, assault rifles, carbines and even an underwater spear. The pistol appeared in the 1967 James Bond film *You Only Live Twice* and even had a limited field test during the Vietnam War, but none of the company's dreams came true. The Gyrojet is now a collector's item and the answer to a trivia question. Best estimates put total production at about 600 pistols. Today a live Gyrojet 13mm rocket can sell for $150.

The Gyrojet wasn't the only attempt to harness rocket power in a firearm, but it is the best known. It's probably pretty much what Philip Nowlan, the creator of Buck Rogers, had in mind.

SILENCERS: NAUGHTY OR NICE?

One of the first commercial silencers was produced in the early 1900s by Hiram Percy Maxim, the son of Hiram Stevens Maxim, the man from Maine who was knighted by England's Queen Victoria for inventing the self-powered machine gun.

Percy Maxim came up with his silencer as a way "to meet my personal desire to enjoy target practice without creating a disturbance. I have always loved to shoot, but I never thoroughly enjoyed it when I knew that the noise was annoying other people."

sional killer" (as someone once testified to a Congressional committee). Somehow Maxim's item of neighborly consideration wound up blacklisted by our feds.

England has very restrictive gun-control laws, while Americans enjoy exceptional firearms freedom. So why this huge difference in attitude about a harmless—beneficial, actually—shooting accessory?

With the National Firearms Act of 1934, the US federal government for the first time regulated machine guns, sawed-off shotguns and rifles, hand grenades and . . . silencers. The activities of notorious gangsters were the motivation for trying to control the guns and explosives, but the reason for going after silencers isn't clear any more. The country was in the Great Depression at the time, with millions of people poor and hungry, and some researchers now think that poaching game animals (for food) with silenced firearms was the problem.

Whatever the reason, the 1934 law required anyone who wanted to own these items to register with the US Treasury Department, to have their background checked for criminal history, and then to pay a $200 tax. The National Firearms Act still stands, and since then some states have added more restrictions and made the penalties

Percy Maxim, son of the man who invented the machine gun, wanted shooters to use silencers so the noise didn't bother the neighbors. Instead, at least in the US, silencers somehow became associated with professional assassins.

Today if you mount a silencer on the muzzle of your rifle in England, you're a considerate sportsman. Do the same thing in the US, though, and you're a "racketeer, drug trafficker or profes-

worse if a silencer is used in committing a crime. So much for Percy Maxim's good intentions.

'TURNING OFF THE NOISE'

Sound is air in motion. The noise when we trigger off any firearm comes from the high-pressure gas of the burning powder leaving the barrel behind the bullet. It travels outward from the gun's muzzle in a wave, which causes sudden changes in air pressure that our ears translate into sound. This is what makes the *bang!* or *boom!*

Sound levels are expressed in decibels, shortened to "dB." Sounds vary from zero decibels to 194 dB, which is the loudest possible sound. A whisper in a quiet library measures 30 dB, while normal conversation reaches 60 to 70 decibels. City traffic runs at about 85 db. Each time the dB level goes up by 10 points, the sound is 10 times louder.

A .338 Lapua Magnum sniper rifle built on a Savage action and outfitted with a synthetic stock, a bipod and a screw-on, can-type suppressor. "Turning off the noise" when you shoot is pretty cool. It also has a lot of benefits.

When noise levels reach 90 to 95 decibels, we suffer at least temporary hearing loss. A loud rock concert registers about 115 dB, but the music can hit 150 dB. At 125 dB we feel physical pain in our ears. Just a quick blast at 140 dB causes permanent damage. Hearing tissue dies at 180 dB.

Firing an air rifle makes a sound that measures only 88 to 94 decibels. But from just three feet away a .22 pistol makes 155 dB and a .223 rifle round reaches 163 dB. In either case, shooters who aren't wearing good ear protection will suffer immediate hearing damage. Maybe only a small amount, but it's permanent and it adds up.

So what does a silencer do? First, it is more accurate to describe it as a "muffler," as the British do. (If your family car didn't have a muffler, the noise would be awful.) Silencers don't create complete silence; they muffle the sound waves to make them less intense. Although federal law in America still refers to these devices as silencers, in the shooting trade they're now better known as suppressors, so that's what we'll call them.

There are two types: integral, which is built into the barrel, and screw-on. The screw-on kind is sometimes called a "can" because that's what it looks like, sitting out on the end of the barrel. Both are fatter than the gun barrel because they have internal chambers that contain sound-absorbent material and baffles, fins that trap the combustion gas of the exploding cartridge.

A suppressor works by slowing and cooling the gasses, and this greatly reduces the pressure wave that we receive as noise. (This is exactly what a car muffler does too.) A suppressor can drop the level of a gunshot by 40 dB or more. That's a lot.

An integral suppressor may reduce the velocity of the bullet somewhat, because the gasses that are pushing it down the barrel bleed out through vents in the bore and then are trapped in the outer baffles.

A can-type suppressor screwed onto the muzzle doesn't slow down the bullet. All the gasses stay in the barrel and push the bullet to its maximum speed as it gets to the muzzle; whatever the

SUPERSONIC BULLETS

In addition to the *bang!*, if the bullet is traveling at supersonic speed—faster than 1,125 feet per second, the speed of sound at sea level—there also will be a *crack!* as it breaks the sound barrier. Most rifle bullets are supersonic; most handgun bullets are not.

If you fire the rifle, you hear both together. If the rifle is fired at you from a hundred yards away, you may hear the crack of the bullet passing by before you hear the bang (if it hasn't slowed to subsonic speed by then). At least we hope you hear it.

SUBSONIC BULLETS

To eliminate the other noise of firing a gun—the sound-barrier *crack!*—the velocity of the bullet has to be reduced to less than the speed of sound. Subsonic versions of some ammunition are available or can be loaded. However, as we say in "How Far & How Hard," the energy of a bullet comes from both its mass and its velocity. If a bullet is slowed down, its energy and impact are reduced. Fortunately, we can get some or all of this energy back by making the bullet a bit heavier.

suppressor does to the gasses after that no longer affects the bullet.

So, the ultimate in a "silenced" rifle is one with an integral suppressor built into its barrel that fires subsonic cartridges loaded with heavier bullets to help compensate for the reduced velocity. No *bang!*, no *crack!*—and a high-powered rifle that makes less noise than some BB guns. If the gun is a semi-automatic, you'll hear the empty shell being ejected and the action opening and closing.

Police officers and soldiers sometimes use suppressed weapons when they're invading a building and don't want to alert the people inside (or scare the neighbors). Military marksmen sometimes put cans on their sniper rifles to help conceal their positions. Very few sportsmen use suppressors, at least in America, but we think this will change as hunters begin to understand the benefits: Less noise means less spooked game and fewer annoyed non-hunters.

Very little research has been done on who owns or uses suppressors in the US, but what there is suggests that legal, licensed suppressors are not a problem and that suppressors, even illegal ones,

are seldom used in crimes. In fact, they show up so rarely at crime scenes that the Bureau of Alcohol, Tobacco, Firearms and Explosives keeps no records on them. Still, the federal penalties for possession and use of unlicensed silencers are severe, even if the "silencer" is nothing more than a plastic soda bottle, a tennis ball or a roll of toilet paper fitted to the muzzle.

We can blame this at least in part on Hollywood. Who hasn't watched a villain on TV or in a movie prepare to whack somebody by screwing a silencer onto the muzzle of a pistol or rifle? (It seems so premeditated and evil.) Unfortunately, a lot of people, including some legislators, base their opinions on what they see in movies.

In a legal case in California (*The People vs. Phen Pal*), the trial judge said, "A silencer is used only for killing other human beings." This makes him eligible for our Montaigne Award. (Lord Michel Eyquem de Montaigne was the 16th Century author who observed: "Nothing is so firmly believed as what is least known.")

The judge might have been surprised to learn that silencers are legal in 37 states if federal requirements are met. In 1996 a survey found that private individuals in the US owned about 60,000 suppressors, and at one point about 2,000 new permits for them were being issued every year.

More than a century ago Percy Maxim got it right. Silencers can enhance our enjoyment of the shooting sports. The best way to improve people's shooting ability is to reduce the noise, which magnifies their fear of recoil. The best way to make shooting less objectionable to the general public is by making it less noisy. This is understood in parts of Europe and Britain, New Zealand and other places where there are fewer restrictions on suppressors. Many British .22 rifles are used to shoot garden pests, and they're suppressed out of consideration for the neighbors.

In the chapter "Cool Guns 4 U" we list our top fun guns to own and shoot. Here we want to add a recommendation to one of our recommendations: If you like the Ruger 10/22, you'll love one that's suppressed. Several companies make complete conversions that include special barrels for subsonic .22 Long Rifle cartridges loaded with heavier, 60-grain bullets. These rifles are so quiet that your first reaction is to laugh in disbelief. "Turning off the noise" when you shoot is pretty cool.

Do Guns Make Heroes?

These days guns often get a bad rap, especially in the news, where they're usually mentioned in connection with some terrible crime like a school shooting. However, guns are only tools, and tools have their proper uses; by themselves, guns are neither "bad" nor "good." If guns are used to commit crimes, guns can also be used to stop crimes. In some cases guns may be the last resort, the only way to defend what's right—and people who use guns to help others sometimes become heroes.

The dictionary defines a hero as "a person of distinguished valor or fortitude." But if you're confused about what it means to be a hero, you're not alone. The word is one of the most misused in the English language. Someone who used a cell phone to report a fire or who rescued a puppy from a swimming pool gets called a "hero." These are worthy acts, but they aren't heroic.

A true hero puts his or her own life on the line for others. Anyone may become a hero, but there are two professions, law enforcement and the military, where this happens most often. When peace officers or soldiers perform exceptional deeds, it is often with the aid of guns. But a weapon alone can't make a hero.

The 19,000 American peace officers who have died in the line of duty since 1791 are remembered on the National Law Enforcement Officers Memorial, in Washington, DC. Individual police departments also recognize the bravery of their officers.

For our armed forces, there are memorials across the country and even the world. Individual acts of military heroism are recognized with medals, the highest of which is America's Congressional Medal of Honor. It is awarded by the President of the United States on behalf of the Congress to a member of the military who "distinguishes himself or herself conspicuously by gallantry and intrepidity at the risk of his or of her life above and beyond the call of duty while engaged in an action against an enemy of the United States." It was established in 1862 and first awarded one year later to Private Jacob Parrott, Company K, 33rd Ohio Infantry, US Army, for action behind enemy lines during the Civil War.

The Medal of Honor has been awarded 3,458 times, most recently (as of this writing) in 2011 to US Marine Corps Sergeant Dakota Meyer, who "personally evacuated 12 friendly wounded, and provided cover for another 24 Marines and soldiers

US Army Sergeant Alvin York, born a Tennessee hillbilly in 1887, became the most decorated American serviceman of World War I. He earned almost 50 medals, including honors from the governments of Italy and France.

Sgt. Dakota Meyer, a scout sniper with the 3rd Battalion 3rd Marines, was awarded the Medal of Honor for his bravery in the Battle of Ganjgal, in Afghanistan, in September 2009. True heroism requires putting your own life on the line.

to escape likely death at the hands of a numerically superior and determined foe."

On October 3, 1993, US forces were engaged in Mogadishu, Somalia, in northeastern Africa. An army Black Hawk helicopter had been shot down over the city. It wasn't known if the crew had survived the crash landing, and there were no friendlies nearby. In another Black Hawk, hovering over the crash site, were snipers Sgt. 1st Class Randall Shughart and Master Sgt. Gary Gordon of the fabled Delta Force. From their elevation they could see hundreds of Somali warriors rushing through the city streets toward the downed helicopter. Twice they asked for permission to land and defend the survivors, if there were any, knowing that, like Lord Macaulay's Horatius, they would face almost certain death.

At first their requests were denied, but they persisted. When their commander was convinced that they fully understood the risks, he granted permission.

Once on the ground, they fought their way to the downed helicopter and removed the only survivor, Chief Warrant Officer Michael Durant, from the wreckage. By then the Somalis were on them. In the firefight that followed, both Shughart and Gordon died—as did at least 25 of the enemy. Durant was taken prisoner but ultimately released. For their "extraordinary heroism and devotion to duty" Shughart and Gordon were awarded the Medal of Honor posthumously—that is, after their deaths. The story of their bravery and that of the other soldiers with whom they fought on that harrowing day is told in the book and movie *Black Hawk Down*.

Other movies tell Medal of Honor stories from wars past. These will give you a better understanding of what it means to be a hero:

We Were Soldiers—Vietnam (1964-1975), Walter J. Marm Jr., 2nd Lieutenant, US Army.

Chosin—Korea (1950-1953), Walter E. Barber, Captain, US Marine Corps.

To Hell and Back—WWII (1939-1945), Audie Murphy, 2nd Lieutenant, US Army.

Sergeant York—WWI (1914-1918), Alvin C. York, Corporal, US Army.

The reason that each Medal of Honor was awarded is described in an official citation. The citations are in a book called *The Congressional Medal of Honor: The Names, The Deeds—Civil War through Somalia,* by Harley Stuart Shane. They tell stories of courage that can produce a tear in the eye or a lump in the throat. In many cases the recipient was killed in the process of earning the Medal of Honor.

As this is written, there are only 81 living Medal of Honor recipients, and that number is shrinking rapidly as elderly veterans die. If you're

Delta Force Master Sgt. Gary Gordon, left, and sniper Sgt. 1st Class Randall Shughart. Heroes both, they died defending their brother soldiers during a horrific prolonged gunfight in the streets of Mogadishu, Somalia, on October 3, 1993.

very fortunate, someday you may have the honor of meeting one of them. If so, shake his hand and thank him for his extraordinary service.

Whenever you use the word "hero," remember these stories and be sure that you are using the word correctly.

POETIC HEROISM

Nineteenth Century high-school students likely had a better understanding of heroism, because they were required to read classical literature that idolized bravery, combat, sacrifice and love of country. One of the most widely read series of poems of that time was the *Lays of Ancient Rome,* by Lord Thomas Macaulay. (He wrote them in India while he was serving in the British colonial administration.) One poem is about an attack on ancient Rome by an invading army that has to cross the River Tiber to reach the city. Rome's only hope is to tear down the bridge, but someone must defend it while this is done. Horatius, "captain of the gate," and two companions volunteer to stay behind while the bridge is destroyed, cutting them off from retreat. It means almost certain death.

For generations of schoolboys this was the very epitome of heroism:

But the Consul's brow was sad,
And the Consul's speech was low,
And darkly looked he at the wall,
And darkly at the foe.
"Their van will be upon us
Before the bridge goes down;
And if they once may win the bridge,
What hope to save the town?"

Then out spake brave Horatius,
The captain of the Gate:
"To every man upon this earth
Death cometh soon or late
And how can man die better
Than facing fearful odds,
For the ashes of his fathers
And the temples of his Gods."

Cool Guns 4 U

All About the .22—and the Right One For You

Our (the authors') ideas of which guns are cool are different now than when we were 14. We talked about this with the kids who helped with this book. No surprise, they're into AKs, sniper rifles, Desert Eagle pistols and all sorts of heavy hardware like that. (Too much TV, too many video games.) Been there, done that. Most of what we used to think were cool guns—guns we just had to have—got shot once or twice and then went into the safe, rarely to see daylight again. Or got traded away.

So there's "cool," and then there's "used and enjoyed a lot." When it comes to your own money, where do you think it's best spent?

Ruger's .22 semi-auto pistol. This is a Mark III Hunter, the direct descendant of the 1949 Mark I, which was the very first Ruger.

Every shooter has to have a .22 rimfire. The lack of recoil and the low noise make it easy to shoot accurately, and the ammunition is really cheap. So why not two .22s—a rifle and a handgun?

Just about every big gunmaker has some sort of .22 in its catalog. To pick just one example, the Ruger 10/22 rifle and Mark I pistol have been around since 1964 and 1949, respectively, and so far Ruger has made enough of them for every resident of New York City and Chicago combined. Both of these guns are highly reliable and not expensive, whether you buy new or second-hand, and plenty accurate. The Mark I pistol has morphed into the Mark III, and there are four models available. There are now six different versions of the 10/22 rifle and even a long-range handgun version. The 10/22 is so popular that we've added a section about it below.

These are both semi-automatics. Until you get some experience under your belt, it's easy to forget to "safe" the gun (decock it, or at least flip on the safety catch) between shots. Remember: A semi-auto reloads itself. And if you also forget about muzzle control, which is the 3rd Commandment of gun safety, you could put a bullet somewhere it wasn't meant to go. Like into your own leg. Or the dog. Or worse.

It depends on how you learn too. If you shoot at a range under the eye of your mentor or an instructor, a semi-auto can be OK. If you live in the country and learn by going out by yourself, the best gun to start with is a pump-, lever- or bolt-action .22 rifle that you have to crank by hand after every shot. New, a lot of these are more expensive than a Ruger 10/22, but good second-hand guns are easy to find and cost less.

Same goes for handguns. Muzzle control is even easier to forget about with a pistol because the barrel is so short and you hold it (or wave it around!) with just one hand. It might surprise you that, at least new, .22 handguns generally cost more than rifles.

A couple of other things to keep in mind about choosing guns for yourself: Until you're 14 or 15 or

The single-action Ruger Bearcat .22 is one of the few revolvers still being made in sizes that fit kids' hands.

so, an adult-size rifle may be too long for you. You won't be able to bring it to your shoulder to fire it safely and accurately. (You won't be able to look down the sights properly.) Some gunmakers, such as Ruger with its 10/22, offer shorter stocks for kids. And when it comes to handguns, the weight of the gun and the size of the grip may also be a challenge for you at first. There used to be a fair number of revolvers, single- and double-action, that kids could manage, but not any more. Well, except for Ruger's Bearcat and Single-Six .22s. (You'd think Ruger wants to be your gun company, wouldn't you?)

THE TERRIFIC .22

The .22 rimfire is very accurate in the right guns, it produces no recoil and not much noise, and it happens to be both useful and great fun to shoot. It has been around for a very long time. In fact, it was the first metallic cartridge made in America, more than 150 years ago.

Rimfire means that, instead of a separate primer, the cartridge has priming compound in the rim of its case. When the firing pin or hammer hits the rim, it sets off the primer, which lights the main powder charge. (The hit also deforms the case, so we can't reload and reuse it.) Louis Nicolas Flobert invented rimfire ammunition in France in the mid-1840s by shaping a percussion cap to give it a rim, and then sticking a ball into it, to make a self-contained round. This became an indoor shooting-gallery cartridge called in English the .22 BB Cap, for "bulleted breech cap." Flobert cartridges have no gunpowder; the bullet (or ball) is driven just by the primer.

Smith & Wesson took this idea a step further and, in 1857, used it in a new cartridge for their first revolver, the Model 1. The S&W .22 had a little 29-grain bullet in a rimfire case, but it was also loaded with four grains of powder, so it had more punch than a Flobert.

The S&W Model 1 was a self-defense "belly gun" meant to be used across a card table, but even for that the original .22 cartridge was pretty puny. A hotter version in a longer case with *five* grains of powder came along in 1871. This was dubbed the .22 Long, so naturally the first one became the .22 Short.

The rimfire .22 Short cartridge was created in 1857 by Smith & Wesson for the company's new Model 1 pocket revolver, above, a hideaway gun meant for self-defense at close range. The gun disappeared, but the .22 cartridge lives on.

Pretty soon someone added one more grain of powder, lengthened the case again, and upped the bullet from 29 to 40 grains. Presto, the .22 Extra Long!

Many shooters' first rifle is the Chipmunk, an inexpensive, single-shot, bolt-action .22 made by Keystone Sporting Arms.

And then in 1887 came yet another version, with the 40-grain bullet of the Extra Long in the slightly shorter case of the Long. This was the .22 Long Rifle. It was converted to the new smokeless powder, and then it went on to become the most popular cartridge in the history of Planet Earth. And never mind its name; the Long Rifle round works in any .22 that's chambered for it, whether they're long guns or handguns.

Many more .22 variants appeared, but by now most of them have disappeared. One that hasn't is the .22 WMR, or Winchester Magnum Rimfire. It fires a 30-, 40- or 50-grain bullet at up to 2,200 feet per second, making it about twice as hard-hitting as the .22 LR. In 2002 the Hornady ammunition company squeezed down the neck of a .22 Magnum case for a .17-caliber bullet. The .17 HMR (Hornady Magnum Rimfire) steps out at 2,350 to 2,550 fps. The bullets are so tiny, though (just 17 and 20 grains) that their energy is a lot less than the .22 Magnum.

But forget the .17 and the Mag. We're here to talk about the .22 LR. The .22 Short and Long are still around, but ammunition-industry experts says that more than *one billion* Long Rifle rounds are sold *every year*—just in the US. That's a lot of tin cans, dump rats, woodchucks, squirrels, bunnies, paper bull's-eyes and other targets.

You'll find all sorts of LR ammunition, labeled Standard Velocity, High Velocity and Hyper Velocity, with bullets from 30 to 40 grains, copper-plated or plain lead, hollowpoint or solid. You can even get .22 tracer rounds and cartridges loaded with tiny shot pellets, for small pests (although they aren't very effective). And finally there is subsonic .22 ammunition, which is quieter.

Some guns shoot one brand more accurately than others, so try a few and see if there's any differ-

ence. If absolute accuracy down to the last eighth of an inch doesn't matter, buy the cheapest ones you can find. Hollowpoints are best for hunting small game because the bullets expand, to kill more quickly.

Steve Helsley

Cartridges (from left, shown actual size): A .22 LR round costs as little as 4¢, factory-loaded .223s are about 60¢ each, and a box of 10 .600 Nitro Express rounds can cost $250 or more.

Twenty-twos (British and Canadian shooters call them two-twos) are really cheap—as little as 4¢ or 5¢ a round. Sometimes even less, if there's a big sale. To compare: A single .223 cartridge costs about 60¢, or 12 times as much, and one factory .600 Nitro Express round can easily cost $40! (Then again, what do you think it costs to hunt an elephant?)

The .22 is the biggest little round of them all.

THINGS TO DO WITH THE .22

Around 1900 a few British companies fastened seven or eight single-shot .22 rifle barrels together in a cluster and added a hammer that fired all of them at once. These "volley guns" could drop a duck or goose at twice the range of even an 8-gauge shotgun. There were safety problems, though, because a .22 bullet can travel a mile or more, much farther than the heaviest bird-shot pellets.

So that idea didn't last long. But it was just one of many things the .22 is good for. For example, it's not only the ideal small-game plinking and hunting round (and poachers everywhere like it because it's quiet and cheap), but it's also used in world-class target competition. There are 15 different shooting contests in the Summer Olympic Games for pistol, rifle and shotgun, and six of them are fired with .22s. There's even a winter event called biathlon, where competitors race around a course on cross-country skis with rifles on their backs, stopping to fire at targets along the way. Norwegian soldiers started doing this in the 1860s as a training exercise called military patrol. It was demonstrated at the Olympics in the 1920s, '30s and '40s, and it got so popular that finally in 1960 it became a regular medal event. At first it was shot with army rifles,

Modern biathlon competition grew out of an old skiing-and-shooting exercise called military patrol. At the 1928 Winter Olympics, the German army team (shown here) finished fifth out of nine. Norway won.

but then the .22 LR became the standard cartridge.

If you want to become a professional shooter (read "Careers"), you're going to burn up a few hundred thousand rounds in practice, and that means .22s. Most of the famous trick shooters in America used .22 rifles and pistols. They preferred to be called exhibition shooters, but to their amazed audiences, what they could do with a gun were tricks, if not outright magic. With her Marlin lever-action .22, Little Sure Shot (Annie Oakley) could hit a dime tossed in the air 90 feet away. Ad and Plinky Topperwein, a husband-and-wife team who worked for Winchester from 1901 till about 1950, also did miraculous things with .22s. Plinky would shoot the buttons off Ad's vest and cigarettes out of his lips.

(Ad's name was Adolph. "Plinky" was a nickname that came from plinking, fun shooting. Mrs. Topperwein's real name was Elizabeth.)

Ad once shot at 72,500 small wooden blocks thrown in the air, and missed only nine of them. His longest run without a miss was 14,540. Plinky once broke 967 out of a thousand clay pigeons. They set these records not with shotguns, but with .22 rifles.

In 1959 a Remington pro named Tom Frye broke Ad's record with a Nylon 66 .22 semi-auto

A biathlon rifle: the Anschutz Model 1827. It's carried on the skier's back in a special sling. He or she cycles the action by flicking the straight-pull bolt back and forth with a finger. Extra magazines, one for each target stage, are mounted in a holder on the stock's forend.

rifle: 100,004 out of 100,010 wooden blocks. It took 13 nine-hour days of shooting. Then in 1987 John Huffer, known as "Chief AJ," used a Ruger 10/22 to set a different wooden-blocks-in-the-air record: 40,060 hits in a row without a miss. (These dudes must have hated wooden blocks.) Actually, he used 18 Ruger 10/22s, which assistants reloaded and handed to him.

Later on you'll see that military forces use Ruger .22s as special sniper rifles. Plenty of cops carry .22 pistols as backup guns or when they're off duty. Blank .22 cartridges provide the power for tools like industrial nail guns and the captive-bolt guns used to kill animals in slaughterhouses.

Long ago, one of the authors was at a remote spot on the Zambezi River in Zimbabwe. At night elephants started coming into camp to feed. This meant destroying the trees—pulling branches down and eating them, leaves, twigs, wood and all. Elephants will push trees over and uproot them to get to the branches. Dennis, the PH (Professional Hunter), yelled at them to leave. The first night they did. Then they ignored him. Next he chased them out of camp with the Land Rover. This worked only once or twice. Finally he said, "If you hear some shooting tonight, it's just me after the ellies again."

Sure enough, late that night came *bang!bang! bang!bang!bang!* And then trumpeting and squealing and running. Dennis was peppering their butts with a .22 rifle. Elephant hide is so thick there that the bullets didn't penetrate, but they sure stung.

The next day the miscreants, three young bulls, were seen huddled together in a dry riverbed, sulking like kids who'd been punished for shoplifting. They stayed out of camp after that.

But never think the .22 is harmless. As you know, where you put a bullet is much more important than how powerful it is. Although the power of a .22 LR is less than five percent of a .30-06, it can do real damage. The bullet leaves the muzzle of a rifle at around 1,250 fps, which generates 140 foot-pounds of energy. This can be deadly on soft tissue out to 250 yards or more. There are many stories of covert agents, from the days of World War II up to today, using .22 pistols to assassinate enemies. (Two shots, at close range and usually low at the back of the head.) Peter Hathaway Capstick, the safari hunter and author, wrote about two adult elephants that were killed with single shots from a .22 rifle. In each case the bullet penetrated the thin skin behind the animal's foreleg and got to the heart, where it caused enough bleeding to lead, eventually, to death. Or maybe they died from embarrassment.

And finally there's this interesting story of survival with a .22 pistol from a friend of ours:

"My personal favorite defense gun has always been a Beretta Jetfire loaded with .22 Shorts. I never go hiking without it in my pocket. My other rule is to use the Buddy System—never hike alone, so one of us can go for help if something happens. One time I was hiking with my brother-in-law in northern Montana. Out of nowhere came this huge brown bear, and man was she mad. We must have been near one of her cubs. Anyway, if I hadn't had my little Jetfire, I wouldn't be here today. Just one shot to my brother-in-law's kneecap and I was able to escape just by walking at a brisk pace!"

Think it's true?

THE AWESOME RUGER 10/22

Ruger's fast-handling, high-tech but ultra-simple Model 10/22 carbine may be the most adaptable gun of all time. Every kind of sight, stock, barrel and firing mechanism is available for it, including some you couldn't imagine.

Back in 1960, Ruger (Sturm, Ruger & Company) came out with its first rifle, a handy semi-auto carbine called the Deerstalker that fired the .44 Magnum revolver cartridge. It was meant for hunting medium-size game at close range in thick woods or jungle. It sold well, but its real claim to fame now is that Bill Ruger made a .22-caliber version of it called the 10/22. When this arrived, in 1964, it was about the most high-tech, fastest-handling .22 anyone had ever seen. It cost $54.50, which wasn't cheap; that's like $450 today.

Ruger knew he was onto something good. Shooters began buying it immediately, and they haven't stopped. The 10/22 must be the most popular .22 rifle in history. The original version was short, with an 18½-inch barrel, and weighed just a bit more than five pounds. The model name came from the fact that it held 10 rounds, and its magazine was unique for a .22. Instead of stacking the cartridges on top of each other in a box, it held them separately in a spool that rotated to feed each one into the action. Very smooth and reliable.

The gun was also ahead of its time because it was completely modular. The main pieces—the trigger mechanism and trigger guard, the barrel and the stock—can be swapped out easily by loosening just one screw. This is part of why the 10/22 has become a best-seller. Ruger now sells a half-dozen

This is a Ruger 10/22 also—dressed up with an aftermarket kit to look like a World War II German MG-42 machine gun.

different 10/22 models, but dozens of other companies make hundreds of accessories for the little Ruger. Every imaginable kind of sight, stock and barrel are available for the 10/22, along with suppressors, 50-round drum magazines and other things you *couldn't* imagine. You can dress up a 10/22 to look like an AR or AK assault rifle or a World War II German MG-42 machine gun. There's even a gadget that turns two 10/22s into a sort of mini-Gatling gun. Crawl around on the Web for a few minutes, and you'll see what we mean.

Most of these things require no alteration to the rifle. Buy the kit or the parts, and you can install them without special tools or skills.

Cool as this stuff can be, the basic goodness of the 10/22 is what makes it so great for kids (kids of all ages, that is). It's light, accurate and reliable. The stock is the right size. It will fire and feed any Long Rifle ammunition, and it requires only the most basic cleaning and maintenance. We recommend learning to shoot well with the factory-installed sights before you add a scope. Your best bet for the first accessory is an extended magazine (unless it's illegal where you live) and a hand-crank tool that will help you stuff ammo into it.

With all these wild, Airsoft-looking accessories, you might start to think that the 10/22 is some sort of toy. Wrong. It's not a fake MP5; it's a real .22 rifle. Real police officers and soldiers, including US Navy SEALs and Israel's Defense Forces, use 10/22s.

Israeli Special Forces reportedly use scoped and suppressed Ruger .22s to kill neighborhood dogs quickly and quietly, to prevent them from barking during undercover operations. (The rifles were nicknamed Hush Puppies.) Israeli marksmen have also used 10/22s for "crowd control" in the West Bank and the Gaza Strip, the territories Israel seized in 1967. The goal was to take out key protestors by shooting them in the legs with something "less deadly" than the 5.56mm assault-rifle round but more effective than a bullet made of rubber, plastic or wood.

This is one of those ideas that may sound reasonable but doesn't always work as planned. Possibly because they're shorter than adults, several children were killed by .22 bullets that were aimed low at grown-up legs. Israel's Judge Advocate General decided that the 10/22 was a true live-fire weapon and should not be used for crowd control. An investigation showed that the .22s were more deadly than the army expected, especially in upper-body injuries. It also turned out that soldiers thought the Rugers were less harmful because of the suppressors—*Hey, how dangerous can it be if it's so quiet?*

Once again: It isn't the size or the energy of the bullet (or the noise) that matters so much as where the bullet hits. Even highly trained snipers can't always guarantee what a bullet will hit, particularly in a crowd. And soldiers don't always understand ballistics, either. But now you do.

An Israeli soldier takes aim with a "Hush Puppy," a scoped and suppressed Ruger 10/22 with a folding bipod on the forend. Used as a crowd-control weapon, the .22 rifle turned out to be more deadly than expected. US Navy SEALs reportedly use 10/22s also.

Careers

You Can Make Money with Guns

Some historians believe that firearms are the single most important man-made item in human history. Guns settled wars and elevated one country over another, "pacified" wildernesses for colonization and civilization, fed and protected families, and both aided and stopped crime. Many modern manufacturing processes were developed to build guns, and the oldest documented manufacturer of anything still in business today is a gunmaker. Beretta, in northern Italy, has a receipt dated October 3, 1526, for 185 musket barrels sold to the City of Venice. The Beretta company is now one of the world's largest and most successful suppliers of sporting, police and military firearms.

In addition to Pietro Beretta, men named Whitney, Lefaucheux, Forsyth, Colt, Winchester, Remington, Gatling, Maxim, Mauser, Lee, Lebel, Whitworth, Mannlicher, Rigby, Browning, Thompson, Kalashnikov, Garand and many more—designers or manufacturers of guns—played crucial roles in history. Cities in England, France, Germany, Austria, Belgium, Italy, Russia, Spain and the United States became centers of gun manufacturing. School systems and professional associations were created to support gunmaking.

In the Digital Age gunmaking is still important, and there are many professions (besides being police officers or soldiers) that involve working with guns. Some of them require the latest in computer technology, while others have hardly changed in 500 years. See if any of these spark your interest.

GUNMAKER: CRAFTSMAN

A gunmaker builds firearms, either mass-production guns or guns that are made one at a time to a buyer's specifications, or something in between. Whether they are individuals or large companies, gunmakers often focus on certain markets: They build only rifles or only shotguns, or a particular type of handgun. They may concentrate on military or police needs, or big-game hunting or competitive trap shooting. A few gunmakers specialize in building replicas of historic old guns.

Gunmaker Dale Tate of California performing the role of a gunsmith: opening the chokes in a pair of shotgun barrels with a hand-operated honing tool.

Silvio Calabi

In one way, gunmaking is like any other kind of manufacturing. There are tools and methods to learn, and some people get into it because they invented a new widget or came up with a better way to do something. In one important aspect, though, building guns is different from producing refrigerators or door hinges. Gunmakers are usually very interested in what they do, proud of what they make, and always looking for ways to improve their products even more.

There's no better way to pick a career. Why would you want to spend 30 or 40 years doing something you didn't like?

In any company that builds guns there are specialists: craftsmen who carve and checker wood stocks, machinists who bore the barrels and cut the rifling, actioners who make and assemble the lock-work, and finishers who put all the pieces together and test them. Whatever they do, these are highly skilled workers who learned their trade in a technical school or as apprentices.

When it comes to super-expensive, custom-made guns, which require a lot of hand craftsmanship, the best of these workers often become self-employed; they set up workshops at home, and gun companies send them jobs. In Europe they're known as "outworkers to the trade." Many of them are in great demand and earn good livings.

GUNMAKER: MECHANICAL ENGINEER

A gun is a machine. If you're interested in how guns function and in creating new guns or improving old ones, you can enroll in a four-year college program to become a mechanical engineer. Designing a firearm that is safe, reliable, accurate and commercially practical—meaning that it can be built at a reasonable cost and sold at a fair profit—is a challenge. It requires knowledge of mechanical forces and the physical properties of all the materials used in a gun and how to produce the various parts and pieces. Whether they create automobiles, household appliances or firearms, mechanical engineers rely on CAD-CAM processes—computer-aided design and computer-aided manufacturing.

All but the smallest companies that manufacture guns also need employees besides those who actually design and produce them, including accountants, managers and salespeople. These people don't specialize in guns, but they have to know a lot about them in order to do their work well.

GUNSMITH

A gunsmith works with used guns instead of building new ones. He repairs faulty guns or modifies them to suit the owners' wishes, or he may restore valuable old guns for collectors. Some gunsmiths are generalists who have learned how to work with a huge variety of guns. They may mount a scope or a recoil pad on a customer's rifle one day, and the next day fix a broken extractor or clean and refinish a shotgun that got rusty. Other gunsmiths become specialists who focus on one type of gun or shooting. For example, they fine-tune competition pistols (known as "race guns") or big-game rifles to make them faster and more reliable. Gunsmiths now even have TV shows and work with computers.

Many gunsmiths work for themselves, and many also buy and sell guns. Some gunsmiths are self-taught tinkerers, but they're a dying breed. Today anyone who wants to work on firearms is well advised to go to a vocational school to learn the trade properly.

ARMORER

Large police departments and every branch of the military service have gunsmiths too, called armorers, who maintain their members' weapons. This can be especially interesting work, as armorers often also customize guns (ammunition and accessories too) for special uses such as sniping or close-quarters combat, Arctic or desert warfare, or match competition. Armorers often advise manufacturers on field-tested improvements to guns, ammunition, sights, even holsters, carrying slings and unusual features like sound suppressors.

The people who design, build and take care of the guns used in movies and TV shows are called armorers also. Many of those guns are real but have been modified in some way, for safety or for special effects. Hollywood machine guns, for example, are often converted to operate on natural gas, so they don't have to fire live ammunition to make them cycle realistically. As you can see, this kind of work takes not only good gunsmithing skills, but also engineering know-how and imagination.

ENGRAVER

These days, more and more of the engraving that decorates guns is being applied with a laser or by acid-etching. The best guns, however, will always be engraved by hand. There are different kinds of engraving, but they all amount to "drawing on steel" and they all rely on the same skills: a steady hand, an artist's eye and a knowledge of metals. The tools are simple: a small assortment of chisels and gravers, used to cut grooves or make dots in the steel; a special padded vise that swivels, to hold the gun; a good chair; strong, even light from a big window or a lamp; and some sort of magnifying lens. Some engravers also use an electric cutter like a dentist's drill.

It's possible to go to school to become an engraver, but many engravers learn by themselves or as an apprentice to an established master. (Naturally, you practice on a piece of scrap metal, not a fine gun.)

Some engravers, especially when they're starting out, work for studios, decorating not just guns but also knives and money clips and other things. If they love the work and show a talent for it, they may go out on their own as independent craftsmen. (Many engravers are women, by the way.) The best engravers become famous artists

A kudu and warthog by Virginia engraver Lisa Tomlin takes shape on the lockplate of what will be a very pricey double rifle. Tomlin also cut the decorative scrollwork. The best engraving artists often have several years' worth of work lined up.

and often have several years' worth of commissions lined up. Their work doesn't make guns shoot any better, but it adds many thousands of dollars of value and satisfaction for their owners.

All engravers, whether self-taught or schooled, have the natural ability to draw. If you have it—and by now you'd know if you do—this can be an interesting, creative and well-paid way to make a living.

FORENSIC SCIENTIST

Crime labs have been supporting the criminal justice system in the United States since the 1920s, but it wasn't until *CSI* started on TV that the public got interested in them. Officially known as criminalistics or forensic laboratories, they are staffed with specialists such as document and fingerprint examiners, toxicologists, crime-scene and laboratory technicians, photographers, firearms examiners and others.

Technicians are generally the ones who gather evidence (strands of hair or fibers, shards of glass, bullets, blood, fingerprints, ashes, tissue and bone, weapons, etc.) at crime scenes. Back at the lab, scientists analyze these materials to try to unravel exactly how a crime happened.

Forensic firearms examiners collect evidence and examine it with optical and electronic instruments, then interpret their findings. Sometimes they testify in court. Often they test-fire guns and then compare bullets and cartridge cases with suspect firearms to see if they can be tied to a crime. Firearms examiners handle all types of guns and ammunition and are very involved in shooting. They work with police officers, prosecutors and other forensic experts who may be examining the same guns for DNA evidence or fingerprints. This can get tricky; lifting a fingerprint from a bloody gun with epoxy fumes might affect the bloodstains, which also need to be examined.

There are about 400 crime labs serving federal, state and local law-enforcement agencies in the United States. A Bachelor of Science degree in biology or chemistry is usually the minimum requirement for getting a job in one of them. If you like firearms and science and the notion of putting criminals in prison, you'd be hard-pressed to find a more interesting and rewarding career.

Steve Helsley

Torrey Johnson using a comparison microscope at a California Dept. of Justice forensics lab. Firearms examiners often test-fire guns and then compare bullets and cartridge cases with suspect firearms to see if they can be tied to a crime.

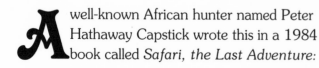

PROFESSIONAL HUNTER

A well-known African hunter named Peter Hathaway Capstick wrote this in a 1984 book called *Safari, the Last Adventure:*

Professional Hunter Wanted:
Young active man interested in low and infrequent pay to play bwana in remote bushveld.

Must be proven raconteur and socialite without liver trouble, expert card player, bartender, caterer, barbecuer, philosopher, African historian. Experience in sanitary engineering, local architecture, labor relations, navigation, medicine and pharmacology, botany, zoology, ichthyology, mineralogy, entomology, butchery, taxidermy, dietetics, optics, photography and radio operation essential. Applicant should speak at least two black African languages fluently as well as English and one other modern European tongue. A solid knowledge of mechanics, driving, gunsmithing, toxicology, ballistics, tracking, marksmanship, hand loading and experience as a professional bodyguard are required.

Benefits are: Twenty-four-hour day, unlimited fresh air, including rain, sun and dust, no medical, dental or life insurance and no retirement benefits. Applicant should supply his own rifles. Vehicles on a per diem basis.

Capstick meant this to be a contrast to the popular impression that people had of a White Hunter as some sort of minor god who looked like a movie star and could sweep both beautiful women and charging elephants off their feet with equal ease. The reality, as Capstick knew very well, was much less glamorous.

They're no longer called "white" hunters. Anything that seems to be a racial term makes people nervous (never mind actual skin color), and many safari professionals these days are, in fact, black. So today they're known as PHs, Professional Hunters, and they have to take certification courses and pass examinations to earn the title.

Most countries in southern Africa have two kinds of PH licenses: plains game and dangerous game. Taking clients after lion, elephant, rhino, Cape buffalo and leopard is a lot more risky than stalking antelope. The PH has to be ready to deal with an animal that can kill his client, him or other people in the vicinity, and this calls for a higher standard of skill.

Anyone can become an African PH, given enough determination and effort. The work, however, only gets harder after passing the test and joining a safari company. The hours are long, the conditions can be awful, the clients can be inept (or worse) and the pay isn't great. But for a certain kind of person, there's no other life.

Joe Coogan

Harry Selby, one of Africa's most famous Professional Hunters, now retired, with his favorite rifle. The hours are long, the conditions can be awful, the clients can be difficult and the pay isn't great. But for a certain kind of person, there's no other life.

In the rest of the world, the regulations governing hunting guides are very different from state to state and country to country. If you think you'd like to guide hunters where you live, log onto your government Website and start clicking around for "becoming a hunting guide." It's not an easy or well-paid life, but it'll keep you outdoors for at least part of each year.

GAME WARDEN

Every state and most countries have game wardens: police officers who are charged with keeping an eye on hunters and fishermen (and sometimes boaters, snowmobilers, hikers, back-country skiers and others who participate in outdoor recreation). Wardens spend much of their time in the field, checking fishing and hunting licenses and enforcing the laws about bag limits and what sorts of game and guns and hunting or fishing methods are legal in their district.

Wardens are government employees, armed and generally well trained and equipped, who work in uniform and have government vehicles (pickup trucks, boats, snow machines, even airplanes and helicopters) for their work. They may use the Internet and forensic investigation techniques to break up a gang of wildlife smugglers or go out on snowshoes with dogs to find a lost hunter or hiker. If dangerous animals have to be dealt with—a bear that's been killing someone's sheep or a mountain lion that attacked a hiker—game wardens are called in. Some states employ professional hunters to track down such problem animals.

PROFESSIONAL SHOOTER

To earn a living by shooting means becoming an exceptional shot, and this requires two things: a certain natural talent and the willingness (and opportunity) to practice for hours each week, if not each day. And then you have to find a company to employ you.

Companies sometimes hire expert shots to help sell their guns by demonstrating them at carnivals and other public events (search for "trick shooting" on YouTube) or at private demos for military or police buyers. Certain world-class competition shooters may get a paycheck for

a few years from a gunmaker. Members of national Olympic shooting teams may have their living expenses paid so that they can practice and compete without the distraction of a job.

Many expert shooters get some sort of support from companies in exchange for using their products. The teaching pro or the club champion at a popular sporting-clays course might get a new gun each season and have his or her ammunition provided. A well-known hunting guide or African PH might get guns and ammunition and maybe even a truck, especially

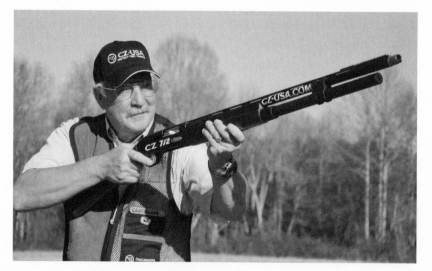

Tom Knapp may be America's best-known exhibition shooter. A great showman and an exceptional shot, he's one of the few people talented and hard-working enough to make a good living as a shooter.

if he's featured in a TV series. But this isn't earning a living; the pro and the guide still have to attract paying clients.

Very few people are full-time professional shooters, and the odds of being one compare to becoming a professional skateboarder or playing in the NFL or NBA.

GUNSHOP OWNER

Many a gunshop owner or gun-department employee at a sporting-goods store such as Cabela's was once a kid fascinated with guns. However, the day-to-day work of retail sales and owning a small business can easily overwhelm the enjoyable aspects of being in the gun trade. Many gunshop owners say, only half-joking, that they used to do a lot of shooting until they got into the shooting business.

Managing cash flow, tax records and employees can be a job unto itself. So is figuring out how to bring in more customers, and then having the right mix of guns, ammunition and other products on hand for them. In addition, in America and most other countries, anyone involved in selling (or manufacturing or repairing) firearms has to be specially licensed. This involves a great deal of paperwork too, as gun and sometimes ammunition sales have to be carefully recorded and reported.

If you think your knowledge of guns and human nature makes you the perfect candidate for a gunshop, get a job at one as soon as you're old enough and see for yourself. If it works out, your boss, the store owner, will be thrilled to find a good employee to whom he can sell the business when he wants to retire.

A rack of double-barreled shotguns on display in a gun shop. Do you know enough about guns, ammunition and shooting to work in a store like this?

SHOOTING WRITER

Worldwide, there are hundreds of magazines, in print and on the Web, and other media that deliver information to shooters—the latest guns, ammunition and gear, shooting techniques, places to shoot or hunt, interesting people, collectible or historic firearms and so on and so forth. Each year books are published on these subjects too. Being an author of such articles and books can be a very interesting career, although not usually a highly paid one.

Successful shooting writers may travel all over the world, get free samples of guns and gear, be invited to tour gun factories or go on safaris, and meet famous people. Some gun writers become famous themselves, in a small way.

(Authors such as Ernest Hemingway and Robert Ruark became famous in a big way. While it's true they wrote about guns and shooting, they weren't gun writers—or at least not only gun writers. They were also great novelists whose stories happened to involve people who were hunters or soldiers.)

Just as in almost every other firearms-related career, simply knowing a lot about guns or being a world-class shot isn't enough. To write successfully about guns (or hunting, or skeet shooting, or firearms history or whatever) means becoming a good writer too.

A writer thinks clearly and then expresses those thoughts in sentences that are equally clear. Don't worry about imagination just yet; focus on vocabulary and grammar. Start paying more attention in English class. The creativity will come.

As the saying goes, if you want to write a book, you have to read one first. Writers read—a lot. After a while, you'll begin to see how books are put together. Some you'll like and some you probably won't. Why? What's the difference? Can you write that way?

Try it. Join the school newspaper or Website. (Whether your work is published on paper or online doesn't matter.) When you think you may be ready for a larger audience, get in touch with the editors of a magazine and tell them your idea. Editors need writers, and publications are always looking for fresh talent.

A day at the office (Namibia's Kalahari Desert) for a lucky shooting writer.

Jofie Lamprecht Photography

ACKNOWLEDGEMENTS

Terry Allen, Mike Ball, Joe Coogan, Lisa Damian, Rich Eastman, Naomi Farmer, George Hoyem, Perry Jones, William King, Jofie Lamprecht, Jim Land, Dan Mayers, Bronwyn McGary, Jay Menefee, Chuck Michel, Harry Selby, Ralph Stuart and Chris Zealand helped us with this book. We are very grateful to the late collector extraordinaire George Swenson, many of whose photographs and guns appear in this book. And once again, our wives—Sue, Marilyn and Kathy—cheered us on and listened to us, for the umpteenth time, tell the stories that we put in this book. (Our own kids are long grown up and have moved away, so they didn't have to listen. But they all got a good grounding in shooting when they were young.)

We are especially grateful to Karim and Hayden Baker and to Lisa and Chris Mayers, mothers and sons who "proof-tested" the manuscript of this book and whose enthusiasm and comments were so helpful.

Silvio Calabi
Steve Helsley
Roger Sanger

BIBLIOGRAPHY

Adams, Cyril and Robert Braden. (1996). *Lock, Stock & Barrel*. Long Beach, CA: Safari Press.

Agnew, M.S.C. *Journal of the Royal Highland Fusiliers*, Vol. 24, No. 2.

Associated Press, (Jan. 3, 2012). "Ohio man cleaning gun killed Amish girl."

Atkinson, John A. (1978). *The British Dueling Pistol*. London, England: Arms & Armour Press.

Ayed, N. (2008). "Mideast Dispatches: Deadly Merriment, the fallout from celebratory gunfire": CBC News.

Baker, David J. (2000). *The Heyday of the Shotgun*. Shrewsbury, UK: Swan-Hill Press.

Baker, Sir Samuel White. (1867). *The Albert N'yanza, Great Basin of the Nile and Explorations of the Nile Sources*. New York, NY: Macmillan and Co.

Baldick, Robert. (1965). *The Duel: A History of Dueling*. London, England: Chapman & Hall.

Ballistic Resistance of Body Armor NIJ Standard-0101.06. (2008). National Institute of Justice.

Barnes, Frank C. (2009). *Cartridges of the World* (12th ed.). Iola, WI: Gun Digest Books.

Barsness, Larry. (1974). *Heads, Hides and Horns: The Compleat Buffalo Book*. Fort Worth, TX: Texas Christian University Press.

Beginner's Digest. (1960). Washington, DC: National Rifle Association of America.

Bell, W.D.M. (1949). *Karamojo Safari*. New York, NY: Harcourt, Brace and Co.

Bell, W.D.M. (1960). *Bell of Africa*. London, England: Neville Spearman & The Holland Press.

Bell, W.D.M. (1960). *The Wanderings of an Elephant Hunter*. London, England: Neville Spearman Ltd.

Berg, Al and Lauren Sherman. (2004). "Pistols at Weehawken." New Jersey: Weehawken Historical Commission.

Blackmore, Howard L. (1961). *British Military Firearms 1650-1850*. London, England: Herbert Jenkins.

Bolotin, David Naumovich. (1995). *Soviet Small-Arms and Ammunition*. Hyvinkää, Finland: Finnish Arms Museum Foundation.

Book of Field Sports. (1863). London, England: Tallis & Co.

Boomgaard, Peter. (2001). *Frontiers of Fear: Tigers and People in the Malay World, 1600-1950*. New Haven, CT: Yale University Press.

Booth, Martin. (1986). *Carpet Sahib—A Life of Jim Corbett*. London, England: Constable and Co., Ltd.

Boothroyd, Geoffrey. (1970). *The Handgun*. New York, NY: Crown Publishers, Inc.

Bradbury, Jim. (1985). *The Medieval Archer*. Woodbridge, UK: The Boydell Press.

Bradford, Charles H. (1996). *The Battle Road: Expedition to Lexington and Concord*. Ft. Washington, PA: Eastern National.

Braun, Jerry et al. (2007). *The Complete Guide to Paintballing* (4th ed.). Hobart, NY: Hatherleigh Press.

Bredero, Adriaan H. (1994). *Christendom and Christianity in the Middle Ages* (1st English ed.). Grand Rapids, MI: Wm. B. Erdmans Publishing Co.

Brophy, William S. (1992). *The Springfield 1903 Rifles*. Harrisburg, PA: Stackpole Books.

Brown, Edwards Jr. (1951). *Rimfire Rifleman*. Harrisburg, PA: Stackpole Books.

Buck, Bruce. "The Eyes Have It." *Technoid Talk*. Retrieved February 23, 2012, from http://www.shootingsportsman.com/technoid-talk/2011/february/the-eyes-have.

Campbell, D. (2011). "Winchester Model 1895: A Look Back." Retrieved March 21, 2012, from http://www.americanrifleman.org/articles/winchester-model-95/.

Campbell, Walter. (1864). *My Indian Journal*. Edinburgh: Edmonston and Douglas.

Capstick, Peter Hathaway. (1984). *Safari, the Last Adventure*. New York, NY: St. Martin's Press.

Carter, Greg Lee. (2002). *Guns in American Society: An Encyclopedia*. Santa Barbara, CA: Oxford.

Charles, Henry, H.P. Howard and F.G. Aflalo. (1911). *The Encyclopaedia of Sport and Games* (IV). Philadelphia, PA: J.P. Lippincott.

Chinn, George M. (1951). *The Machine Gun* (I & III). Washington, DC: Bureau of Ordnance—Dept. of the Navy.

Chivers, C.J. (2010). *The Gun*. New York, NY: Simon & Schuster.

Clark, P.A. (2007). "Criminal Use of Firearm Silencers." *Western Criminology Review*, Vol. 8 No. 2, 44-57.

Conan Doyle, Arthur. (1902). *The Great Boer War*. Hinhead, UK: Undershaw.

The Congressional Medal of Honor. (1984). Forrest Ranch, CA: Sharp & Dunnigan Publications.

Cooch Behar, The Maharajah of. (1908). *Thirty-Seven Years of Big Game Shooting in Cooch Behar, the Duars, and Assam*. Bombay, India: The Times Press.

Corbett, Jim. (1946). *Man-eaters of Kumaon*. New York, NY: Oxford University Press.

Corbett, Jim. (1947). *The Man-Eating Leopard of Rudraprayag*. New Delhi, India: Oxford University Press India.

Corbett, Jim. (1952). *My India*. New York, NY, and Bombay, India: Oxford University Press.

Corbett, Jim. (1953). *Jungle Lore*. London, England: Oxford University Press.

Corbett, Jim. (1954). *The Temple Tiger and More Man-Eaters of Kumaon*. New Delhi, India: Oxford University Press India.

Corbett, Jim. (1955). *Tree Tops*. New Delhi: Oxford University Press India.

Crudgington, I.M. and D.J. Baker. (1989). *The British Shotgun, Volume II: 1871-1890*. Hampshire, UK: Ashford.

Dater, Philip H., MD. (1993). *The Art of Silence*. Boise, ID: ATI Star Press.

Dater, Philip H., MD. (2000). *Sound Measurements*. Boise, ID: ATI Star Press.

Davidson, Steve. (2009). *A Parent's Guide to Paintball*. Vancouver, British Columbia: Liaison Press.

Davis, Tenney L. (1943). *The Chemistry of Powder & Explosives*. Hollywood, CA: Angriff Press.

De Calzo, Nick and Peter Collier. (2003). *Medal of Honor*. New York, NY: Artisan.

Dixon, Olive K. (2005). *The Life of Billy Dixon*. Abilene, TX: State House Press.

Ellis, John. (1975). *The Social History of the Machine Gun*. Baltimore, MD: The Johns Hopkins University Press.

Esper, T. (1965). "The Replacement of the Longbow by Firearms in the English Army." *Technology and Culture*, Vol. 6, No. 3, 382-393.

Ezell, Edward Clinton. (2001). *Kalashnikov—The Arms and the Man*. Ontario, Canada: Crown Grade Publications.

Farquharson, W.J. (1977). ".45-70 at Two Miles." *Rifle*, Vol. 9, No. 6, 36-40.

Farrow, Edward S. (1895). *Farrow's Military Encyclopedia* (2nd ed.). New York, NY: Military-Naval Publishing Co.

Farrow, Edward S. (1904). *American Small Arms* (First ed.). New York, NY: The Bradford Co.

Fischer, David H. (1994). *Paul Revere's Ride*. New York, NY: Oxford University Press.

Flayderman, Norm. (2007). *Flayderman's Guide to Antique American Arms* (9th ed.). Iola, WI: Gun Digest Books.

Fleming, Bill. (1993). *British Sporting Rifle Cartridges*. Oceanside, CA: Armory Publications.

Fox, Richard Allan Jr. (1993). *Archaeology, History, and Custer's Last Battle*. Norman, OK: University of Oklahoma Press at Norman.

Freemantle, T.F. (1901). *The Book of the Rifle*. London, England: Longmans, Green & Co.

Gangarosa, Gene Jr. (1999). *FN Browning—Armorer to the World*. Wayne, NJ: Stoeger Publishing Co.

Geibig, Alfred. (1995). *Die Kunst der Konstrukteure*. Coburg, Germany: Kunstsammlungen der Veste Coburg.

Geibig, Alfred. (2002). *Die Kunst der Konstrukteure*. Coburg, Germany: Coburger Landesstiftung.

Geibig, Alfred. (2005). *Der Herzöge Lust*. Coburg, Germany: Kunstsammlungen der Veste Coburg.

Gilbert, Miles, Leo Reminger and Sharon Cunningham. (2003). *Encyclopedia of Buffalo Hunters and Skinners*. Union City, TN: Pioneer Press.

Gordon, James D. (1997). *Winchester's New Model of 1873: A Tribute*. Self-published.

Greener, William W. (1910). *The Gun and Its Development* (9th ed.). New York, NY: Bonanza Books.

"Gyrojet Handgun." *American Rifleman*, Vol. 113, Issue 12, 80-81.

Hackley, F.W., W.H. Woodin and E.L. Scranton. (1967). *History of Modern U.S. Military Small Arms Ammunition*, Vol. I, 1880-1939. New York: The Macmillan Co.

Hamilton, Douglas T. (1916). *Cartridge Manufacture*. New York, NY: The Industrial Press.

Hanger, Gen. George. (1816). *Hanger to All Sportsmen*. London, England: J.J. Stockdale.

Hardy, Robert. (1992). *Longbow: A Social and Military History*. Goldthwaite, TX: Bois d'Arc Press.

Hatcher, Julian S. (1962). *Hatcher's Notebook*. Mechanicsburg, PA: Stackpole Books.

Hawkins, George Walter. (1897). *Treatise on Ammunition*. London, England: Harrison & Sons.

Held, Robert. (1957). *The Age of Firearms*. New York, NY: Harper & Brothers.

Herne, Brian. (1999). *White Hunters: The Golden Age of African Safaris*. New York, NY: Henry Holt & Co.

Howe, W.J. (1960). "The Quick-Draw Craze." *American Rifleman*, Vol. 107, No. 2, 14.

Howe, W.J. (1961). "Nonmercuric, Noncorrosive Primers." *Beginner's Digest*, Vol. 109, No. 1, 34.

Howell, C.G. (1959). "Fast Draw—No Bloodshed." *Guns*, Vol. 5, No. 9-57, 14-41.

Hoyem, George A. (1981). *The History and Development of Small Arms Ammunition* (I-III). Tacoma, WA: Armory Publications.

Humphry, A.P. and Lt. Col. T.F. Fremantle. (1914). *The History of the National Rifle Association During its First Fifty Years, 1859 to 1909* (First ed.). Cambridge, UK: Bowes & Bowes.

"Israeli Ruger 10/22 Suppressed Sniper Rifle." Retrieved March 26, 2012, from http://www.ruger1022.com/docs/israeli_sniper.htm.

Jaleel, Jerry A. (2001). *Under the Shadow of Man-Eaters/The Life and Legend of Jim Corbett*. Hyderabad, India: Orient Longman, Ltd.

James, Edward C. (1951). *A Boy and His Gun*. New York, NY: A.S. Barnes & Co.

Jonas, George. (2005). *Vengeance: The True Story of an Israeli Counter-Terrorist Team*. New York, NY: Simon & Schuster.

Keith, Elmer. "Elmer Keith on Combat Quick Draw." *Guns*, Vol. VI No. 2-62, 22-44.

Kent, Daniel W. (1990). *German 7.92mm Military Ammunition 1888-1945*. Ann Arbor, MI: self-published.

Kirkland, K.D. (1990). *America's Premier Gunmakers*. New York, NY: Mallard Press.

Klein, J. "Another Made in USA 'less-lethal' weapon kills in Palestine." Retrieved March 26, 2012, from http://mondoweiss.net/2011/01/another-made-in-usa-"less-lethal"-weapon-kills-in-palestine.html.

Kontis, G.E. (2011). "Enemies of the Gun Barrel." *Small Arms Review*, Vol. 15, No. 3, 37.

Korwin, Alan. (2003). *Gun Laws of America*. Scottsdale, AZ: Bloomfield Press.

Lenk, Torsen. (1965). *The Flintlock: Its Origin and Development* (G.A. Urquart, Trans.). New York, NY: Bramhall House.

Little, John and Curtis Wong. (2001). *Ultimate Guide to Paintball*. New York, NY: McGraw-Hill.

Logan, Herschel C. (1959). *Cartridges*. Harrisburg, PA: The Stackpole Co.

Marcot, Roy M. (1989). *Hiram Berdan*. Irvine, CA: Northwood Heritage Press.

"Market Hunting." Retrieved January 2012, from http://www.museum.state.il.us/RiverWeb/harvesting/harvest/waterfowl/industry/market_hunting.html.

Mattenheimer, A. (1868). *Cartridges for Breech-Loading Rifles*. Darmstadt & Leipzig: Eduard Zernin.

McIntosh, Michael. (1990). *The Big-Bore Rifle*. Traverse City, MI: Countrysport Press.

McKee, Thomas Heron. (1918). *The Gun Book for Boys and Men*. New York, NY: Henry Holt & Co.

McPherson, M.L. (1997). "Replicating Billy Dixon's Legendary Long-Shot." *Precision Shooting*, Vol. 42, No. 9, 74-85.

Mention, Philippe and Christian Ramio. (1988). *Cartridges of the Gras System* (H. Bernard Malric, Trans.). Oceanside, CA: Armory Publications.

Michel, C.D. (2011). Michel & Associates, PC, Attorneys at Law. Personal communication.

Money, Albert. (1896). *Pigeon Shooting*. New York, NY: Shooting & Fishing Publications.

Mottelay, P. Fleury. (1920). *The Life and Work of Sir Hiram Maxim*. London, England: John Lane.

Mueller, Chester and John Oldson. (1968). *Small Arms Lexicon and Concise Encyclopedia*. Hackensack, NJ: Shooter's Bible, Inc.

Murcot, Roy M. (1989). *Civil War Chief of Sharpshooters Hiram Berdan*. Irvine, CA: Northwood Heritage Press.

Neal, W. Keith and Back, D.H.L. (1969). *Forsyth & Co.: Patent Gunmakers*. London, England: G. Bell & Sons, Ltd.

Nedelin, Alexei. (1999). *Kalashnikov Arms*. Moscow, Russia: Military Parade, Ltd.

Norton, Charles B. (1880). *Breech-Loading Small Arms*. Springfield, MA: Chapin & Gould.

NRA Staff (1961). "Did Body Armor Protect?" *American Rifleman*, Vol. 109, No. 10, 28.

NRA Staff. (1961). "How Far Will a Gun Shoot?" *American Rifleman Beginner's Digest*, Vol. 109, No. 9, 22-24.

Ordog, G.J. MD, Peter Dornhoffer, MD; Greg Ackroyd; Jonathan Wasserberger, MD; Michael Bishop, MD; William Shoemaker, MD; Subramanium Balasubramanium, MD. "Spent Bullets and Their Injuries: the Result of Firing Weapons Into the Sky." *The Journal of Trauma—Injury, Infection, and Critical Care*, Vol. 37 Issue 6.

Partington, J.R. (1960). *A History of Greek Fire and Gunpowder*. Cambridge, England: W. Heffer & Sons, Ltd.

Payne-Gallway, Sir Ralph. (1882). *The Fowler in Ireland*. London, England: John Van Voorst.

Payne-Gallway, Sir Ralph. (1892). *Letters to Young Shooters (First Series) on the Choice and Use of a Gun*. London, England: Longmans, Green & Co.

Peterson, Harold L. (Ed.). (1967). *Encyclopedia of Firearms*. London, England: The Connoisseur.

Phillipps-Wolley, Clive. (1894). *The Badminton Library* (II). London, England: Longman, Greens & Co.

Plaster, John L. (1993). *The Ultimate Sniper*. Boulder, CO: Paladin Press.

Poole, Eric R. (Ed.). (2010). *Complete Book of the AK-47*. New York, NY: Intermedia Outdoors, Inc.

"Puntgunning: An Introduction to the Sport and Code of Practice." Retrieved January 4, 2012, from http://www.wildfowling.com/Puntgunning/puntgunning.htm.

Reid, R.J. Maj. (ret.) (2005). "*The Development of Artillery Ammunition*." Paper presented at the Winter Meeting, Larkhill, UK.

Rod and Gun in Canada. (1914). Vol. XVI, No. 9.

Rorabacher, J. Albert. (1970). *The American Buffalo in Transition*. Saint Cloud, MN: North Star Press.

Ruark, Robert. (1966). *Use Enough Gun: On Hunting Big Game*. New York, NY: The New American Library.

Ruark, Robert C. (1987). *Horn of the Hunter*. Long Beach, CA: Safari Press.

Rush, Robert, USA (ret.). (2006). *NCO Guide* (8th ed.). Mechanicsburg, PA: Stackpole Books.

Sandoz, Mari. (1960). *The Buffalo Hunters*. London, England: Eyre & Spottiswoode.

Sapp, Rick. (2005). *The Gun Digest Book of Sporting Clays*. Iola, WI: Gun Digest Books.

Sapp, Rick. (2009). *The Gun Digest Book of Trap and Skeet Shooting* (5th ed.). Iola, WI: Krause Publications.

Schreier, J. and F. Konrad. (1967). "The Origin of the .22 Rim Fire." *The Gun Report*, Vol. XIII, No. 1, 30-32.

Schuster, M.A., Todd M. Franke, Amy M. Bastian, Sinaroth Sor and Neal Halfon. "Firearm Storage Patterns in U.S. Homes with Children." *American Journal of Public Health*, Vol. 90, No. 4, 588-594.

Scoffern, John. (1858). *Projectile Weapons of War and Explosive Compounds* (3rd ed.). London, England: Longman, Brown, Green and Longmans.

Selby, H. (2011). "Harry Selby's Rigby.416." *Sports Afield*, Vol. 234, No. 3, pp. 44-49.

Senich, Peter R. (1988). *The Complete Book of U.S. Sniping*. Boulder, CO: Paladin Press.

Senich, Peter R. (1982). *The German Sniper 1914-1945*. Boulder, CO: Paladin Press.

Skennerton, Ian. (1984). *The British Sniper*. Australia: Self-published.

Smith, Anthony. (2003). *The Machine Gun*. New York, NY: St. Martin's Press.

Smith, W.H.B. (1964). *Small Arms of the World* (7th ed.). Harrisburg, PA: Stackpole Books.

Smith, W.H.B. (1957). *Gas, Air & Spring Guns of the World*. Harrisburg, PA: The Telegraph Press.

Stevens, R. Blake. (1998). *The FAL Rifle* (Classic ed.). Ontario, Canada: Collector Grade Publications, Inc.

Stonehenge (Walsh, John H.). (1870). *British Rural Sports* (9th ed.). London, England: Routledge.

Strickland, Matthew and Robert Hardy. (2005). *The Great Warbow: From Hastings to the Mary Rose*. Stroud, UK: Sutton Publishing, Ltd.

Sweeney, Patrick. (2008). *AK & SKS*. Iola, WI: Gun Digest Books.

Swenson, George W.P. (1972). *The Pictorial History of the Rifle*. New York, NY: Bonanza Books.

Taylor, John. (1994). *African Rifles and Cartridges*. Huntington Beach, CA: Safari Press.

Temple, B.A. (1977). *The Boxer Cartridge in the British Service*. Brisbane, Australia: Watson Ferguson & Co.

Toepperwein, Adolph. *Handbook of Texas Online*. Retrieved March 29, 2012, from http://www.tshaonline.org/handbook/online/articles/fto09

Trench, Charles Chenevix. (1972). *A History of Marksmanship*. London, England: Longman.

Upton, E. Maj. Gen., USA. (1878). *The Armies of Europe and Asia*. London, England: Griffin & Co.

VanGelder, Arthur Pine and Hugo Schlatter. (1927). *History of the Explosives Industry in America*. New York, NY: Columbia University Press.

Venola, R. (2005). "Iraq: Lessons from the Sandbox." *Combat Arms*.

Venturino, M. (1993). "How Far Will a Sharps Shoot?" *Black Powder Cartridge News*, Vol. 1, No. 3, 9-11.

Walker, John Frederick. (2009). *Ivory's Ghosts: The White Gold of History and the Fate of Elephants*. New York, NY: Atlantic Monthly Press.

Webster, D.B. (1963). "American Wall Guns." *American Rifleman*, August.

Wilson, R.L. (1986). *Colt: An American Legend*. New York, NY: Abbeville Press.

INDEX